D1546225

Erotic Liberalism

Erotic Liberalism

Women and Revolution in
Montesquieu's *Persian Letters*

Diana J. Schaub

Rowman & Littlefield Publishers, Inc.

ROWMAN & LITTLEFIELD PUBLISHERS, INC.

Published in the United States of America
by Rowman & Littlefield Publishers, Inc.
4720 Boston Way, Lanham, Maryland 20706

3 Henrietta Street
London, WC2E 8LU, England

British Cataloging in Publication Information Available

Library of Congress Cataloging-in-Publication Data

Schaub, Diana J., 1959—
Erotic liberalism : a reading of Montesquieu's Persian letters /
by Diana J. Schaub.
    p.   cm.
Includes bibliographical references and index.
1. Montesquieu, Charles de Secondat, baron de, 1689–1755. Lettres
persanes.   2. Eroticism in literature.   I. Title.
PQ2011.L6S33 1995   843'.5—dc20   94–45438   CIP

ISBN 0–8476–8039–8 (cloth : alk. paper)
ISBN 0–8476–8040–1 (pbk. : alk. paper)

Printed in the United States of America

To my parents

Contents

Preface

For Americans, the first acquaintance with Montesquieu usually comes through study of the nation's founding. The drafters of the Constitution were assiduous readers of Montesquieu—"the celebrated Montesquieu" is cited more than any other author in the *Federalist Papers*. While our indebtedness to Montesquieu for such constitutional mechanisms as the separation of powers, and especially the independence of the judiciary, is readily acknowledged, nonetheless it is John Locke who is generally given the honor of being America's philosopher. Among the English-speaking peoples, at least, Montesquieu tends to be characterized as a Continental version of Locke, a Frenchified Locke.

It seems to me that that characterization does not do justice to Montesquieu's uniqueness. Certainly, Montesquieu felt his uniqueness and frequently drew attention to it. He does so, for instance, in the concluding lines of his preface to *The Spirit of the Laws*. With a very characteristic mix of humility and hubris, Montesquieu speaks of his relationship to his predecessors and contemporaries:

> If this work meets with success, I shall owe much of it to the majesty of my subject; still, I do not believe that I have totally lacked genius. When I have seen what so many great men in France, England, and Germany have written before me, I have been filled with wonder, but I have not lost courage. "And I too am a painter," have I said with Correggio.[1]

The line "And I too am a painter" is an apocryphal one, attributed to Correggio on seeing Raphael's painting of the martyrdom of St. Cecilia (Roman virgin and patroness of music). Raphael, it should be remembered, was a contemporary of Machiavelli. In other words,

Montesquieu has looked upon the great mural of modernity, begun by a Renaissance Italian, extended by the European Enlightenment, and is yet undaunted. He does not apprentice himself in the workshop of either the ancient or the modern masters; instead, like the anomalous Correggio, Montesquieu takes up his own canvas and seeks to represent the modern world (and in such a way as not to require the sacrifice of the musical Cecilia).

In this book, I have tried to capture something of Montesquieu's distinctive genius. Of course, Montesquieu owes much to his predecessors, and I do not mean to deny the existence of very large areas of agreement. But there are significant differences, and it is the differences that tell. Again, in the preface of *The Spirit of the Laws*, Montesquieu explains that once the spirit is laid hold of, one is able to see the differences in things that otherwise appear similar. The first production of Montesquieu's pen, and the work that claims my attention here, is the *Persian Letters*. Surely no one could imagine this racy novel coming from either of the sere-souled English bachelors (Hobbes or Locke); indeed, many have expressed shock that a Frenchman of such evident sobriety as Montesquieu could have written it. I take both the novelistic form of the work and its sexual content very seriously. If Montesquieu is Frenchified Locke, perhaps we had better look more closely at what Frenchification means.

With Montesquieu, "the woman question" rises to prominence. My reading of the *Persian Letters* suggests that part of the problem with the Enlightenment, from Montesquieu's perspective, was that it had been blind to the woman question. While it thought of itself as a rationalization in the service of the passions and sought to secure a vastly expanded private realm, it had not been terribly insightful about the nature of those private passions. According to Montesquieu, man is not a solitary being, but a coupling being. A philosophy of man that fails to take account of woman is inadequate to the task of guiding humankind's common life. The early liberals, in keeping with their individualist premise, had been on the whole unconcerned with the bearing of sexual difference on political life; that very indifference, of course, spoke in favor of sexual equality and was the theoretical forebear of equal-rights feminism. Montesquieu's treatment of women is considerably more complex: more aware of the pivotal role of women, more appreciative of sexual differences, and at the same time more impressed with the difficulties of harmonizing the domestic and political realms. For anyone interested in liberalism and/or feminism, the *Persian Letters* is a pregnant text.

Believing it to be a mistake to read an old book by placing over it a contemporary template, I have tried to take the *Persian Letters* very much on its own terms. By proceeding in this fashion, however, it is often possible to gain an elevation that allows the current situation to be seen in a new light. Our own public life is increasingly occupied with matters of a sexual or familial nature: in the courts, the legislatures, the churches, and the media, the issues of the day are domestic abuse, abortion, child care, gay rights, and family values. Even internationally, issues such as child prostitution, female genital mutilation, and population planning have become prominent. I only occasionally allude to such contemporary concerns and at no point discuss them systematically; nonetheless they should often spring to mind. We cannot look to Montesquieu for direct prescriptions, but he can deepen our reflections upon our lives and institutions.

Just as he highlights the natural bifurcation of humankind into sexes, Montesquieu focuses attention on the diversity of regimes, the variety of the ways of life. His political science is much less doctrinaire, legalistic, and universalistic than that of Hobbes and Locke. Hobbes and Locke sought to elaborate a universally valid public law— a constitutional law meant to be applicable to every possible society, that is, if it wants to be a legitimate and stable political society. Montesquieu, however, is interested not so much in the law as in the spirit of the law, or really the many different spirits animating the many different codes of laws. Political life is marked by variety, due to the variety of circumstances, and that fact affects political theory decisively.

The extent of Montesquieu's revision of liberalism is an important issue, given the serious challenges to "Lockean" liberalism that begin with Rousseau and continue unabated. For the protomoderns, the embrace of nature was not enslaving. For subsequent thinkers, the news of no *imperium in imperio* meant bondage; some egress to a realm outside of nature had to be found, for the sake of the human spirit. Thus began the flight from nature, with the baton being passed from Spinoza to Rousseau, Kant, Hegel, Marx (who carried the baton upside down), and Nietzsche. They ran fast and far, but the visible, political terminus of this course of theoretical flight has not been freedom, but totalitarianism and the abyss, communism and fascism. We must wonder if there is not some more adequate understanding of both the nature of humankind and the nature of the world, and the relation between the two over time. Montesquieu may be the only thinker whose correction of the early moderns did not take the form of a dangerous radicalization.

In vatic fashion, Joseph Cropsey has told us that "our prospects in our third century appear to depend on the possibility that our moral resources will incline to fortify themselves at the spirited wells of modernity."[2] It seems to me that we could not do better than take a draft of Montesquieu. Particularly at this juncture, as the nations of Eastern Europe and the former Soviet Union attempt a liberal reordering of their polities, Montesquieu ought to be our resource, for he offers a liberalism responsive to circumstances, history, and national differences, while avoiding the perils of relativism and historicism. Because of the weight that Montesquieu assigns to the general spirit of a nation, there can be no standard blueprint for moderate government. The advent of a liberal order will not look the same in all countries. Instead of dictating rules, Montesquieu teaches us how to fathom for ourselves. He teaches the art of legislation and statesmanship rather than the science of public administration. For the newly released East, Montesquieu may provide the best equipment for the arduous journey toward moderate, constitutional government; but for the West, Montesquieu is even more indispensable—as a tonic for a debilitated liberalism.

The *Persian Letters* can be a baffling book, and a commentary that simply followed its odd twists and turns might baffle also. Instead of proceeding in the usual tagalong fashion of an *explication de texte*, I have pursued a method that Montesquieu himself hints is necessary; I have grouped and regrouped pairs, sets, and series of letters, often widely separated in the text, being attentive to the presence of connecting links and correspondences of various sorts (including author, subject, and chronology). A brief overview of the chapters may give a sense of the territory ahead.

Chapter 1, "Dis-Orientation," begins with an account of the reception accorded the *Persian Letters*, then and now, and moves to a discussion of Montesquieu's manner of writing and the difficulties it presents. What does it mean for a philosopher to write a novel? Speculation on Montesquieu's rhetorical strategy leads to some preliminary reflections on the work's design and its interlocking chains of sexual, political, and religious despotism.

Chapter 2, "Montesquieu's Untraditional Despotism," turns from questions of form to examine more closely Montesquieu's concept of despotism, a concept at the heart of all his writing. This chapter explores Montesquieu's quarrel with both the ancient and modern understandings of rule, setting Montesquieu against both Hobbes and Aristotle, with a particular focus on the question of human sociality and the account of the passions. It closes with a reading of the Troglodyte series and related letters.

Chapter 3, "Venus in the Cloister," focuses on the women of the harem and traces the results of the attempt to coerce virtue in the face of nature's opposition. Through his careful delineation of the wives and their varying responses to Usbek's despotism, Montesquieu conducts a study on the origins of revolution.

Chapter 4, "The Politics of Fecundity," examines the extended series of letters on population and the reforms recommended there. In every instance, Montesquieu aims at decentralizing power and reversing interference with the family in the interest of both affectional freedom and civic prosperity. Here Montesquieu forwards a politics of fecundity, propitiating nature rather than conquering her.

Chapter 5, "Impotence Tyrannus," returns us to the seraglio to examine its overseers (the eunuchs) and the master they serve. The various forms of eunuchism, and its meaning for the governance of both church and state, are explored.

Chapter 6, "Paradise Regained," examines the two tales, by far the longest letters of the book, that serve as counterpoint to the dystopia of Usbek's seraglio. The first is the history of the incestuous lovers Aphéridon and Astarté; the second is the fable of the heavenly rule of the philosopher-queen Anaïs. In both tales, religious and domestic revolution are linked. The successful reclamation of the household is shown to depend upon the abandonment of the reigning religious orthodoxy.

Chapters 7 and 8, "The Parliament of Women" and "Continuation of the Same Subject," turn toward France. Through Montesquieu's careful interweaving of events in the harem with events in France, we learn of European monarchy's tendency toward despotism. Having expressed his doubts about the stability or sufficiency of the monarchical principle, Montesquieu considers how moderate republics might be made to emerge out of the wreckage of monarchy. The role that women play in this transformation is highlighted, particularly through the letters of Rica.

At no point have I been hesitant about turning to *The Spirit of the Laws* for confirmation and elaboration of points first made in the *Persian Letters*. I hope that my occasional forays in this direction will indicate the possibility of (and the need for) new ways of thinking about that even more daunting work.

* * *

It was Joseph Cropsey who suggested that I read the *Persian Letters*. Although I immediately bought the book, I didn't actually follow up on his suggestion until a year or two later, when it happened to catch my eye while I pondered writing a dissertation on Aristotle's *Rhetoric*. An afternoon spent with Montesquieu was sufficient to displace Aristotle (not permanently perhaps, but for the time being) and to give me a new project. In retrospect I believe Mr. Cropsey meant his seemingly offhand suggestion to acquire such significance, but in any case I wish to acknowledge his matchmaking role. More importantly, I wish to acknowledge the force of his example. He presents his students with a vision of benevolence and wisdom, quite beyond my power to emulate. My thanks also to Ralph Lerner and Nathan Tarcov for their help and encouragement.

Before The University of Chicago, however, there was Kenyon College; and it was there that the life of the mind first showed itself as choiceworthy. My debt to my teachers and friends there, especially Robert H. Horwitz and Pamela K. Jensen, is deeply felt. They opened up a wondrous world to me; in person and in spirit, they remain my guides.

A grant from the Robert H. Horwitz Memorial Fund, with the sponsorship of Robert Strong, allowed me to travel to libraries in Paris and Bordeaux and to commune with the ghost of Montesquieu at the chateau La Brède. The Lynde & Harry Bradley Foundation supported me through the writing of this study and did the additional good turn of putting me in contact with Gertrude Himmelfarb. The time spent as her research assistant constituted a valuable apprenticeship to a master scholar and a great lady.

I am obliged to Kathleen Endlein at the University of Michigan-Dearborn for her labors in preparing the manuscript for publication.

My friend Daniel J. Mahoney was ever at the ready with good fellowship, an inexhaustible fund of learning, and sound advice. Also, my thanks to all the participants in various reading groups over the years, whose conversation, while not on the subject of Montesquieu, often fortified me for my own endeavors.

At my side from Kenyon on, joining in what Aristotle calls συναισθάνεσθαι (a consciousness of one another's existence, attained by living and conversing together), has been Lauren Weiner. She has shared in every word written and every word crossed out. Without such a partner, the book would not have been finished, nor the life complete.

Note on Texts

References to the *Persian Letters* are by number in the text (e.g., #51). In general, I have relied on the translation of George R. Healy (Indianapolis: Bobbs-Merrill, 1964) though occasionally I have preferred that of C. J. Betts (New York: Penguin, 1973). I have emended both translations wherever I thought greater literalness imperative. References to *The Spirit of the Laws* use capital roman numerals for books and arabic numerals for chapters (e.g., IV.7). I have used the translation of Anne M. Cohler, Basia Carolyn Miller, and Harold Samuel Stone (Cambridge: Cambridge University Press, 1989), making only very rare emendations of my own. References to other works by Montesquieu are to the two-volume *Pléiade* edition of the *Oeuvres complètes*, edited by Roger Caillois (Paris: Librairie Gallimard, 1949–51), cited by volume and page number (e.g., 2:39), with the exception of *Mes Pensées*, which are by number in the text (e.g., no. 115). Translations from these works are my own.

Chapter One

Dis-Orientation

In 1754, Montesquieu at last came to the defense of the *Persian Letters*, a work he had written some thirty years before. In response to the abbé Gaultier's pamphlet *Les "Lettres persanes" convaincues d'impiété*, Montesquieu wrote "Some Reflections on the Persian Letters," published as a supplement to a new edition of the letters. In the concluding paragraph of the first draft, Montesquieu apologized for the numerous error-ridden editions of the *Persian Letters*, explaining that "this work was abandoned by its author from its birth."[1] Three other unpublished versions of this confession expand on his reasons for orphaning the *Persian Letters*: he says (with his customary third-person reference) "the author took part in its making only to repent having done so, . . . devoted himself to some more serious things, . . . wrote at a time when he was quite young, and published his work at a time when all the world was young."[2]

In approaching the *Persian Letters*, we need to take seriously these indications of authorial chagrin. Why should we read the *Persian Letters* at all if it is only a youthful bagatelle regretted by the mature author of *The Spirit of the Laws*? Should we not bow to what Henry James calls "the artist's presumptive desire to limit and define the ground of his appeal to fame"?[3]

The *Persian Letters*, however, was not quite the foundling that Montesquieu describes. It was indeed published anonymously—but that manner of desertion was standard practice and simple prudence in eighteenth-century France. Regardless of the nameless publication, the paternity of the *Persian Letters* was soon ascertained and there were those who thought such literary extravagance unsuitable for a provincial magistrate. Montesquieu had predicted just such a reaction in his original preface to the *Persian Letters*: "If it were known who I was, it

1

would be said: 'His book is inconsistent with his character; he ought to employ his time with something better: this is not worthy of a grave man.' The critics never pass up reflections of this sort, since they can be made without overtaxing one's intellect." In other words, Montesquieu was aware from the beginning that he could be accused of writing a *plaisanterie*. The self-accusation found in the various drafts of "Some Reflections on the Persian Letters" (1754) was one that he had already raised and dismissed in the preface of 1721.[4]

Despite whatever disproportion was felt between the gravity proper to a *président à mortier* of the Bordelaise *parlement* and the gaiety of the *Persian Letters*, the book was a *succès de scandale*, bringing the thirty-two-year-old Charles Louis de Secondat, Baron de La Brède et de Montesquieu, fame and entry into the salons of Paris. Seven years later in 1728, the *Persian Letters* was both the only grounds for and the main impediment to his entry into *l'Académie française* (neither the *Considerations on the Causes of the Greatness of the Romans and Their Decline* nor *The Spirit of the Laws* was published yet). Despite his being the only candidate standing for election, it took the careful stewardship of the *faction Lambertine* and a delicately handled interview between Montesquieu and Cardinal Fleury to overcome the opposition—from academicians, clerics, and the court. It was not the book's supposed lightheartedness or licentiousness that provoked, but rather the pointedness of its political and social satire. (Indeed, one letter, #73, was given over to ridicule of the Academy itself.) One suspects that a carefully cultivated reputation as a harmless *jeu d'esprit* could only serve to protect the *Persian Letters* from future attacks.

Whereas Montesquieu had insisted upon anonymity in the preface to the *Persian Letters* (warning his readers that "if my name comes to be known, from that moment I will be silent. I know a woman who walks well enough, but who limps when watched"[5]), late in life he laid claim to the productions of his pen, including the *Persian Letters*, with a vengeance. It seems to have been the vehement and concerted attacks upon *The Spirit of the Laws* that galvanized him. The quarrel surrounding *The Spirit of the Laws* led to Montesquieu's publication of his *Défense de L'Esprit des lois* and his *Eclaircissements sur L'Esprit des lois* in 1750 and later still, in response to the Sorbonne's contemplated censure, Montesquieu submitted to the Faculty of Theology his *Réponses et explications*. Despite Montesquieu's strenuous efforts, *The Spirit of the Laws* was placed on the Index of Prohibited Books in 1751. His confidence in a book's ability to go it alone shaken by the quarrel surrounding *The Spirit of the Laws*, Montesquieu seemed to feel that some new provision must be made for the *Persian Letters*.

Gaultier's 1751 pamphlet received its response in the "Reflections" of 1754. At about the same time, Montesquieu took up the text itself, preparing a notebook of corrections for a final edition.

In the original preface, Montesquieu had not only separated himself from his work, he had ostentatiously refused the protection of a patron, declaring that the *Persian Letters* "will be read, if it is good; and, if bad, I am not anxious that it be read." An entry in *Mes Pensées*, Montesquieu's private collection of jottings and reflections, expresses a similar policy of benign neglect: "I would say: 'I have not time to trouble myself with my works; I have resigned them into the hands of the public'" (no. 102). But given the advent of both radical literary politics and increased literary persecution (book bannings and burnings, the imprisonment of Diderot, the suppression of the *Encyclopédie*), the public in the mid-1700s was no longer a safe repository. If, as Montesquieu says, he first published the *Persian Letters* "at a time when all the world was young," the world had changed; it was carefree no more. The ministry of Cardinal Fleury had replaced the regency of the duc d'Orléans. Montesquieu acknowledges this altered atmosphere in yet another of his belittling late apologias for the *Persian Letters*:

> When this work appeared, it was not regarded as a serious work: it was not. Two or three temerities were pardoned in favor of a completely open conscience, which bore criticism toward all but malice toward none. Every reader was his own witness. He remembered only the gaiety. One was angered heretofore just as one is angry today; however, one knew better heretofore when it was necessary to be angry.[6]

Part of Montesquieu's new provision for the *Persian Letters* seems to have been to deflate interest in his early work among both the *philosophes* and their enemies. He sought to protect his writings from overzealous appropriation by the *philosophes*, and simultaneously protect them from official denunciation. Although the publication of the *Persian Letters* virtually inaugurated the French Enlightenment, Montesquieu's own relationship with the younger *philosophes* of the "movement" was reserved.[7] Montesquieu for instance declined to write essays on despotism and liberty for the *Encyclopédie*, claiming—quite rightly, but also perhaps prudently—to have said all he had to say on those subjects elsewhere.[8]

Even when Montesquieu was on his deathbed, the partisans of the Republic of Letters and the soldiers of monarchic and religious orthodoxy did not want to let Montesquieu transcend their war. A febrile Montesquieu was forced to decide the contest between the assembled *philosophes* and Jesuits for possession of the notebook of corrections, and thus control over the fate of the *Persian Letters*. Montesquieu gave the Society of Jesus the satisfaction of receiving his confession; but the *philosophes*, in the person of the duchesse d'Aiguillon, received the manuscript. (The Vatican expressed its dissatisfaction with this division of the spoils by placing the *Persian Letters* on the Index in 1761.) By this disposition of his affairs, Montesquieu may have thought to secure for himself a double immortality, on earth as in heaven. But whatever its otherworldly fate, Montesquieu's rational soul is vividly present to us today in his writing. Montesquieu's determination to keep the final redaction of the *Persian Letters* out of priestly hands—his refusal, in effect, to repudiate literary sins—does not suggest that he regarded the *Persian Letters* as an unworthy or discreditable legacy.

Neglect and Recovery

And yet, for the better part of the last two and a half centuries, the *Persian Letters* has been underappreciated. During Montesquieu's lifetime, it was celebrated; as Desmolets predicted, "Président, cela sera vendu comme du pain."[9] There were ten editions in the first year and twenty-eight French editions during the years 1721–84.[10] Critical acclaim was not unanimous, however, even apart from those who felt themselves the butt of satire. Voltaire called it a "trumpery book, . . . which anybody might have written easily."[11] The depreciation of the *contes philosophiques* (La Harpe deemed *Le Temple de Gnide* "a mere trifle, an ingenious bagatelle")[12] gradually extended to the *Persian Letters*, until the nineteenth and early twentieth centuries found it seriously out of favor. Dissatisfaction centered on the harem plot. Sainte-Beuve, the great French literary critic, pronounced the novel's end "voluptuous and delirious" with "nothing relating to us in it. All this sensual part is dry and hard, showing that Montesquieu's imagination lay solely in the direction of historical and moral observation."[13] Sainte-Beuve's strictures were taken as authoritative by generations of scholars. Sorel affirmed of the Persian elements: "This is the most questionable part of his book. It was then quite the fashion, but is now wholly out of date."[14] This line of criticism culminated in the conclusion that the *Persian Letters* is a failure as a novel—according to F. C. Green, a "rather unhappy experiment in the use of the new form."[15] The aestheticians were pleased to turn the *Persian Letters* over to the political scientists and historians; but the towering majesty of *The Spirit of the Laws* prevented much consideration being accorded it in that camp. The political scientists, although willing to credit it a literary masterpiece, were interested in the *Persian Letters* mainly as a prefiguration of the theoretical analysis of the later works. With neither humanists nor political scientists convinced of its independent worth, the *Persian Letters* became a distinctly marginal work. If the fiction was "so much pill-gilding,"[16] and the gilding now tarnished and distasteful, then why not take the political pill straight; in other words, why read the *Persian Letters* when one could read *The Spirit of the Laws*?

It was not until the mid-twentieth century that both groups began to reclaim their prerogatives. This reconsideration of the *Persian Letters* was contingent on a fresh look at those very passages that had prompted earlier critics to dismiss the *Persian Letters* as a piece of exoticism, a literary concession to the Regency's libertine taste. Roger Oake, one of the first to recover the seriousness of the harem framework, pleaded the case thus:

> If we feel that the touches of *gauloiserie* with which admittedly Montesquieu enlivened his work are so shocking to tender sensibilities that they constitute a defect, let us at least give him the credit of believing that they were not put in for their own sake alone, arbitrarily and salaciously. Montesquieu contributed so much to the dignity of man that it seems a poor reward to thank him by reducing his stature and censoring his text merely to satisfy a still-lingering *pruderie huguenote*.[17]

In part, it was revolutionary intellectual lenses like Freudianism and feminism that allowed readers to see politics where only pornography had been seen before. Where once critics had claimed that "[t]here is not a shadow of psychological penetration in the *Lettres persanes*"[18] and "particularly so in regard to the psychology of love,"[19] they now found the domestic dynamic to be most skillfully explored. Oake declared that "the series of self-revelations on the part of the eunuchs, as well as that of Usbek in Letter 6, offer an extraordinary study in abnormal psychology."[20] Likewise, Pierre Testud described the *Persian Letters* as possessing a psychological order: "the adventure of a conscience."[21] Along with the new sensitivity to the work's psychological complexity, there was an attempt to uncover personal elements in it. After all, it was known that upon publication of the *Persian Letters*, Montesquieu's friends took to calling him "Usbek"; and in the index to the 1758 edition (overseen by Montesquieu's son), Montesquieu's name was entered with the annotation: "He paints himself in the person of Usbek." These intuitions now received a full psychosexual workup. Franz Neumann suggested that the *Persian Letters* might be

interpreted as an "autobiographical attempt, . . . a kind of self-analy-
sis."[22] Pierre Barrière and Jean Starobinski, among others, followed that
trail, with Starobinski going so far as to declare that: "The 'voluptuous' images are described with too much complaisance not to corre-
spond to the imaginary lusts of Montesquieu."[23] Others, most notably
Aram Vartanian, declined to read the *roman du sérail* as symptomatic
of erotic obsession on the author's part, suggesting instead that "there
is no reason why a literally erotic fiction, especially in an artistic
context, should not on occasion symbolize a veiled non-erotic content—
to the point even of prefiguring some abstract idea with which its
author might be philosophically obsessed."[24]

Once the psyche had been sexualized by Freud, feminism politicized
that sexual self. The feminist pioneers, while generally welcoming of
the Enlightenment—Kate Millett, for instance, speaks of "the subversive impact of its agnostic rationalism upon patriarchal religion, the
tendency of its humanism to extend dignity to a number of deprived
groups, and the invigorating clarity which the science it sponsored
exercised upon traditional notions both of the female and of nature"[25]—
said little specifically about Montesquieu.[26] Recent feminist investigations of the treatment of women in political philosophy have tended to
concentrate on Plato and Rousseau. Susan Moller Okin, for instance,
in her *Women in Western Political Thought*, makes only one (largely
negative) reference to Montesquieu.[27] Nonetheless, we may say that the
consciousness-raising has had its effect: no modern reader of the *Persian Letters* could fail to be struck by the theme of sexual politics.
While the harem sequence may have titillated the eighteenth century
and repulsed the nineteenth, it seems destined to be appropriated by
the twentieth.[28]

Intellectual developments other than sexual psychology and sexual
politics have also been important in reviving critical interest in the
Persian Letters. In recent years, authors belonging to the Western tradition have come under attack for their handling of the "Other." Their
interest in the Orient has been denounced as intellectual imperialism
rather than genuine openness. With respect to Montesquieu, the charge
of "Orientalism"[29]—Edward Said's term for an ethnocentric appropriation of the other[30]—is misconceived on several grounds. First, Montesquieu is in part responsible for the respect that we now accord to ways
of life and forms of social and political organization different from
our own. He is, of course, not a thoroughgoing cultural relativist; for
Montesquieu, there are some regimes and some folkways that are un-
acceptable, that run contrary to human nature. But there is considerable latitude in his judgments. Moreover, because he accords such

importance to the unique general spirit of a nation, Montesquieu is a most determined foe of imperialism. This appears most forcefully in his writings on the exploration of the New World, where he castigates the Spanish for their plundering and pillaging, as well as their prose-lytizing. Between them, the conquistadors and Jesuits have despoiled South America. Montesquieu does what he can to ensure that this is not the model of Western involvement with the world. He shows not only how the conquered have been exterminated, but how Spain itself has been ruined through its quest for gold and empire. Judged by the anti-imperialist litmus test, Montesquieu (despite being a dead, white, European male) turns the right color.[31] Moreover, to the extent that Montesquieu deploys a particular stereotype of the East, he does so in such a way as to undercut the reader's faith in Western superiority. He takes an available stereotype and redirects it against the West; his presentation of Eastern despotism is not intended to buttress the pride and arrogance of the West. There is, for instance, no suggestion in the *Persian Letters* that the East is doomed to despotism. Even in *The Spirit of the Laws*, where Montesquieu makes large concessions to the role of climate and other physical circumstances in his discussion of civil and domestic slavery, Montesquieu holds out the possibility that proper laws and institutions, together with the liberating potential of technology, could overcome the despotic tendency of hot climates.

More fundamentally, however, Montesquieu could not be said to endorse this abstraction, this anti-matter of the self, called the Other. While Montesquieu is more than usually cognizant of other peoples and other ways of life, he still believes in a common human nature. For him, the philosophic dictum "Know Thyself" embraces humanity and inspires his far-reaching attempts to understand the articulation of the universal and the particular in human affairs. It is the very aspiration to comprehend the particular within the universal that is denounced by the latest academic radicalism. The exercise of reason itself has become suspect, denounced as phallogo-Eurocentrism. When the quest for knowledge is understood on the model of power politics rather than the erotic model of old, then reason is inevitably seen as a tool of domination. Thus, despite the international carnival aspect of multiculturalism, its deeper tendency is toward the impenetrability of cultures (witness the rapid transformation of the call for curricular pluralism into a call for a new centrism: Afro-centrism). If the academic separatists have their way, the "inscrutable East" will return.

On the literary front, once the evolutionary view of the novel began to be questioned, forms like the epistolary that had been thought quaint were reexamined and proclaimed hypersophisticated: "This genre prefigures a technique of the ultra-modern novel, which cultivates discontinuity, the fragmentary vision and 'the indicative present.'"[32] Eventually, one imagines, deconstructionists will revel in the polyphonic possibilities of a work like the *Persian Letters*. Thus, the renewed interest in the *Persian Letters* has been spurred in part by new academic fashions, some of which, like deconstruction, are in principle hostile to the text, others of which, like feminism and the critique of Orientalism, tend to approach the book with an agenda or litmus test, asking whether Montesquieu is guilty of Western or aristocratic or male *parti pris*. Even if Montesquieu is acquitted of such charges, the prosecutorial method may not be the best by which to ascertain Montesquieu's intention.[33] While wishing to acknowledge the service such approaches have performed in rescuing the *Persian Letters* from oblivion, I believe there remains a need for a more openhearted and openminded approach to the work.

In the preface to the *Persian Letters*, Montesquieu says that he has "issued these first letters to gauge the public taste." Clearly, both public and critical tastes have shifted since Montesquieu's day. However, we should not forget that reading is still a two-way street. While we strive to render judgment upon the *Persian Letters*, it takes our measure in return. In his *Pensées*, Montesquieu admitted: "I like to read a new book after the public has rendered its judgment, which is to say that I like to judge the public more than the book" (no. 81). If we would gain a favorable ruling from Montesquieu, we must suspend our prejudices and enter into the spirit in which Montesquieu himself writes. The fault is ours if we fail to decipher his intention. Until we possess ourselves of that intention, criticism is foreclosed; understanding must precede judgment.

Political Philosophy in Novel Form[34]

Making sense of the jigsaw assembly of the book's 161 letters is not an easy task. The interpretation of the *Persian Letters* poses unique difficulties—difficulties tied to the epistolary form of the work. Although the novel of letters was not Montesquieu's invention, he was one of the genre's pioneers and aware of himself as such.[35] In both preface and "Reflections," Montesquieu makes slighting reference to his precursors and successors. In the original preface, where Montesquieu claims only the office of a translator, he says that he offers an abridgment of the letters, purged of trifles: "If most of those who have produced collections of letters had done the same, they would have seen their work evanesce." In the later supplementary preface, where Montesquieu drops the pretense of editorship and emphasizes authorial design, he speaks somewhat condescendingly of "several charming works which have appeared since the *Persian Letters*" (Samuel Richardson's *Pamela* and Mme. de Graffigny's *Lettres péruviennes* are referred to in the manuscript draft). Montesquieu thinks of himself as exploiting certain potentialities of the epistolary form that were unknown to its more traditional novelistic practitioners. The latter, although they avail themselves of the heightened immediacy of letters over narrative, do not appreciate the real superiority of the novel of letters. In the "Reflections," Montesquieu explains that superiority by saying that "the author is given the advantage of being able to join philosophy, politics, and morals to a story, and to link the whole by a secret and, in some manner, unknown chain."

Rousseau, in *La Nouvelle Héloïse*, was to follow Montesquieu's literary lead. Rousseau often receives kudos as the first poetic modern philosopher—his poetry intimately connected to his dissatisfaction with the unerotic liberalism of Hobbes and Locke. According to Allan Bloom:

> Modern philosophy . . . could not inspire a great poetry corresponding to itself. The exemplary man whom it produces is too contemptible for the noble Muse; he can never be a model for those who love the beautiful. The fact that he cannot is symptomatic of how the prosaic new philosophy truncates the human possibility. . . . Rousseau, a philosopher-poet like Plato, tried to recapture the poetry in the world.[36]

Despite Montesquieu's reputation as the philosopher of commerce and other such unerotic pursuits, his literary activity would seem to indicate that he, unlike his fellow liberals, does possess a poetic sensibility. In *The Spirit of the Laws*, Montesquieu even begins the section on commerce with an invocation to the Muses and affixes a poem—"O Venus, O Mother of Love"—to the head of the book on population. The purpose of these poetic flights is not, I believe, to point up the distance between eros and such mundane matters, in other words, to beg the bored reader's pardon, but rather to show the erotic foundation of Montesquieu's brand of liberalism. Montesquieu reminds us that family and property—those institutions generally regarded as the cornerstones of the liberal polity—are rooted in a particular disposition of sexual passion. Montesquieu's poetry may be in the service of the bourgeoisie in a way that Rousseau's is not.[37]

Montesquieu regarded Plato as among the four greatest poets and the epistolary form as conceived by Montesquieu bears some resemblance to that older poetic/philosophic form, the Platonic dialogue.[38] It too is philosophy made dramatic, philosophy enacted. Accordingly, both forms call for a particular kind of reading: attention must be paid to the dramatic situation, to the verdict that the deeds render on the words; the characters of the interlocutors or correspondents must be taken into account and the possible distance between the author and his protagonist gauged. In both cases, the communication between the participants must be understood as crafted to further an indirect communication between author and reader. Because of their mediated presentation, it may be that both forms also yield a particular kind of understanding. If there are some works that stand as vast peaks to be scaled, with methodical effort, there are others that lie outstretched like great cities, dauntingly multitudinous.[39] On this analogy, Montesquieu, like Plato, is more cosmopolis than mountain.

While the similarity between the dialogue and the epistolary novel is marked, the difference is perhaps more so.[40] A Platonic dialogue, as its name indicates, operates dia-logos: through the word. This is not to say that a Platonic dialogue operates on a purely dianoetic or intellectual level, but it is to say that even the dialogue's mimetic or dramatic elements are tied to the spoken word. The drama occurs entirely within the conversation; it consists in who speaks to whom, how, when, and in what context. For instance, the forcible entry of Thrasymachus into the discussion of the *Republic* and his subsequent silencing constitute the dramatic refutation of the Thrasymachean argument. Thrasymachus, we might say, engages in speech-acts that elucidate his speech proper.

In the *Persian Letters*, although words are unavoidably the medium through which the story is presented, the drama itself occurs in large part independently of the written exchange, in the lives of the characters, in their erotic attachments and their political actions. Speaking loosely, we might say that the dialectic of the *Persian Letters* is as much material or passional as noetic. In the preface Montesquieu stresses that the success of the work's dramatic component lies in its fidelity to the passions of the characters and its appeal to the passions of the readers. In a similar vein, one of his characters justifies the use of fables on the grounds that "there are certain truths with respect to which persuasion is not sufficient; they must be felt as well" (#11).

Modernity could be said to begin in a revaluation of the rank of passion and reason in the human constitution. Reason suffers a self-administered demotion, becoming instrumental, a pimp for the passions. Understanding their activity as a rationalization in the service of the passions, the early modern philosophers retained the old modes of argumentation; but one might wonder whether their discourses and treatises, by their very form, did not belie the substance of their claim about human nature. Montesquieu experiments with the epistolary novel as a new vehicle for the new philosophy. He fashions a poetry proper to modernity.

By encompassing a wider audience through a literary form that appeals to the passions, Montesquieu forwards, and redirects, the project of enlightenment. He aims at a reform of opinion. Of course, the Socratic consideration of questions like "what is justice" takes common opinion as its point of departure; but whatever Socrates' reasons for participating in any particular conversation, the Platonic account of the exchange cannot be said to have a purpose primarily corrective or hortatory.[41] There is thus a vast difference between the rhetorical strategies of the Montesquieuan novel and the Platonic dialogue. The two forms envision different audiences. One need only note the care with which Montesquieu cultivated female readers to sense the contours of the difference. Not only did Montesquieu develop a genre—the novel—in which women figure prominently—as authors, as readers, and as heroines—but he did such apparently frivolous things as order specially and expensively bound editions of his writings for bluestocking friends. A copy of the *Persian Letters* in green moroccan leather on display in the salon of Madame Duplessy, one of the powerful women who shaped the cultural life of the French nation, was welcome publicity. In addition to promoting himself through female acquaintances, Montesquieu actually wrote some of his works at the instigation of women, for instance the philosophic/erotic tales *Le Temple de Gnide* and *Arsace et Isménie*. Again, Rousseau was to follow Montesquieu in this feminization of philosophy. Montesquieu's attention to securing a female audience is one of the more intriguing indications of the fact that Montesquieu has a different view than Plato of the philosopher's relationship to the political community.

In *The Spirit of the Laws*, in a one-paragraph chapter titled "Of Legislators," Montesquieu addresses this question of the philosopher's relationship to the regime. He speaks of Plato and Machiavelli among others. The implicit suggestion of the chapter is that the true legislators are those philosophers who make themselves the teachers of the actual lawgivers. What Montesquieu explicitly says of his philosophic predecessors is curious, however. He makes a series of what seem unfair, even trivializing remarks about the passions and prejudices that motivate such ordering intelligences. "Plato," he says, "was indignant at the tyranny of the people of Athens. Machiavelli was full of his idol, Duke Valentino" (XXIX.19). Despite the seeming persiflage, Montesquieu is on to something. The central event for Platonic political philosophy is, after all, the death of Socrates at the hands of the city. Socrates is reincarnated, so to speak, in the Platonic corpus. Plato's dialogues, which offer a deathless imitation of Socrates, could thus be read as depriving the city of its ill-gotten victory over philosophy. According to Montesquieu, they constitute an act of philosophic revenge upon the body politic. While criticizing Plato for his philosophic partisanship, Montesquieu criticizes Machiavelli for partisanship of an opposite sort. Machiavelli was an apologist not for Socrates, but for Duke Valentino, Cesare Borgia. His philosophizing, Montesquieu suggests, was in the service of tyranny.

In the opening chapter of book XXIX—the book of *The Spirit of the Laws* that concludes with the criticisms of Plato and Machiavelli—Montesquieu begins: "I say it, and it seems to me that I have written this work only to prove it: the spirit of moderation should be that of the legislator" (XXIX.1). Montesquieu demonstrates the moderation of his own attitude toward political power by rejecting both Platonic indignation and Machiavellian adoration. His works are addressed neither to potential philosophers nor to potential princes, but to the public, to Everyman and, as we have seen, Everywoman.

In the *Persian Letters*, Montesquieu makes patent his departure from his predecessors, and particularly Machiavelli, by refusing to write the customary epistle dedicatory. It is the one sort of letter that has no place in his experiment with epistolary fiction. The opening lines of the preface announce his independence: "I am not writing an epistle dedicatory here, and I seek no protection for this book." Montesquieu abandons the prince and his patronage for the republic of letters. Public opinion becomes the new sovereign. To serve as adviser to this fickle and untutored force, the philosopher must write not a *speculum principis* but a *speculum publicus*. Dena Goodman, in her fine book, *Criticism in Action*, also recognizes Montesquieu's literary revolution. She describes the *Persian Letters* as "the first attempt at political writing for the modern age. With the *Lettres persanes*, Montesquieu turned his back on the king as the basis of political reform and set a new direction for practical political criticism in the eighteenth century."[42] Neither the Platonic dialogue, premised on an understanding of human being that accords primacy to the activity of the mind, nor the Machiavellian mirror of princes, with an audience almost as select, was a suitably public conveyance for Montesquieu's political philosophizing. He fashioned a new form: "*une espèce de roman*" ("Reflections").

Chain Letters

Despite its emphatically popular character, attested by the "prodigious sale" Montesquieu boasts of in the "Reflections," the *Persian Letters* is by no means a simple or transparent work. It is in fact notoriously elusive—"this enchantingly mysterious creation,"[43] in the words of one commentator. The sheer variety of the letters, with respect to both correspondents and topics, is a source of aesthetic pleasure and critical frustration. Even when the import of an individual letter seems straightforward (as in the more boldly satiric letters), the place of that letter in the overall construction is difficult to ascertain.

This impression of brilliant disarray is the natural consequence of Montesquieu's manner of presentation. As he explains in his *Pensées* (no. 802): "In order to write well, it is necessary to skip the intermediary ideas, enough so as not to be boring; not too much, from fear of not being understood. These are the happy suppressions which have caused M. Nicole to say that all good books are double." Even in a work as weighty as *The Spirit of the Laws*, Montesquieu employs the abbreviated, epigrammatic style first displayed in the *Persian Letters*. Witness the famous quip that the book should have been called *De l'Esprit sur lois* (*Wit about the Laws*), rather than *De l'Esprit des lois* (*The Spirit of the Laws*); the pun on the double entendre of *esprit* captures something of the connection between Montesquieu's procedure and his principles. This massive volume is composed of 605 short chapters, some only a sentence or two in length, the majority under a page, with transitions seemingly absent. How to get one's bearings amidst what Montesquieu himself admits to be "the infinite number of things in this book"? Given its multiplicity, there has long been a question about the order of *The Spirit of the Laws*, or rather a conviction of disorder.[44] In the preface to *The Spirit of the Laws*, however, Montesquieu avers a "design." He says further that "[m]any of the truths will make themselves felt here only when one sees the chain connecting them with others." In his *Réponse à des observations de Grosley sur L'Esprit des lois*, Montesquieu sheds additional light on the chain construction: "That which renders certain articles of the book in question obscure and ambiguous, is that they are often separated from others which explain them, and that the links of the chain that you have remarked are very often separated the one from the other" (2:1197). As the chain imagery indicates, the design he speaks of is not a matter of logical hierarchy and categorization, but of complex interrelationships, of links and correspondences (not surprisingly, twenty-two of the thirty-one books of *The Spirit of the Laws* have *rapport* in their titles).

The supplementary preface added to the *Persian Letters* in 1754 (that is, after the publication of *The Spirit of the Laws*) is even more laden with references to chains, links, liaisons, and designs—testimony to a certain similarity of conception between the two works, the youthful *jeu d'esprit* and the masterpiece of Montesquieu's maturity. In attributing the pleasure one takes from the *Persian Letters* to its novelistic unity, Montesquieu says, "One sees in it a beginning, a progress, an end. The diverse personages are placed in a chain which links them." And again, in speaking of the advantage of the novel of letters over "ordinary" novels, he cites the ability to join what would normally be "digressions"—that is, reasonings on philosophy, politics, and morals—to a story, "and to link the whole by a secret and, in some manner, unknown chain." Characters, ideas, and drama are all enchained.[45]

The *Persian Letters* is made up of 161 letters written and received by two Persians—Usbek, the master of a plentiful harem, and Rica, a young unmarried man—who leave Persia together to travel to Paris in search of Western enlightenment. The letters fall of themselves into two broad categories: the Persian and the Parisian. The Parisian letters, accounting for three-quarters of the whole, detail Usbek and Rica's adventures abroad and convey their observations on all facets of French, and more generally European life, from the latest Paris hairstyles to the relations between king and pope. These letters are written to friends in Persia and elsewhere—mostly elsewhere; in fact, half of these Parisian letters are exchanges between Usbek and Rica and their Turkish counterparts, Ibben and Rhédi, whom they meet in Smyrna enroute to Paris. (During the course of the novel, Rhédi will also set out on a voyage of self-instruction, but to republican Italy rather than monarchic France.) The remaining quarter of the letters traces the growing dissatisfaction and disorder in Usbek's seraglio, consequent upon his absence. This correspondence is limited to Usbek, his wives, and the eunuchs, both white and black, who are charged with overseeing the harem.

What I have called a Persian/Parisian division is thus the same division that Montesquieu referred to when he claimed to have mixed *raisonnements* and *roman*. The Persian clutch of letters can be said to constitute the *roman* proper, the drama. It tells a tale of sexual violence, jealousy, and intrigue. Usbek's seraglio is an erotic nightmare; its operation entails the rape of the women, the castration of the men, and the slavery of all save the absent master, Usbek. Despite severe precautions, Usbek's absence leads to sexual revolt of varying degrees, culminating in the seraglio's destruction through murder and suicide. By contrast, the "digressive" Parisian letters, with their freethinking philosophic speculation, political regime analysis, and social commentary on the comedy of French manners and mores, breathe a very different spirit.

There are two different motions or lines of development in the book: the travelers' assimilation to Parisian ways and the doomed attempt to enforce Persian ways in the rebellious harem. In the opening paragraph of the "Reflections," Montesquieu describes the seesaw effect of the voyage: "In proportion as their European stay lengthens, the mores of this part of the world take on in their minds an air less marvelous and bizarre, . . . On the other hand, disorder grows in the Asian seraglio in proportion to the length of Usbek's absence, that is to say, in proportion as frenzy increases and love declines."

Usbek is clearly the fulcrum for both motions. In his very first letter, written to a Persian friend, Usbek claims for himself and Rica the distinction of being the first Persians to leave their country for the sake of philosophy. "We were born," says Usbek, "in a flourishing kingdom, but we did not believe that its boundaries were those of our understanding, nor that the light of the Orient should alone illuminate us." Usbek's second letter, giving orders for the guarding of his wives to his chief black eunuch, includes a command to put to death any man who encounters the women as they journey to the countryside. Enlightenment and cruelty are juxtaposed. Far from abating, this split between Usbek's head and his heart, his wisdom and his women, increases as the novel progresses. Even in remove, he remains a captive of the harem's dynamic. Despite the laments of the wives and eunuchs, even they understand that Usbek, the man for whom this claustral world exists, is the most miserable of human beings. As Zélis, one of his wives, writes to him, "In the very prison in which you hold me, I am more free than you: you can only redouble your efforts to guard me, that I may enjoy your uneasiness; your suspicions, your jealousy, and your vexation are so many marks of your dependence" (#62). In one of his *pensées*, Montesquieu says: "It is not with declamations that despotism needs to be attacked, but by showing that it tyrannizes the despot himself" (no. 1818). This I take to be an apt description of the method of the *Persian Letters*. Despotism is refuted in the person of the despot.

The conflict that Usbek experiences between his Persian patriarchalism and his French enlightenment demonstrates the self-contradiction and impossibility not only of despotism simply, that is, Oriental despotism, but also of the hybrid version, "enlightened despotism," which was beginning, in Montesquieu's time, to find advocates and practitioners in the West. When Montesquieu spoke of a "chain, linking the whole," he chose his metaphor well, for the chain that links the Persian and the Parisian components of the novel, the drama and the digressions, is the chain of despotism. The *Persian Letters* is a thoroughgoing analysis and critique of despotism in all its forms.

Persia, of course, has from ancient times been synonymous with despotic rule. But interestingly, Montesquieu does not examine in any detail the government of the shah of Persia and his viziers; Usbek and his eunuchs stand in their stead, representative of the privatization of politics that despotism entails. In Persia, no real public life exists; there are only households of varying sizes. Politics has been reduced to sexual politics, the politics of the body.

For Montesquieu, as for Aristotle, the Orient is the locus of despotic rule. Occidental governments, however, are not immune to despotic degeneration. As summarized most bluntly by Usbek: "[European monarchy] is a violent state, invariably degenerating into either despotism or a republic" (#102). What seemed to be a Persian/Parisian dichotomy looks more and more like a convergence as the novel progresses. Usbek, for instance, reports that Louis XIV, the king of France, "has often been heard to say that of all the world's governments, that of the Turks, or that of our august sultan, pleased him most. So highly does he esteem Oriental statecraft" (#37). In France, such actions as the withdrawal of the court to Versailles, with its resulting harem-like claustration, and the exiling of the *parlement* of Paris, are symptomatic of a despotic privatization of politics. The caprice of the ruler replaces the rule of law. The debility of the intermediate corporate bodies and the absentee authoritarianism of the king leaves Paris in an odd state of ferment. Paris presents a spectacle analogous in many ways to the erotic escapades of Usbek's wives. It is Rica, not Usbek, who chronicles the formation of this new social world, a world of cafes, of literary politics, a world governed by the insurgent force of public opinion. For the moment, the enterprises of this new world are largely frivolous (the fickle absolutism of fashion), but Montesquieu senses its revolutionary potential. Montesquieu presents a France in which the political garment has been separated from its social lining. Montesquieu's account of the rent between politics and society makes the *Persian Letters* a sort of before-the-fact version of Tocqueville's *The*

Old Regime and the Revolution, but with a practical premonitory intent.

While the harem has its political analogue at Versailles/Paris, its religious analogue is found at Rome. By deploying the naiveté of the Persian visitors, who call the pope a "mufti" and dub the Jesuits "dervishes," Montesquieu is able to indicate the problematic Eastern origin and character of Christianity—problematic because the Christianization of Europe has resulted in a certain Orientalization of Europe. Then by presenting the harem itself as a sexualized version of the kingdom of God—an absent lord who demands obedience and love, his priestly intermediaries (the eunuchs) and a community of devoted (or, as it turns out, not so devoted) women—Montesquieu is able to dramatize the detrimental psychological and political effects of the notion of Christian virtue. The deepest level of Montesquieu's critique of religion in the *Persian Letters* is not directed at rites and ceremonies, or even the temporal power of the Church, but at the claim of miraculous revelation itself—the claim common to the three great revealed religions: Judaism, Christianity, and Islam. Thus, in the very first letter, when Usbek mentions his "devotions at the tomb of the virgin who gave birth to twelve prophets," we understand that Montesquieu is lampooning the Catholic cult of the Virgin Mary and the status of miracles, as much as he is Islamic worship. Both Jean Starobinski and George R. Healy, in their editions of the *Persian Letters*, inform the reader that Montesquieu has confused the venerated virgin Fatima with another Fatima, the wife of Ali and mother of the Alid line.[46] Far from making a mistake as these editors claim, Montesquieu has deliberately confounded the two Fatimas in order to produce a ridiculously exaggerated version of Christian beliefs. The parallels Montesquieu draws between Islam and Christianity may seem initially to play upon the anti-Islamic, parochial prejudices of his audience, but they do so in order to tame prejudice, temper fanaticism, and promote toleration. Just as Montesquieu inaugurates the modern study of comparative government, he discovers the use of comparative religion for the purposes of disenchantment.

There are in the *Persian Letters* essentially three levels of despotism: the sexual despotism of Usbek's harem, the political despotism of Louis XIV's increasingly Orientalized France, and the spiritual despotism of the biblical God and his earthly viziers. Put simply (albeit paronomastically), Montesquieu's overarching purpose in the *Persian Letters* is to disorient—to dis-Orient Christianity, France, and the patriarchal family.

Chapter Two

Montesquieu's Untraditional Despotism

Because the *Persian Letters* is concerned with the articulation of despotic government (and the interrelationship between domestic, religious, and political despotism) more than with its positive alternative, moderate government, it might be described as having a largely "negative" character.[1] However, it is not negative in the sense of being a separate and merely preliminary undertaking; rather the *Persian Letters* is like the film negative from which Montesquieu's masterpiece, *The Spirit of the Laws*, was developed. Indeed, the concept of despotism might be said to hold together Montesquieu's entire corpus. The *Persian Letters*, while treating despotism comprehensively, takes up in particular the question of Christian monarchy's relation to despotism and Montesquieu's doubts of the stability or sufficiency of the monarchical principle. The *Considerations on the Romans* then traces the relation of ancient republicanism and despotism. Like monarchies, republics too (especially those which attain political greatness) are subject to collapse into despotisms. Moreover, the moral greatness of ancient republics bears a certain resemblance to despotism proper, such that we may speak of a despotism of virtue. Accordingly, the movement in *The Spirit of the Laws* is from these three traditional regimes toward a new regime, one devoted explicitly to liberty. In other words, Montesquieu explores the possibility of a regime with a greater resistance to the gravitational pull of despotism. (Tocqueville, in his elaboration and correction of Montesquieu, will look more closely at the dark side of this regime and discover that there is a despotism of liberty as well—what Tocqueville calls "democratic despotism.")

The concept of despotism is central to Montesquieu's political project. Moreover, by means of it, one can locate his achievement vis-à-vis both ancient and modern thinkers. Despite its familiarity to us

19

today, Montesquieu's usage of the term *despotism* was unique and constituted a significant departure from both ancient and early modern
usage. Unlike the ancients, whose search for the best regime was guided by a view of man's natural end; and equally unlike those moderns,
namely Hobbes and Locke, whose elaboration of a universally valid
public law was guided by a view of man's natural beginnings, Montesquieu takes as his starting point the most prevalent political situation:
despotic government. He begins in medias res, amidst human history
and human convention. Perhaps no other thinker has so documented
the ways in which individuals are unfree: under the power of climate
and geography, of passion and prejudice, of custom and law. Montesquieu's sociological inquiry, however, is not undertaken with a view to
establishing determinism. Rather, he seeks room for maneuver within
the conditions of life; he seeks to increase the potential for politics.
In the *Pensées*, Montesquieu offers this startling summation of the
difference between despotic and nondespotic government: "For me, good
laws are like great nets in which fish are caught but believe themselves free, and bad laws are like nets in which the fish are so con-
strained that they sense immediately they have been caught" (no. 1798).
For Montesquieu, liberty is in a very real sense a state of mind, an
opinion of one's security—an opinion fostered by mild laws and unob-
trusive institutions. More than any other thinker, Montesquieu is guided by a negative standard. Liberty itself is understood not as the
opposite of despotism (that is, as the absence of constraint), but rather
as a relaxation of it. The constraints of liberty should be invisible.

Like Machiavelli, Montesquieu could claim to take men as they are.
Montesquieu, however, does not reach Machiavellian conclusions; he
is in fact a most determined opponent of Machiavellian policies and
practices. It is Montesquieu who more than any other thinker is responsible for the onus that now attaches to despotism. Although *despot* and *despotic* were part of the political lexicon of the Greeks, their
meaning was not always pejorative. *Despotēs* was the Greek term for
master and despotic rule proper was that exercised by a master over
his slaves. To the extent that slavery was regarded by the Greeks as
just, despotic rule had its legitimate sphere in the household. It was
only when a ruler sought to treat free men as slaves that *despot* became a term of abuse. Aristotle, for instance, in his categorization of
regimes, refers to all three corrupt regimes as despotic.[2] In general,
however, the ancients spoke much more frequently of tyranny than of
despotism. One of the great achievements of classical political science
was its analysis not simply of the tyrannical regime, but of the tyrannical soul. Although the ancient authors gave memorable accounts of

the methods of tyranny, those accounts were in some sense ancillary to the more fundamental inquiry into the motivations to tyranny. Through such works as Plato's *Republic* and Xenophon's *Hiero*, we come to understand in just what way "tyranny is a danger coeval with political life."[3]

Given the power of ancient analysis of tyranny, perhaps it is not surprising that, of all the Greek words for political things, *tyrant* and its cognates were the only ones to be adopted into Latin. For the duration of Latin's sway, *despot*—that other Greek term of political corruption—languished. It was known of course to those who read Aristotle in the Greek; in Latin and Latin-influenced vernaculars, however, despot was translated into other terms: *dominus, seigneur*, or master.[4]

After this long neglect, it was Thomas Hobbes who reintroduced the original Aristotelian terminology into political discourse.[5] His intentions in writing of "dominion paternal and despotical" were, however, very un-Aristotelian. Just as Machiavelli had dissolved the Aristotelian distinction between kingship and tyranny, Hobbes, as the foremost apologist of absolute sovereignty, redefined *despotic*, attempting to relieve it of any negative connotations. Hobbes's restoration of the term *despotic* was thus accomplished on the ground of a significant moral abdication. According to Hobbes, despotical dominion is founded on the consent of those vanquished by force; and for Hobbes, that extracted consent does not differ from the consent of those who agree together to submit to a sovereign. Both types of consent are prompted by fear—whether it be fear of a conqueror or fear of one another. Hobbes concludes that "the rights and consequences of . . . *despotical* dominion, are the very same with those of a sovereign by institution; and for the same reasons."[6]

Montesquieu was unwilling to follow the Hobbesian progression from the primacy of individual natural right to the doctrine of absolute sovereignty. He expressed his disagreement with the Hobbesian argument throughout his career, from his earliest to his latest writings. Of course, John Locke also departed from Hobbes; but his departures—despite their tremendous practical significance—could be described as on the order of refinements, qualifications, and corrections. For Locke, individuals do not cede to the civil sovereign the full natural power that each person in the state of nature possesses to be his own judge and executioner. Natural right is inalienable. In Locke's view, individuals cannot be said to transfer their natural power to the sovereign; rather, in moving out of the state of nature they create a new kind of power: political power. On the basis of the distinction between natural and political power—the one unlimited, the other limited and divided into executive and legislative—Locke establishes more stringent standards for legitimacy. Unlike Hobbes, he denies the legitimacy of governments founded on conquest and usurpation and, accordingly, allows people recourse to a collective right of revolution against despotic or tyrannical authority. (It is true that Hobbes permits the man on the way to the gallows, whether justly condemned or not, to try to make off or otherwise resist. This may be an exercise of an inalienable right to self-defense, but as to its efficacy, we must judge it "too little, too late.") As a theorist of limited government, Locke took the first steps to make *despotic* once again a term of opprobrium.

Montesquieu's differences with Hobbes are more thoroughgoing than Locke's. Montesquieu rejects both elements of the Hobbesian paradox: the absolute liberty of the individual in the state of nature and the absolute power of the sovereign in the state of civil society. He rejects as well the mediating term between the extremity of liberty and the extremity of power: namely, the social contract. Whereas Locke sought to avoid the despotic Hobbesian outcome while retaining in large measure the Hobbesian account of man's origins, Montesquieu was duly impressed by their inseparability. He accepted the Hobbesian linkage of fear and absolutism. He did not, however, regard fear as the originating passion of all government. For Montesquieu, fear is the spring of one particular form of government: despotism. In effect, Montesquieu turns Hobbes's terminological innovation back upon him. Hobbes had retrieved the adjective *despotic*, thinking to render it value-neutral; but Montesquieu appropriated it, and by capitalizing on its transformation into the noun *despotism*, forged a powerful weapon against absolute monarchy.

Montesquieu was the first political philosopher to embrace the neology *despotism* and to make it central to his thought.[7] Although the Church had been employing the *ism* suffix for some time, producing such words as *paganism, exorcism, Thomism*, and *atheism*, and although both *humanism* and *Machiavellism* existed, there had not as yet been an -ism designating a system of government.[8] *Despotism* was the first. The study of political science today is largely a study of -isms; in the midst of our current welter of -isms, it is worth remembering and reflecting upon the beginnings of this branch of nomenclature in the thought of Montesquieu.

We might wonder, for instance, at the significance of the shift from tyranny to despotism. Why does Montesquieu need a new word? What makes tyranny no longer serviceable? The ancient critique of tyranny was connected to a particular understanding of the human soul according to which the naturally superior element of mind ought to govern spiritedness and desire. The tyrant possesses a soul gone awry, a soul lacking the proper articulation of its elements. His tyranny is but the simulacrum of his disordered soul. Tyranny is then a phenomenon traceable to the individual; it is the structure of the tyrant's soul writ large. Despotism, by contrast, is understood by Montesquieu as systemic or institutional. The despot himself is not the culprit. To put it in terms we are all too familiar with: he is a product of the system. Montesquieu's protagonist Usbek is just such a reluctant despot, a despot not by his own desire or design. Usbek is presented to us as an enlightened and virtuous man whom we nevertheless see authorizing and perpetrating horrible cruelties. We may say that Montesquieu's use of the term *despotism* in preference to *tyranny* acknowledges the ideologization of politics; in other words, Montesquieu finds the source of the political problem not in rulers, but in ruling doctrines. His critique of despotism is able to encompass the doctrines of both Christian divine right and Hobbesian natural right—no small feat, given the virulent anticlericalism and thinly disguised atheism of Hobbes. But Montesquieu saw that the Hobbesian system shares something fundamental with Christian dogma: the principle of fear. In the Christian dispensation, the fear of God is the beginning of all wisdom; in the Hobbesian dispensation, the fear of death is the beginning of all wisdom. Montesquieu implies that for people who have rejected the religious justification of rule, Hobbes's views are a likely and dangerous replacement.[9] (Rousseau, by the way, in his *Social Contract*, showed his understanding of Montesquieu's critique by classing Hobbes among the "Christian authors."[10])

For Montesquieu, the alternative to despotism is not a different -ism; it is moderate government, of which there are many varieties in accordance with the many varieties of the human spirit. Montesquieu, the most nondoctrinaire of thinkers, would not have welcomed our proliferation of -isms. Despotism was his only -ism, the one that should have discredited all others.

Through his concept of despotism, Montesquieu pursues his quarrel with both the ancient and the modern view of rule. The ancients, and Aristotle in particular according to Montesquieu, made the mistake of distinguishing among regimes on the basis of what Montesquieu calls "accidental things, like the virtues or the vices of the prince" (XI.9). The ancients believed, if not in the possibility, then at least in the theoretical desirability of rule by one preeminently virtuous man: Aristotle's *pambasileus*, or king over-all. However, the practical import

of Aristotle's ideal king was a lesson in moderation, not absolutism.
For Aristotle, the politically-available approximation of the all-king's
complete virtue was to be found in the mixed regime, wherein demo-
crats and oligarchs moderate their respective claims to possess the
whole of virtue. By combining the partial virtue of these two groups,
the mixed regime achieves the best available approximation to the rule
of the best man. As so often in ancient thought, contemplation of the
best prepares the way for compromise with the existing.

Machiavelli's revolution, by exploding the distinction between kingship and tyranny, did away with the Aristotelian standard, and thereby
eroded the "ideal" support for political moderation. Modern thought,
from the realism of Machiavelli on, has believed itself more effica-
cious. Indicative of this, one speaks, quite spontaneously, of the modern political "project" and of the various rehabilitations it has undergone
(in a certain sense, modern men all may be said to live, like the res-
idents of Cabrini Green, "in the projects"). Paradoxically perhaps, the
utopian impulse has been given much more scope in modern times than
in antiquity.

Although Montesquieu agrees with Machiavelli in rejecting Aristotle's manner of thinking, he is concerned about the disappearance of
moderation and its replacement by a philosophic incitement to extrem-
ism. In a passage deleted from the final proofs of *The Spirit of the
Laws*, Montesquieu blamed "the delirium of Machiavelli" for having
"given to Princes, in order to maintain their grandeur, principles which
are necessary only under despotic government, and which are unuse-
ful, dangerous, and even impracticable under monarchy." He concludes
that Machiavelli, despite "his great spirit," has "not understood well
the nature and the distinctions" of regimes.[11] Montesquieu does not
endorse the immoderation of the Machiavellian prince; nor does he
endorse either the Hobbesian sovereign or the Lockean executive, both
of which are formalized, legalized, constitutionalized versions of Machiavelli's prince.[12] The routinization of the Machiavellian prince undertaken by Hobbes and Locke is regarded by Montesquieu as an
insufficient response to the danger of Machiavellian immoderation. In-
stitutionalization is not a cure.

Montesquieu's own response is to seek a recovery of moderation
and prudence, albeit on modern grounds, which is to say, not on the
grounds of classical virtue but on the grounds of security and liberty
for the individual. This moderation undoubtedly gives Montesquieu's
political science something of the aspect of Aristotle's. It possesses an
equivalent breadth and flexibility. However, we ought not to forget that

whereas Aristotle's moderation is supported from above, by a conception of human virtue, Montesquieu's moderation is supported from below, by a conception of elemental human needs and passions.

Contra Hobbes

Having seen something of the unique form and content of the *Persian Letters*—its unusual epistolary style and untraditional notion of despotism—we can begin to explore the particular understanding of the passions that accounts for that uniqueness.

Classic liberalism begins from an insight into man's asocial concern for self-preservation in the face of other men's animosity and nature's stinginess. Hobbes places more stress on the former, Locke on the latter. But whether it is the fear of violent death, or the problem of scarcity that is primary, Hobbes and Locke are alike in presenting a fundamentally optimistic rendering of the human situation. For despite the fact that "nature should thus dissociate, and render men apt to invade, and destroy one another,"[13] the art and artifice of man can supply the defect. Man can bring together, or convene, what nature fails to; convention can remedy the inconvenience of nature. According to the guns and butter diagnosis, the human problem is soluble. The Leviathan neutralizes strife among men; and once the world has been made safe for the industrious, the bare endowment of nature can be rendered productive.

For Hobbes, the movement from the state of nature to the state of civil society depends on the ascendancy of man's most powerful (and most rational) passion—the fear of violent death, which inclines men toward peace—over the welter of desires and appetites which leads to vain contentiousness. Natural law is derivative from passion, but not from all passion indiscriminately. In keeping with his conviction of man's solitary life in the state of nature, Hobbes does not accord any socializing significance to sexual passion. Even the existence of the family does not really mitigate the essential character of the state of nature. According to Hobbes, "For the savage people in many places of America, except the government of small families, the concord whereof dependeth on natural lust, have no government at all; and live at this day in that brutish manner, as I said before."[14]

Montesquieu is generally reticent about the state of nature; however, in the opening book of *The Spirit of the Laws*, he does take one chapter to consider the human constitution "before the establishment of societies." Montesquieu there criticizes Hobbes by name:[15]

Hobbes asks, "If men are not naturally in a state of war, why do they always carry arms and why do they have keys to lock their doors?" But one feels that what can happen to men only after the establishment of societies, which induced them to find motives for attacking others and for defending themselves, is attributed to them before that establishment. (I.2)

In propounding his new conception of natural law, Hobbes mistakes nurture for nature. Just as primitive man, concerned with self-preservation, would be incapable, according to Montesquieu, of speculative ideas (like the idea of a creator), so too "the idea of empire and domination" would be beyond him. By discounting first the traditional Christian natural law teaching and, in the next breath, the Hobbesian teaching, Montesquieu indicates that Hobbes shares with his Aristotelian and Christian opponents a certain overestimation of human capacities.[16] Contrary to the assertion of Hobbes, prepolitical men are not bellicose and prideful: they are weak and fearful and timid. "Everything makes them tremble, everything makes them flee." Peace is indeed the first law of nature, but not in the Hobbesian sense of a dictate of reason. Rather, peace is the immediate consequence of subrational sentiment; peace is not a desideratum, something that must be sought and followed, but simply a fact of the solitary, uncivilized life.

According to Montesquieu, however, the pattern of mutual flight is temporary. Men have other, potentially more unifying, inclinations. Hunger inspires men to seek nourishment. Although Montesquieu does not say so, obedience to this second natural law may, in an incidental way, bring men into contact with one another. It is possible to imagine this contact as peaceful, even cooperative. Montesquieu does say that men's very timidity conduces in the end to acquaintance. Although fear initially keeps men separated, the perception of reciprocal fear is an assurance of safety and encourages approach. Montesquieu's third natural law concerns sociability directly. Montesquieu discerns a force in our nature that considerably mitigates the radical isolation and individualism of the state of nature. Like other species, human beings feel the pull of animal attraction; they take pleasure in others of their kind and are especially charmed by those of the opposite sex: "The natural entreaty [*prière naturelle*] they always make to one another would be a third law" (I.2). In other words, the prayers of natural man are directed not to God but to natural woman. In addition to fellow feeling and sexual passion, Montesquieu describes the emergence of a fourth natural law: the desire to live in society—a desire motivated by the specifically human bond of acquired knowledge.

According to the Thomistic understanding, the natural law prescribing man's duties draws upon three natural inclinations: self-preservation, sociality, and knowledge. Hobbes dispenses with the latter two, restricting natural law to a deduction from the right of self-preservation. Montesquieu, it seems, preserves all three, albeit in drastically altered form. His mention of natural incentives to association should not be taken as a pious harking back to an earlier tradition of natural sociability. According to Montesquieu, our sociability is in large part animal—gregarious and carnal—not political, as the ancients would have it. And while Montesquieu's laconic presentation leaves it unclear just what he means by knowledge serving as a "new motive for uniting," it is clear from his earlier remarks that the knowledge of God—the keystone of Thomistic natural law—is not meant. Montesquieu folds knowledge into a discussion of sociality; he does not consider it as an inclination to transcendence.

Although sexual and social alliances take shape naturally, those very alliances serve to divide as well as unite men. Men join themselves not to some universal society, but to societies—particular and plural. As soon as men are allied in this way to others, "they lose their feeling of weakness; the equality that was among them ceases, and the state of war begins" (I.3)—war between nations and between individuals within nations. Thereafter, "these two sorts of states of war bring about the establishment of laws among men." In Hobbes, the movement is from individual, anarchic natural right to universal natural law; in Montesquieu it is from universal natural law to the multiple forms of positive right: the right of nations, political right, and civil right. These contain, so to speak, the disciplines of war, the rules of men's engagement with one another. On Montesquieu's explanation, the state of war is the product of society, not the condition of nature; it is born of developed inequalities, rather than original equality. Thus, it seems that Montesquieu's correction of radical individualism, which had looked so favorable to the social virtues, may chasten our expectations of community as much as embolden them. Man's bodily desires and intellectual capacities drive him into human connectedness, but it may well be that those very desires and capacities are incapable of fulfillment within or any easy reconciliation with a social, political, or familial order. Montesquieu suggests the ambiguous character of an instinctual sociability rooted in drives and desires rather than reasoned consent. Human sexuality and human knowledge (libido and *libido sciendi*) are soon transformed into the desire for distinction and domination—*amour-propre* to use the familiar language of Rousseau. (Indeed, Rousseau's debt to Montesquieu for the outline of his conjectural account of humanity's prehistory, the *Discourse on the Origin and Foundations of Inequality among Men*, should be obvious.)

Whereas Hobbes sees men, or would like to see men, moving from vanity to fear, Montesquieu describes the reverse movement, from fear to vanity. For both thinkers, these primary passions have great political significance; they are in fact correlated to specific regimes. The public life of a democratic or aristocratic citizenry elevates considerations of honor and reputation over mere life. Thus, according to Hobbes, republics are like hothouses for the noxious growth of vainglory. In monarchies, on the other hand, salutary fear retains its prominence, both for the sovereign, aware of his solitary position, and for his subjects. By Hobbes's account, monarchy preserves the sense of exposedness necessary to real security.[17]

The correlations set forth in Montesquieu's politics of passion are more complex, for Montesquieu divides rule by one into two distinct forms of government: monarchy and despotism. According to Montesquieu, fear is the principle, the psychic animus, of despotism. "As the principle of despotic government is fear, its end is tranquillity; but this is not a peace, it is the silence of the towns that the enemy is ready to occupy" (V.14). Montesquieu is not impressed by the supposed political beneficence of fear. Montesquieu prefers a regime with spirit. For him, a monarch governs by fundamental laws rather than by his will alone, which is to say that monarchy depends on the existence of intermediate powers (as for instance, the nobility, the clergy, and municipalities), with prerogatives and rights of their own. Honor, or "the prejudice of each person and each condition" (III.6), is the soul of monarchy. Montesquieu admits that "philosophically speaking," monarchic honor is "false" (III.7)—a delusive refinement upon self-preference. As such, honor is susceptible of various incarnations and, as we shall see later, Montesquieu speaks more favorably of some national codes of honor than others (preferring, for instance, the French to the Spanish, and it seems the English to the French). But in general, Montesquieu speaks well of the political effects of the striving for rank and preferment in monarchies:

> You could say that it is like the system of the universe, where there is a force constantly repelling all bodies from the center and a force of gravitation attracting them to it. Honor makes all the parts of the body politic move; its very action binds them, and each person works for the common good, believing he works for his individual interests. (III.7)

These thoughts on the differing passional springs of despotism and monarchy, which appear in *The Spirit of the Laws* with Montesquieu's characteristic compression and economy of thought, receive their preliminary, and in many respects, fuller and more profound elaboration in the *Persian Letters*. Just as the harem sequence of letters is an investigation and tragic dramatization of what it means for fear to be the predominant passion of life, so the French letters, or more accurately, that subset of letters that treat of social life, provide an analysis of honor, the predominant passion of monarchical subjects. This understanding of Montesquieu's intention would, I believe, account for the odd double character, both satiric and appreciative, of the observations made about French social life. On the one hand, Montesquieu does not spare the French. Honor is shown to be a fundamentally artificial or theatrical passion. Moreover, when kept from its proper political exercise, honor is susceptible of degeneration into the most anserous forms of personal vanity. On the other hand, through its role in producing civility, politeness, and taste, honor is instrumental in creating and protecting a preserve of personal freedom (what Montesquieu calls the "liberty of the subject"). At its best, honor can work to secure political freedom also ("the liberty of the constitution")—though it must be said that the fate of the *parlements*, which Montesquieu discusses in two very importantly placed letters (#92 and #140), does not augur well for the political efficacy of honor in absolutist France.

Sons and Lovers

Unlike *The Spirit of the Laws*, the *Persian Letters* contains no direct mention of Hobbes. Nonetheless, there are two places in which state-of-nature theorizing is touched upon (#94 and #11-14). Analysis of these letters (and those immediately adjacent to them) reveals Montesquieu's complicated take on the question of human sociability, and offers, as well, a good portal to the work as a whole.

In #94, prior to criticizing the prevailing *realpolitik* conception of public or international law, Usbek mocks inquiries into society's beginnings:

> I have never heard a discussion of public law which was not preceded by a careful inquiry into the origin of societies. This appears absurd to me. If men did not form into society, if they avoided and fled from one another, then it would be necessary to find the reason why they kept apart. But they are all born linked to one another. The son comes into the world beside his father and stays there: here is society and the cause of society.

The differences between this passage and that of *The Spirit of the Laws* (I.2) are instructive. Usbek asserts the naturalness of patrilineal society. When speaking in his own name, Montesquieu made no such statement. He offered, in very brief compass and preliminary to his investigation of positive law, an anticontractualist account of the evolution or derivation of society. Society was shown to be natural in the sense of being the outcome of certain natural mechanisms and impulses, prime among them the operation of sexual passion. Montesquieu said nothing, however, as to the form of these early associations: fleeting or permanent, monogamous or polygamous, patriarchal, matriarchal, or fatherless (i.e., mother alone with children).

Usbek's version of the familial origin of society does echo a passage from Montesquieu's *Pensées* (no. 615).[18] There, after savaging Spinoza, Montesquieu launches into Hobbes, a philosopher "much less *outré* and, as a result, much more dangerous" than Spinoza:

> Hobbes says that, natural right being only the liberty that we have of doing whatever conduces to our conservation, the natural state of man is a war of all against all. But, beyond the fact that it is false that defense must entail the necessity of attack, it is not necessary to suppose men, as he does, fallen from heaven or sprung fully armed from the earth, almost like the soldiers of Cadmus, for the sake of destroying one another: this is not the state of men.
>
> The first and only would fear no one. This man alone, who would come upon a woman alone also, would not make war on her. All the others would be born into a family, and soon into a society. There is no war here; to the contrary, love, education, respect, recognition: each breathes peace.

Montesquieu's account, although reminiscent of Usbek's, begins from the conjugal rather than the paternal relation; he stresses mutuality rather than obedience. Moreover, in the remainder of the passage, Montesquieu grants Hobbes's starting point, but argues that Hobbes's reasoning from that premise is incorrect:

> It is not even true that two men fallen from the clouds into a wilderness, would seek, out of fear, to attack and subjugate one another. A hundred circumstances, joined to the particular nature of each man, would enable them to act otherwise. The air, the gesture, the bearing, the particular manner of thinking would make for some differences. First, fear would lead them, not to attack, but to flee. The marks of mutual fear would soon lead them to approach. The boredom of being alone and the pleasure that every animal feels at the approach of another animal of the same species would lead them to unite, and the more they were miserable, the more they would be determined toward it. Up to this point

one sees no aversion. It would be with them as with other animals, who make war on those of their species only in particular cases, although they are found everywhere in the forests, almost like Hobbes' men. The first sentiments would be for the true needs that one would have, and not for the commodities of domination. It is only when Society is formed, that individuals—in abundance and peace, having at every instant occasion of sensing the superiority of their spirit or their talents—seek to turn to their favor the principal advantages of this society. Hobbes wants to cause to be done among men what lions themselves do not do. It is only by the establishment of societies that they abuse one another and become the most powerful; before that, they are all equal. (no. 615)

This portion of the refutation of Hobbes was, as Montesquieu indicates in a margin note, "placed in large part in *The Spirit of the Laws*" (I.2, discussed above). The more harmonious, monogamous account of the first man and woman was dropped.

In judging Usbek's pronouncements, and particularly those on the family, we must not lose sight of Usbek's domestic situation. Montesquieu admonishes the reader against such forgetfulness by juxtaposing to these two letters on public law (#94-95) a letter detailing the method by which a harem, including Usbek's own, is formed (#96). The first eunuch writes Usbek boasting of his procurement of a new wife—part of a shipment of women just arrived from Visapour, a once-independent kingdom conquered in 1686 by the Grand Mogol Aureng Zeb. Although this wife was bought for Usbek's brother, a provincial governor, the first eunuch promises to do as well by Usbek. After Usbek has just stated in the previous letter that "[c]onquest in itself does not establish right" and moreover, "if the people are destroyed or dispersed, it is the monument of a tyranny," we learn that Usbek acquires his wives via conquest and the international slave trade. In his ridicule of state-of-nature reasoning in #94, Usbek spoke of sons being born near to their fathers; however, he was silent as to how men secure women to bear them sons. The sequel (#96) reveals his own and his brother's method: rape or, in its institutional form, domestic slavery. The context shows this to be one of the most elemental and pervasive violations of both natural law (the law of "natural entreaty" between the sexes) and public law (the principles of just war).

Interestingly, the letter on the other flank of #94 is written by Usbek to a different brother, a monk at the Casbin monastery. Other than these two letters (#93 and #96) surrounding Usbek's declaration of father/son solidarity as the definition and cause of society, the novel contains no other mention of Usbek's male relatives. Letter #93 describes the anchorites, both Moslem and Christian, who hid themselves in the desert to pray: "Ten entire years sometimes passed without their seeing a single man." So apparently there have been men—indeed, men honored above others—who avoided and fled human contact. They were not entirely alone however: "day and night they lived with demons and were ceaselessly tormented by malignant spirits who sought them out in bed and at table; no asylum from them was possible." As Usbek wryly observes, "If all this is true, venerable santon, it must be admitted that no one ever lived in worse company." Eremitism just lands you in bed with a host of incubi and succubi. Despite his fulsome praise of his brother ("I humble and prostrate myself before you, holy santon"), Usbek manages to convey his criticism of monasticism. For instance, he presents the conclusions of "sensible Christians," who look on the lives of the saints as allegories about the ineradicability of the passions. "In vain do we seek tranquillity in the desert." Moreover, it turns out that, even in the desert, the early hermits did not live completely alone with their visions and phantoms. Usbek says "they took refuge by the thousands in the fearful Theban deserts and had for chiefs Paul, Anthony, and Pachomius." In other words, these hermits formed themselves into communities. Even those who regarded the passions as evil could not suppress the urge for a common life. Pachomius, the last named, organized a cenobitic community (the very word "cenobitic" means common life, from the Greek *koinos-bios*) and wrote a very influential monastic rule. Monasticism represents a profound recasting of the desire to live in society.

Usbek's confidence in an unproblematic natural sociality based on the patriarchal family, as expressed in #94, is qualified by Montesquieu through the information about Usbek's brothers in the neighboring letters. Usbek's brothers, one a monk, one a despot, present the extremes of enforced sexual abstinence (the denial of the natural law of entreaty) and forceful sexual indulgence (the violation of the same law). The social life of one is founded on celibacy, that of the other on rape. We might conclude that these social orders not begun by proper sexual coupling have some connection to the theory of society expressed by Usbek. With his inattention to the role of women as partners and mothers, Usbek made society a matter of intergenerational male bonding. The monastery and the harem are embodiments of that neglect.

Usbek's scorn for speculative reconstructions of man's original condition also manifests itself in his history of the Troglodytes (#11-14). In place of "subtle philosophizing," Usbek prefers to present this "morsel of history," the first installment of which (#11) reads like a parody of the Hobbesian state of nature. Although they were the descendants of ancient cave dwellers who "more resembled beasts than men," the Troglodytes themselves, Usbek says, "were not that deformed; they were not shaggy like bears, nor did they hiss, and they had two eyes. However, they were so wretched and ferocious that there was no principle of equity or justice among them." Usbek's history of this Arabian tribe is a fable-like demonstration that men constituted along Hobbesian lines could not construct the great Leviathan, but could only destroy themselves. The Troglodytes are ungovernable. In a reversal of the Hobbesian progression, the Troglodytes move from kingship to anarchy—not just ordinary anarchy, but contractually based asocial anarchy. After murdering a succession of their rulers, from a foreign king to freely elected magistrates, the Troglodytes agree among themselves to obey no one; each will attend to his own interests, without consulting the interests of others. The Troglodytes consent not to associate, but to dissociate.

The self-destructive results of this radical individualism are spelled out in a series of vignettes. The denial of mutual dependence leads quickly to famine, as the Troglodytes are unable to survive agricultural failure or to operate, or better, co-operate, a market. The insecurity of all holdings, whether women or land, unleashes a destructive cycle of desire, usurpation, and revenge. Production of any kind is impossible. All those Troglodytes who lack *humanité* eventually perish—"victims of their own injustice," Usbek concludes.

As the sequel (#12-14) reveals, only two men remained. These two "singular" men possessed of humanity, justice, and virtue are linked to one another by the pity they feel at the surrounding desolation. Pity is "the motive of a new union." In #12, Usbek outlines the idyllic life that flows from this alternative germ of society: loving marriages, the education of the young in virtue (an education based on the negative example of the lost Troglodytes), the advent of natural religion among them, and the practice of communism (shared meals and commingled flocks). In #13, Usbek presents a new sampling of anecdotes, parallel to those of #11, illustrative of the unfailing thoughtfulness of the Troglodytes toward others, from family members to the gods, extending even to criminals and strangers.

Despite an impression of pastoral insipidity, there are a number of interesting features in Usbek's description. We note the singularity of the new nation's beginnings—a fact that suggests that the history of the Troglodytes is not paradigmatic. It is not, for instance, intended as a demonstration of man's natural goodness in the state of nature. While the virtue of the founders may have been exceptional and unexpected, the virtue of their offspring is not; it is laboriously instilled. Usbek indicates that the image of the first Troglodytes' misery is kept constantly before them. Although Usbek does not spell out the principles of this education, we may see that it depends on the evocation of a sympathy grounded in superiority. By keeping uppermost in their minds a comparison to other men favorable to themselves, the Troglodytes are kept both self-contented and tender toward others. Envy and other hostile passions have slim purchase upon hearts given up to the action of pity. However, despite its adept tutoring of sentiment, this education is not always successful; there are, for instance, thieves among the Troglodytes (although to judge by one of the anecdotes, no recourse in law is taken against them). There are other hints that self-interest is not completely subsumed into the common interest. Thinking of themselves as one family, the Troglodytes kept their flocks "almost" always commingled and "ordinarily" spared themselves the trouble of separating them.

Knowledge of the gods is a late development among the Troglodytes—the ratification of their happiness rather than its source. However, once introduced to fear of the gods, the Troglodytes believe in "[the gods'] inevitable anger toward those who do not fear them," regardless of the fact that their own virtuous forebears did not fear and the earth nonetheless "seemed to fructify of itself" for them. When the subject is first mentioned, religion is credited with softening Troglodyte mores, left rude by nature. Yet, in the immediately succeeding description of their religious celebrations, which seem largely to be occasions for the chaperoned courtship of the young people, Usbek says that "it was in these assemblies that naive Nature spoke." In the same letter (#13), after recounting their daily invocation of "the grandeur of the gods, their unfailing aid to men who implored it," Usbek sums up their happy existence by saying that "Nature supplied their desires as well as their needs." This repeated alternation of gods and nature, or more accurately this substitution of natural explanation for divine, suggests Usbek's (and/or Montesquieu's) correction of the Troglodyte self-understanding.[19]

The halcyon days do not last. The Troglodytes are the envy of neighboring peoples who, moreover, regard them as easy prey because of their generosity and innocence. Despite their conciliatory diplomacy, war is forced upon them. They fight successfully in self-defense, not least because "a new ardor took hold of their heart." This new ardor finds its inspiration beyond the common cause; each Troglodyte, we learn, has particular reasons for fighting and, before too long, particular deaths to avenge.

The final letter of the series (#14) has them choosing a king. The

Troglodytes felt it was appropriate to abandon their leaderless state since "the People were growing greater every day." However, it is questionable whether size is a sufficient explanation for the turn to monarchy. Earlier it had been said that numbers had no effect on the bond of union; "virtue, far from dispersing in the crowd, was instead strengthened by a very great number of examples" (#12). Perhaps the people are now swelling not so much in number as in reputation and ambition. The man whom they select to be the new king, the most just among them, laments their choice. He claims the Troglodytes have indeed tired of their virtue and that under a prince they will indulge in ambition, wealth, and pleasures.

Usbek does not explicitly link the Troglodytes' experience of war and their desire for a king. In fact, by concluding one letter with the Troglodyte victory and reserving their election of a king to the next, he seems to sever any connection. But as always in the *Persian Letters*, we must be attentive to juxtapositions sharpened by suppressed transitions. We might speculate that war has eroded the pity that served to unite the Troglodytes. While the image of the ancient, wicked Troglodytes cemented their virtue, an encounter with the real thing—men whose injustice astonishes them—undermines their virtue. In vowing to treat their enemies as wild beasts, the Troglodytes reveal themselves to have lost their sense of common humanity. Universal pity is no match against the martial spirit and, particularly, the desire for revenge. By heightening the prospect of individual suffering and individual glory, war also threatens to introduce inequality among the Troglodytes. It is not that the Troglodytes become selfish, say, by refusing to hazard their lives for others; quite the reverse, they sacrifice themselves readily, but for private reasons. Once the distinction between private causes and the common cause makes itself felt, it can act as a wedge further forcing them apart.

Along with a connection between foreign war and monarchy, Usbek's account suggests (albeit equivocally) some relation between monotheism and monarchy. The Troglodyte chosen to be the first king swears by God and indicates his belief in an afterlife. His monotheism seems to be exceptional; the speech of the Troglodyte ambassadors on the eve of the war indicates that, at that time, the Troglodytes were still polytheists. The king is exceptional also in his justice, and in his reluctance to see monarchy instituted. His decidedly antimonarchic speech, reproving the Troglodytes for their wish to adopt "a yoke other than that of virtue," would seem to debunk the notion that there is any natural connection between belief in one God and rule by one on earth. Interestingly, this first monotheist among the Troglodytes is the first to admit that virtue is difficult. The education of the Troglodytes was initially described as instilling the feeling that "virtue is not something which ought to cost us; and it is not necessary to regard it as a painful exercise" (#12). The lesson of the first monotheist, who "inveighs in a stern voice," is just the reverse. The first monotheist may be averse to the establishment of kingship, but in a deeper sense, the details of the Troglodyte history show a connection between monotheism and monarchy; the advent of both divine and human law is symptomatic of decline from the easy virtue of old. Monotheism and monarchy are distinct responses to the problem of virtue that the popular will insists on amalgamating.

Although the history of the Troglodytes is presented by Usbek in illustration of his view that "men were born to be virtuous," the history's final installment introduces the thought that virtue can be effectually dispensed with under monarchy. Betraying some bitterness, the new king acknowledges that political institutions allow for a relaxation of the moral demands on men: "You know that, so long as you avoid falling into great crimes, you will not need virtue." Usbek concludes his history of the Troglodytes with the king's lamentation for virtue; and by doing so, Usbek implies that he bemoans this political/moral divide as much as the king does.

However, it is by no means certain that Montesquieu sheds a tear with them. Commentators have tended to take Usbek as a mouthpiece for Montesquieu,[20] particularly when it comes to the serialized letters, of which the Troglodyte set is the first.[21] Some attention to the dramatic setting would reveal more interesting possibilities. Usbek writes his history of the Troglodytes in response to a query from Mirza, a Persian associate who has renounced orthodox religious belief, but who finds his own reason insufficient and therefore seeks instruction from Usbek. To judge by Mirza's letter, Usbek had apparently been the central figure of a sort of Persian salon or academy (Mirza remembers him as "the soul of our Society"). In order to decide the question now before the group—whether it is virtue or sensual pleasure that makes for happiness—Mirza asks Usbek to explain his oft-expressed view that virtue is integral to existence. The caption of Mirza's letter reads "Mirza to his friend Usbek, at Erzeron."[22] Usbek's reply is captioned simply "Usbek to Mirza, at Ispahan." In Usbek's first letters to both Rustan and Nessir (#1, 6, 8), the designation "his friend" was used. Its absence here suggests some disproportion in the relationship. Although Usbek professes himself flattered by Mirza's friendship and good opinion, he does not say that the feeling is reciprocated. Indeed, he refers to his response not as an act of friendship but as a performance that has been prescribed. (Mirza's name means "son of a prince"—an etymology not unknown to Montesquieu, one imagines.)

The setting for the Troglodyte letters seems almost Socratic: a man whose reputation for wisdom makes him a sought after and occasionally (as in the *Republic*) a prevailed-upon interlocutor. Taken together, the intellectual difference between Mirza and Usbek, the compulsory character of the discourse, and Usbek's choice of myth over argument raise the possibility that the story of the Troglodytes is intended by Usbek as an exoteric teaching. In other words, there may be some ironic distance between Usbek's full views and those he expresses here. Pauline Kra has shown the extent to which the Troglodyte letters might be read as a naturalized account of biblical history.[23] Such an account would be suitable for a man like Mirza who has expressed religious doubts, but who clearly remains pious with respect to country and family, a patriot and a patriarch. There is no letter in reply from Mirza; whether that is indicative of Mirza's complete satisfaction would be difficult to say.

Even if we determine that Usbek has not deliberately sophisticated his speech, Montesquieu has surely done it for him. Among the second race of Troglodytes, the conflict between the pleasant and the good seemed to be obviated, for a time at least. However, we have already noted some of the complexities and difficulties of the Troglodyte history. Whether Usbek is aware of them is unclear, but Usbek's creator could not be ignorant of them.

This preliminary exposition of Usbek's views on the relation of the passions and virtue is subject to both an internal commentary—that buried in the details of the history—and, more significantly, an external commentary—that provided by the surrounding letters. Usbek's concern for virtue and its imperiled state had already been made very evident, both in the letter to the chief black eunuch charging him with the wives' virtue (#2) and in the letter to Rustan detailing Usbek's uncompromising devotion to virtue while in the service of the shah (#8). Usbek's gloom at the Troglodytes' eventual desire to become like all the nations, with a king over them, would seem to be justified by his experience as a courtier; Usbek's "grand design"—daring to be virtuous even at court—earned him ministerial enmity without securing princely favor. The sincere voice of virtue disconcerted both idol and idolaters. Whereas the first letter to Rustan (#1) had blazoned Usbek's voyage as a quest for wisdom (*sagesse*), this second letter to his friend (#8) lays bare "the true motive" of his travels: under threat by the flatterers whom he had exposed, Usbek flees Persia out of care for his life. It is sagacious self-preservation that determines his self-exile, rather than desire to be a sage. Usbek admits that he feigned an interest in science in order to facilitate his escape. Confronted with the feebleness of moral virtue, but unwilling to make any accommodation to the ways of the world, Usbek took refuge in intellectual virtue. He claims, however, that what began as protective coloration became intrinsic.

As the letters proceed, we will be able to judge the extent to which Usbek's enlightenment is genuine and the extent to which it remains a blind, a place from which he views the world, but in which he lies concealed, undisclosed to himself as well as others. While his dedication to the life of inquiry is yet unproved, we know from letter #8 that Usbek's turn to inquiry is the result of the incompatibility he experienced between his intransigent virtue and Persian rule.

Although Usbek seems so pessimistic about virtue's chances, Montesquieu has him sketching the outlines of a virtuous monarchy in an unpublished continuation of the Troglodyte chronicle.[24] In this sequel, the Troglodytes are once again in the midst of a societal debate. Within a generation of their decision to establish monarchy, they are considering the idea of establishing commerce and the arts. Both king and people believe they can meet the threat to virtue posed by this further sophistication of their way of life. According to the people's spokesman, the Troglodytes' immunity to the blandishments of wealth and luxury will depend on the king's example. The king, in turn, hinges his virtue on the incorruptibility of the people. Thus, the hope for a virtuous monarchy rests on the reciprocal virtue of king and people. It seems a very delicate foundation, inasmuch as a misstep by either side would initiate a downward spiral. In place of the countervailing influences and powers that maintain equilibrium in a Montesquieu-styled monarchy, the Troglodyte version prescribes mutual dependence and mutual exhortation.

Given what we have seen of Usbek's longing for virtue, as well as his belief that virtue's natural locus is in the family, we might expect Usbek's homelife to be a showcase for his views, with his domestic arrangements on the Troglodyte model: "They loved their wives, and were beloved by them. Their entire attention was directed toward educating their children to virtue" (#12). However, instead of tender and virtuous natural relations, we encounter the institution of the harem, wherein we see immediately and most starkly the results of an attempt to realize virtue in the face of nature's opposition. Six of the novel's first nine letters, prior to the Troglodyte series, deal with the harem. By presenting the different perspectives of the parties involved, Montesquieu creates a three-dimensional view of the harem: Usbek writes to the chief eunuch (#2) and to a friend (#5) about his wives; three of the wives write to Usbek (#3, 4, 7); and the chief eunuch writes to a fellow eunuch who has accompanied Usbek on his travels (#9). Moreover, the letter that follows the Troglodyte series is also from the chief eunuch to one of his subordinates (#15). Of the 161 letters constituting the novel, there are only four that do not involve either of the two main characters, Usbek and Rica, as author or recipient. All are written by eunuchs to other eunuchs.[25] Two of these unusual letters—elaborating the plight of men separated from nature and from themselves—appear here, as the frame for the Troglodyte episode. Usbek has sacrificed these men on the altar of virtue. In the harem, moral virtue has been reduced to a species of physical (and specifically "gendered") virtue: namely, female virtue understood as sexual modesty, either virginity or fidelity. Claustration and castration are the sex-specific means of securing that virtue. Set within the context of the surrounding letters, the Troglodyte utopia begins to appear as the Potemkin village for Usbek's dystopia.

Before beginning the real tour, behind the walls of the seraglio, let us return for a moment to Hobbes. He too conducted a critique of virtue, directing himself against the male virtue of courage or the manly disposition of one's body with respect to death. By contrast, Montesquieu's critique of virtue focuses on female rather than male virtue, continence—or the disposition of the body with respect to pleasure—rather than courage. For Montesquieu, the passion for life is positive and linked to sexuality, rather than negative and linked to the fear of death. Montesquieu turns individuals away from such life-denying ethics as ancient manliness and Christian martyrdom, but not, like Hobbes, by directly advocating cowardice. An at least residual admiration for human high-heartedness may be quite indispensable to political life.

Chapter Three

Venus in
the Cloister[1]

Let us assume for a moment that the fickleness of spirit and indiscretions of our [French] women, what pleases and displeases them, their passions, both great and small, were transferred to an Eastern government along with the activity and liberty they have among us: what father of a family could be tranquil for a moment? Suspects everywhere, enemies everywhere; the state would be shaken, one would see rivers of blood flowing. (XVI.9)

The East–West exchange that Montesquieu here assumes only for a moment had, a quarter of a century earlier, formed the working assumption of the *Persian Letters*. Although usually described as the story of two Persian travelers in Europe, in fact the novel is characterized by a double transference: while the Persian men, Usbek and Rica, journey to Paris in search of Western enlightenment, the Persian women, in their absence, acquire Parisian ways, tutored only by their passions. It is the distaff revolution that provides the novel's climax and that Montesquieu seems to allude to in this chapter of *The Spirit of the Laws*, appropriately titled "Liaison between domestic government and politics." The link between the condition of women and political freedom or unfreedom is examined throughout the *Persian Letters*, but particularly in the harem sequence, which frames the work (#1–9 and #147–61).

Fully forty percent of the 161 letters that constitute the *Persian Letters* concern the behavior or treatment of women: sixteen letters are exchanged between Usbek and his wives (Zachi, Zéphis, Zélis, Fatmé, and Roxane); seventeen letters are exchanged between Usbek and the eunuchs who guard the wives; and another thirty-four letters discuss women other than Usbek's wives. Many of these discuss French women, their relative freedom, their vanity, their influence on all aspects of French life, and their legal status; some discuss women in other regimes, from despotic Russia to republican Venice; and there are two very significant letters that recount tales of sexual paradise gained— one tells of the utopia brought into being by a philosopher-queen, the other recounts the travails and eventual happiness of an incestuous love match.[2] More significant than the sheer number and variety of letters devoted to consideration of "the woman question" is the character of the novel's conclusion. It ends with the adulterous betrayal of Usbek by Roxane, his favorite wife and the only one he had never suspected of infidelity. After her lover is detected and killed, she takes the life of her guards and then her own. The novel's final letter reads like a manifesto of sexual revolution. Roxane writes Usbek:

> How could you have imagined me credulous enough to believe that I existed only to adore your caprices, that in permitting yourself every- thing, you had the right to thwart my every desire? No! I have lived in slavery, but I have always been free. I reformed your laws by those of Nature, and my spirit has always held to its independence. (#161)

Montesquieu is, I believe, the first political philosopher to accord such prominence to women. Of course, profound reflections on the question of the relation of the sexes and the role of the family in the polity can be found in the writings of earlier political philosophers. In the *Republic*, Plato famously provides both for the sex-neutral educa- tion of the guardian class and for state-administered sexual commu- nism. Xenophon addresses the vexed question of how to handle a wife in the *Oeconomicus*. In opposition to the Platonic/Xenophontic reduc- tion of politics to home economics, Aristotle carefully distinguishes household management from political rule. Among the moderns, Ma- chiavelli offers instruction in mastering the lady Fortuna, while Hobbes and Locke acknowledge the equality of individuals in the state of na- ture and thereby call into question the naturalness and legitimacy of paternal rule. In the *Persian Letters*, Montesquieu shifts the focus of the liberal critique of patriarchy from paternal to conjugal relations. He is the first to use the conjugal relation as the vehicle of his phi- losophizing and to give the final word to a female *porte-parole*.

Perhaps the only comparable conjunction of women and wisdom in the history of political philosophy is when Socrates lays claim in the *Symposium* to the knowledge of erotica, a knowledge he credits a woman, Diotima, with imparting to him. Since elsewhere he consis- tently claims to possess no knowledge other than the knowledge of his ignorance, one can only surmise that the knowledge of his ignorance and the knowledge of erotic matters are identical. Eros is longing, the longing to overcome human incompleteness (sexual passion is only one manifestation of eros). Socrates' knowledge of erotica, like his knowledge of his ignorance, is the philosophic awareness of human incompleteness and the limitations upon human striving. For Socrates that is a feminine insight, a feminine wisdom—hence his frequent identification of himself in feminine terms: Socrates speaks of philosophy as midwifery, he swears by the goddess Hera rather than by Zeus, and he describes himself as *anthropos* rather than *aner*, thus emphasizing his humanity rather than his manliness.

Although both Montesquieu and Socrates employ a spokeswoman, the messages are radically different. Diotima speaks of eros and immortality, Roxane of her desires and the laws of nature. The meaning of eros is radically terrestrialized. What are we to make of the presence, and even the primacy, of this sexual element that so distinguishes Montesquieu both from the ancients and from earlier liberals, especially the notably anerotic Hobbes and Locke?

Gynaecography

The harem is designed to further two supposedly complementary goals: the protection of female virtue and the pleasure of the husband. But in fact neither goal of the harem is realized. The confinement of women, the denial to them of a legitimate measure of sexual choice, is shown to be an inherently self-contradictory enterprise. Although it is the wives and the eunuchs who live in closest proximity to one another, the reader learns of their way of life only through the letters they respectively exchange with Usbek during his nine-year voyage. As was mentioned earlier, sixteen letters pass between Usbek and his wives, seventeen between Usbek and his eunuchs. Accordingly, a survey of the harem must proceed by a sort of triangulation, in which these two subsets provide the bearings.

Usbek's wives send more letters than they receive. Of the sixteen in which they participate, eleven are from the wives, and only five to them. This disproportion is in keeping with Usbek's lack of interest in them as individuals, even as he is obsessed with them as possessions (hence his preference for mediated contact, through the eunuchs). Of course, the disproportion is also explicable by the simple fact that they are five, while he is but one. However, even among the five, there is disproportion: Zélis writes four letters, Zachi three, Roxane two, and Zéphis and Fatmé one each. Usbek sends one letter apiece to the three more prolific wives (Zélis, Zachi, and Roxane) and two letters to the wives collectively; he does not send an individualized letter to Zéphis or Fatmé. Thus, there is no instance of a one-for-one exchange; in each correspondence between Usbek and a particular wife, as well as in the overall conjugal correspondence, Usbek sends fewer letters than he receives. Moreover, in all but one case (that of Roxane), the wives initiate the correspondence.

On first acquaintance, the wives seem indistinguishable from one another. Montesquieu's choice of "z"-alliterative names (Zachi, Zéphis, Zélis, also the slave-girl Zélide and the mythical Zuléma) reinforces this impression of similarity, in addition to adding a suggestion of serpentine exoticism. Not surprisingly, once in the West, Usbek and Rica are struck by the tremendous variety of the female character in contrast to the uniformity typical of Persian women. The harem, however, despite its aspirations, has not succeeded in reducing the women to mere odalisques—presenting Usbek with a cosmetic diversity of colors, faces, and figures from which all individuality has been expunged. Montesquieu delineates distinct characters among the wives, and distinct understandings of and responses to their situation. Given the brevity and paucity of their letters, this is a remarkable feat of characterization.[3]

The letters of the wives share a common subject. Mirza's question— are human beings made happy by pleasure, and the satisfaction of the senses, or by the practice of virtue?—is also, in less explicit fashion, the women's question.

Zachi, the most overtly wanton among the wives, is the first to write Usbek. Indeed, Zachi's is the earliest dated letter altogether, written two days after Usbek's departure. If the letters were arranged in strict chronological order, this letter, perhaps the most salacious of the book, would be the very first; but because the letters are grouped, with a few notable exceptions, in the order in which Usbek either writes or receives them, taking scrupulous account of how long it takes a letter to travel by caravan from Ispahan in Persia to the various points of his journey, it appears as #3. Montesquieu's placement of letters according to Usbek's timelines can be misleading. Letter #2 from Usbek to the chief black eunuch, written almost a full month after Zachi's letter and not received by the eunuch until another month after that, closes with a grant of permission for the wives to go to the country; Zachi begins her letter by informing Usbek that they have made a trip to the country. If readers are not attentive to the dates, they might simply conclude that the women have taken the excursion authorized by Usbek, missing the fact that within hours of Usbek's departure the women had already managed to procure such entertainment (and release from confinement) for themselves.

Montesquieu does not make it easy to piece together the lines of the plot. In addition to his deceptive sequencing of the letters, Montesquieu has devised a system for dating the letters that ingeniously combines Moslem lunar months with Christian solar years. Accordingly, without some knowledge of Mohammedan chronology, a reader cannot know, for instance, that the twenty-first of the moon of Maharram 1711 (#3) precedes the eighteenth of the moon of Saphar 1711 (#2). Through the creation of this calendrical hybrid, Montesquieu is able to perplex or conceal his meaning somewhat. While some readers may be unaware of the full significance of Zachi's statement, Usbek is all too aware. His next letter (#6) is the first of a number of despairing letters to his friend Nessir, detailing his consuming jealousy and fears for the safety of his wives (i.e., their fidelity). Of course, at the novel's conclusion, the revolt of the women becomes perfectly apparent to all readers. Only the most inquisitive will have realized that the revolt was in preparation from the beginning. To the degree that the fate of the harem offers a study in the origins of revolution (political as well as sexual), that interstitial insight—the insight buried between the two letters—grows in importance.

In informing Usbek of the wives' journey, Zachi sought to put the best construction on it, attributing it not to a desire for freedom, but to the impossibility of staying in apartments filled with the enflaming memory of Usbek. Later, in her second letter, #47, Zachi will be much more frank in acknowledging that the wives' continued trips to the country are motivated by a desire for freedom and adventure. But for now, Zachi simply bemoans her lost pleasure, recounting scenes of erstwhile sensual delight to entreat Usbek's return ("Ah, dear Usbek, if only you knew how to be happy!"). In particular, Zachi recollects the "beauty contest" between the wives, presided over by Usbek. Her description reveals how the laws of decency, shame, and modesty that the eunuchs are directed to enforce had been shattered by Usbek's own conduct with his wives. Initially, the wives presented themselves before Usbek imaginatively and artfully attired. Usbek, however, soon "destroyed all [their] work; . . . it was necessary to appear to [his] view in the simplicity of nature."

This is the introduction of the theme of nature and convention, a theme that Montesquieu frequently discusses in terms of clothing, especially robes and veils. Montesquieu's choice of metaphor is interesting. Compared with Plato's metaphor of the cave, it suggests that the environing of convention is closer, right next one's skin, but also more changeable (see #30 where Rica switches from Persian to Western garb), with more potential perhaps for idiosyncratic departures. It also suggests that the quest for unadulterated nature is not an ascent; nature is body, not the sunlight of truth. Although convention can be laid off, it is never permanently dispensed with. In social life, men do not appear as the "poor, bare, forked animals" they are; just like clothing, convention is second nature to us. Convention is the result of humanity's cosmetic impulse, which seeks to order and adorn the world, attempting to make of it a cosmos. Usbek, however, rejects the arrangements made by his wives. One can certainly see in Usbek's demand for "the simplicity of nature" his ingrained distaste for vanity and pomp. His judgment will be based not on the evening gown or the talent portion of the show, but on a more radical version of the bathing suit competition. Perhaps he believes that in deciding "the famous quarrel between the women" on the basis of the body alone, he decides philosophically.

Yet one cannot help wondering whether Usbek does not do some injustice to the claims of beauty through his reduction of female beauty to measurement or proportion. Moreover, it is not the noble nakedness of a Greek statue—the bodying forth of the soul's character—that Usbek requests: "[His] curious gaze penetrated to the most secret places; [he] made us take a thousand different positions; ever new commands brought ever new compliance." This is the nudity of Hugh Hefner's *Playboy*, not Praxiteles' *Aphrodite*. The fact that Zachi, the most degenerate of the wives, is the winner of the beauty contest should give the reader pause. Under Usbek's regime, the empire of beauty—an empire rooted in nature—is stripped of its moral power. (Montesquieu's *Le Temple de Gnide*, with its very different beauty contest, shows this empire at its civilizing best.) In recollecting the lewd poses she and the other contestants assumed for his delectation, Zachi tells Usbek, "I counted modesty as nothing"; and she expects that confession to please. It is not just Usbek's absence that endangers virtue; the virtue of the women is undermined and outraged by Usbek himself.

This is shown even more clearly in another of the most sexually explicit letters of the book (#26). This letter might be described as the male counterpart to Zachi's letter, for while one is a woman's account of her exhibitionism and virtual prostitution, the other is a man's account of an act of violation. Usbek writes to Roxane without any prompting; he is not responding to word of her misdeeds or to an explicit inquiry from her, as he is in all the other letters written to his wives. Instead, he writes because the license of French women appalls him and makes him think fondly of Roxane, the exemplar as he sees it of Persian modesty. In the letter, he fondly remembers the early months of their marriage, during which she resisted him first with tears and stratagems, and finally with a dagger. Even after his conquest, she denies him "a tranquil possession." If we don't realize it at the time, we realize by novel's end that Usbek's only "love letter" recounts the rape of Roxane. The concluding letter (#161) delivers Roxane's written slap to Usbek: "You were surprised not to find in me the transports of love. Had you known me well, you would have found all the violence of hate."

Those wives, like Zachi, who desire to please Usbek utterly cast aside the veil of modesty; those, like Roxane, who want only to escape him assume it as their shield. While not sufficient to protect her indefinitely from Usbek's advances, Roxane's modesty does serve her well. It provides cover for her adultery. Usbek, in his letter to Roxane, had asserted—whether naively or with some pedagogical intent—that even the impudent French women are not actually unfaithful. According to Usbek:

> There are few women so abandoned as to go that far; for they all have engraved in their hearts an impression of virtue, which is given at birth, and which education weakens but cannot destroy. They can be lax in the external duties that modesty requires, but nature revolts when it comes to the question of taking the final step.

Roxane, punctilious in her observance of all external duties, fools even Solim, the most suspicious of the eunuchs. In writing Usbek of the harem's disorder since the death of the chief eunuch, Solim claims that "Roxane alone respects her duty and retains her modesty" (#151). One year later, after finally discovering Roxane in the arms of a young man, Solim must inform the deceived Usbek that "her fierce virtue was a cruel imposture, the veil of her treachery" (#159). Roxane herself regards as shameful not her adultery, but rather her pretense of fidelity. The veil is perfidious, not the passions behind it. She tells Usbek: "I have profaned virtue, by permitting my submission to your fantasies to be called by that name" (#161). Roxane counters Usbek's conception of virtue and nature with one of her own, telling Usbek, "I reformed your laws by those of Nature, and my spirit has always held to its independence." Roxane's nature is not engraven modesty, but the inviolability of her individual desires.

Female virtue as Usbek understands it and as it has traditionally been understood, that is, as obedience to the laws of decency and modesty, is nowhere to be found in the harem. Zachi and Roxane are opposites in many ways, but both deceive Usbek. Zachi, the first female voice we hear, adoring and arousing, professes her immodest love for Usbek. Nonetheless, Zachi is caught on two occasions taking liberties with a slave-girl; another time a white eunuch is found in her apartments, a forbidden liaison also. As both the language of her letter and the character of her attachments reveal, Zachi is the most corrupt of the wives—and the most content. At the novel's close, when Roxane makes clear her thoroughgoing rejection of the seraglio system, and Zélis also writes to denounce Usbek's tyranny, only Zachi, who has found ways to accommodate her desires within the context of the seraglio, continues to profess love for Usbek (#157). Zachi is a true creature of the seraglio. In his letter to Roxane, Usbek had contrasted the French women's adornment of themselves unfavorably with that of his own wives. He found the French practice whorish, because public; whereas the perfumes and coloring and ornamentation of Persian women are reserved for their husbands alone. In the Persian case, female vanity is not given public scope; it is directed toward one subject, rather than many. Zachi presents a study in such sequestered vanity. The key to her character is her extreme sexual competitiveness, vividly displayed when she recounts her victory in the beauty contest: "My triumph and my rivals' despair were complete. . . . Would that my rivals had had the courage to witness the proofs of love that I received from you! If they had seen my ecstasies, they would have appreciated the difference between my love and theirs." In other words, Zachi wishes for public attendance at her marriage bed. Because her vanity is so closely confined, the scene of her victory must be a private scene. The assault on privacy and sexual discretion is more thoroughgoing in Usbek's harem than in the French salons, where men and women, in flirting with one another, flirt also with the boundaries between the public and the private, but in such a way as to preserve at least the distinction between them.

Zachi's later homosexual involvement might seem to imply that she has renounced vanity or exchanged female rivalry for female solidarity. However, no such character transformation is discernible; rather, in Usbek's absence, Zachi's rivalry with the other wives extends beyond the affections of Usbek to whatever other sexual objects the seraglio might be thought to contain. Her lesbianism is very much *faute de mieux*. It is significant that her lesbian dalliances are not with other wives, but with a slave-girl, Zélide, who belongs successively to Zéphis, Zachi, and Zélis (#4, 20, 53). In fact, there are indications that Zachi gained possession of the slave-girl by falsely accusing Zéphis of improprieties, thereby causing the eunuchs to deprive Zéphis of her female attendant (#4) and award her to Zachi. Following Zachi's familiarities with the girl, for which Usbek reproves Zachi in #20, she is safely entrusted to Zélis, who speaks in #53 of her slave Zélide's proposed marriage to a eunuch.[4] The origin of Zachi's lesbianism is homopolemic, not homoerotic; it follows from her contest with the other wives—a contest that, with Usbek away, must perforce take place on other sexual fronts. While we tend today to think of lesbianism as the most radical rejection of the male, Montesquieu suggests that, at least in the context of the harem—that is, of women organized communally for the pleasure of a man—lesbianism is less revolutionary than adultery.[5] Lesbianism takes place within the walls of the seraglio; adultery involves a breach of the walls. It is Roxane's introduction of an unmutilated man into the premises that results in the overthrow of Usbek. Accordingly, the last female voice we hear is that of Roxane: "Yes, I deceived you; I corrupted your eunuchs, made sport of your jealousy, and learned how to make your frightful seraglio into a place of delight and pleasure" (#161).

Montesquieu's attention to structure is evident in the spacing of the wives' letters (see fig. 3.1). There is an initial laying out of the wives' situation by Zachi, Zéphis, and Fatmé (neither Zéphis nor Fatmé is heard from again). This series of letters (#3, 4, 7, 47) begins with Zachi's mention of the trip to the countryside and her account of the beauty contest; it concludes with another letter from Zachi, also on the twin subjects of travel and female rivalry. However, in this letter (#47), the emphasis is reversed. Zachi briefly announces her reconciliation with Zéphis and then proceeds to an account of the women's river-crossing "adventures." The chief eunuch refused to order the women's release from their enclosed sedan-chairs when a violent wind arose, even though the women's lives might have depended upon their freedom of movement. The river crossing brings home to the reader, and to Zachi herself, the conflict between virtue and self-preservation. One gathers that Zachi has indeed begun to change. I said earlier that Zachi's lesbianism was not a sign of emergent, politically conceived

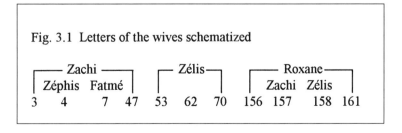

Fig. 3.1 Letters of the wives schematized

sisterhood; her reconciliation with Zéphis, on the other hand, does suggest a new solidarity among the women. (The two wives had presumably been at odds over custody of the slave-girl Zélide. Their reconciliation takes place only when neither wife is in possession of the contested slave-girl, in other words, only when the sexual element has been disposed of.)

There is a parallel foursome of letters at the end of the novel (#156, 157, 158, 161), framed this time by Roxane rather than Zachi. These are Roxane's only letters, written within two months of one another, after a silence of nine years. The first is written on behalf of all the wives, objecting particularly to the treatment that Zachi and Zélis have suffered at the hands of the eunuchs. No other wife writes a generalized protest. On the same day as Roxane's public-spirited defense of her fellows, Zachi and Zélis each write to complain of their corporal punishment, which takes the belittling form of a sound spanking— "a chastisement that begins by alarming modesty; . . . a chastisement that takes one back, so to speak, to childhood" (#157). Zachi blames the proximate cause of her humiliation, the eunuch, and pleads for Usbek's return: "If I am innocent, return to love me; if I am guilty, return that I may die at your feet" (#157). Zélis, more far-seeing, blames Usbek: "I am outraged by the tyrant, not by him who exercises that tyranny" (#158). Although all three women are moved to write Usbek at this point of crisis, they are animated by different spirits. The shared expression of insult in these concluding letters should not lead one to gloss over the individual differences in the women's approaches to their situation. Zachi's fawning protestation of love is quite unlike Zélis's calm, dignified, almost philosophical declaration that she can no longer love Usbek. Roxane's final letter, making clear that she never did love Usbek, presents yet a third response. Her tone is fierce and spirited: "No doubt this language seems new to you. Is it possible that after crushing you with sorrow, I may yet force you to admire my courage?" (#161).

While Zachi and Roxane appear as the two poles—one the lover, the other the hater of Usbek—respectively dominating the opening and closing sets of wifely letters, Zélis represents something of a third way. Situated between the two series of four at the start and finish—that is, situated between obedience and revolution—are, not surprisingly perhaps, three letters by Zélis (#53, 62, 70). These letters are remarkable for their self-consciously forthright speech. Zélis consults Usbek on questions of household management as an equal, giving her own opinion and reasoning first, then soliciting his. Within her limited domain, Zélis demonstrates a capacity and taste for rule. Her first letter (#53) concerns a grant of permission to marry. Since it is a eunuch who sues for the hand of her maidservant, Zélis broaches the subject of poly-morphous perversity. After expressing her repugnance at such mock marriages (in terms that could as well describe her own relations with Usbek for the past two years—"a man able solely to guard and not to possess"), she then softens her opposition by recalling statements she has heard Usbek make about nature's compensatory operations. Rather like blind men whose other faculties are heightened, eunuchs, accord-ing to Usbek, develop "a third sense" and enjoy with women certain voluptuous pleasures unknown to others.[6] Zélis seems to have been a privileged listener to her husband's speculations. Although she certain-ly seems the most mature, and perhaps the first, of his wives, it is surprising that Usbek would have thought it suitable or prudent to dis-cuss with her such questions as the adaptability of the senses and na-ture's directedness toward pleasure. Usbek makes no reply to this letter.

Zélis's second letter (#62) concerns the education of her daughter, who, on her mother's initiative, is about to enter upon her novitiate in the harem. Zélis does not write seeking Usbek's consent to this course. On this subject, Zélis seems to speak with full authority, both judicial and executive. She does, however, explain the reasoning behind the seven-year-old girl's somewhat premature incarceration (ten being the usual age). "It is never too early," she says, "to deprive a young girl of the liberties of childhood, and to give her a holy education within the sacred walls where modesty resides." Habituation must be relied on, for both reason and nature are insufficient guides to female vir-tue. According to Zélis, "[i]t is *en vain* to talk to us of the subordina-tion in which we are put by Nature." Here, the adverbial phrase has a double force, meaning that such speeches are both "in vain" or inef-fectual and that they proceed from male vanity. Submission must be-come customary because it is not natural; moreover, it must become customary before the onset of the passions, which, according to Zélis, "encourage [women] to independence." But even long-ingrained habit is insufficient to guarantee virtue; habit must be buttressed by coer-cive law. "When the laws give us to one man," Zélis says, "they screen us from all others and place us as far from them as if we were a hun-dred thousand leagues away."

From what Zélis says in the first half of her letter, there would appear to be no agreement between nature and the laws instituted by men. However, she directly asserts the opposite in the second half of her letter: "Nature, active in men's favor, . . . has willed that . . . we be the animated instruments of their felicity." Nature accomplishes this dependence through the very agency of the passions that Zélis earlier claimed encouraged women to independence. She says, "[Nature] has set us afire with passion, that men might be tranquil; if men emerge from their insensibility, nature has destined us to restore it to them, though it is never possible for us to enjoy this happy state into which we put them." Nature grants women, as well as men, desires, but apparently it is not an equal grant. Zélis implies that the desires of women are greater or deeper or, in some other sense, insatiable. We must of course wonder how much her conclusions on this score depend on her experience of polygamy; Usbek himself will readily admit that one man cannot satisfy many wives (#114). Moreover, when women are viewed as the "animate instruments" of another, their pleasure may not be attended to very assiduously. Nonetheless, we must also wonder whether Montesquieu, through the aptly named Zélis, intends to make a more general statement about the disproportionate sexual zeal of men and women. Rousseau will develop this argument about women's insatiability (and even more importantly, the complementary insecurity of male desire), using it to authorize the double standard—female modesty being prerequisite for the emergence of romantic (imagination-based) love. Although shut out from the "happy state" of sexual contentment, Zélis—executing a sort of Rousseauean U-turn—goes on to speak of her situation as "happier" than Usbek's, for "imagination" has supplied her with "a thousand pleasures [Usbek] could never understand." "I have lived," she tells him, "while you have only languished."[7] Zélis claims not only superior pleasures, but greater freedom as well. "In the very prison in which you hold me, I am more free than you: . . . your suspicions, your jealousy, and your vexation are so many marks of your dependence." Translated to the political plane, the point would be that the tyrant is more dependent on the people than vice versa.[8]

Zélis's third letter (#70) continues the theme of nature and virtue. She relates the story of Soliman, a friend of Usbek's exposed to public humiliation because of a son-in-law's wedding-night repudiation of the bride, Soliman's daughter. Here, Zélis's interest in household affairs expands to take in more than her own charges (her daughter and her attendants). Soliman's misfortune reveals the social ramifications of the harem ethic, whereby a man's standing among men is made dependent on a woman's hymenal condition. Zélis concludes that "[f]athers are truly unfortunate to be exposed to such affronts." Having ignored Zélis's two previous letters—letters devoted to the disposition of his own household—Usbek responds to this letter, engaged it seems both by pity for his friend and by the medical question at issue. His reply finds fault with the law, derived from the Old Testament (Deuteronomy 22:13–21), which allows such repudiations. According to Usbek, it is a law based on faulty medicine. The study of nature cannot verify virtue; the supposed proofs of virginity are "chimerical." Moral significance cannot be read into doubtful physical signs.[9] Once again, Usbek shows no hesitancy in sharing his enlightened views with at least this particular wife. Despite his openness, Usbek concludes his letter with a fulsome endorsement of the harem tradition, commending Zélis for her care of her daughter, and praying for the girl's purity.

I have said that Zélis's letters are all concerned with household management, and I would add that they give evidence of an active and expansive concern with one's own. They are not, however, concerned with matters of wealth and estate; rather, they are exclusively concerned with matters hymeneal and gynecologic (in both the narrow, medical sense and the larger sense of a science of women). The very meaning of "household" is constricted under despotism. (By contrast, approximately one-fifth of Xenophon's *Oeconomicus* is given over to *gynaikologia*.) Throughout the correspondence with his wives and eunuchs, Usbek, quite unlike Zélis, manifests a remarkable unconcern with family and property in the conventional sense. Usbek gives no directions for the care of his estate or the education of his children; indeed, so far as we know, this plethora of wives has produced only the one daughter. Under the dynamic of despotic jealousy, Usbek gives no thought to either the continuance of life or the commodiousness of life. His household holds only women, who in turn hold him in the grip of erotic fear. As Zélis taunts him, "Proceed, dear Usbek. Have me watched night and day: do not trust in merely ordinary precautions" (#62). The harem is a regime dedicated to love, but founded on fear. The absence of the women's lord and master, Usbek, only makes more pronounced that essential fault line.

Before Zélis writes her final letter (#158) denouncing Usbek's tyranny, the reader is given one more insight into her character. The chief eunuch writes to inform Usbek that Zélis, on her way to the mosque, "allowed her veil to fall and appeared before all the people with her face almost entirely exposed" (#147). In light of the conflagration that erupts soon after this, the significance of Zélis's mode of rebellion can all too easily pass unnoticed. Whereas the rebellions of Zachi and Roxane are private and venereal in nature, that of Zélis is public and sexual in a very different sense; indeed, one might even say it is anti-sexual. Her action involves the eyes; she wishes to see and be seen clearly. Given that the purpose of the veil is to shroud the face itself with the sexual taboo, her action might be described as an attempt to desexualize her face, to claim it as a publicly presentable and shareable feature of herself. Thus, she unveils herself not so much as a woman, but rather as an individual. (Interestingly, the habit of a nun, which wraps the hair and the body, at least leaves the face unobstructed. Indeed, it concentrates attention on the face—the eyes of the soul. The nun's habit, by blocking off the body, might be said to direct the eyes heavenward, to free them for transcendence. Despite the similarities Montesquieu intends us to see between Islam and Christianity, Christianity does not deny the soulfulness of woman to the same extent.) In opposing the veil, Zélis denies that women are entirely creatures of the body.

Just as the modern women's liberation movement is compounded of two elements—sexual emancipation and sexual equality—so too the rebellion in the harem. Roxane, spurred by her specific dissatisfaction as a woman, commits adultery. She seeks a private freedom for the impulses of nature. Zélis, by contrast, seeks not sexual freedom so much as freedom from sex, or more accurately, from an exclusively gender-based definition of the public self. Roxane's act looks toward a liberal celebration of the bodily difference between male and female; Zélis's act looks toward a liberal devaluation of that same bodily difference.

Given Zélis's preference for political expressions of her dissatisfaction, it is not surprising to learn that Montesquieu contemplated having Zélis sue for divorce. In a letter that Montesquieu wrote but did not include in the final text (presumably because the existence of such an option would have weakened the book's portrait of despotic power), Usbek berates and threatens Zélis for seeking a public and judicial remedy for her domestic woes.[10] Had this letter been included, the date it bears would have caused it to be inserted between letters #147 and #148, in other words, right at the start of the concluding harem sequence (#147–61). Thus, we would have witnessed Usbek peremptorily rejecting a legal and orderly dissolution of his harem immediately before the spectacle of murderous, suicidal revolution unfolds. On the eve of revolution, Usbek's suspicions are directed to Zélis, the eldest of his wives, forthright in her speech and deed, with some experience of a share in rule. The more dangerous and unperceived threat, however, is from Roxane, his newest and favorite wife, duplicitous in her speech and deed, governed by passion.

There is a telegraphed message for other rulers in Usbek's misjudgment, a message about the direction and pace of the coming change in France, a message to heed articulate reformers before revolution sweeps all aside.

Chapter Four

The Politics
of Fecundity

Mahomet, who came in glory, established dependence everywhere. His religion having spread into Asia, Africa, and Europe, prisons were formed. Half of the world was eclipsed. Only the iron grates and the bolts were to be seen. All tended to night in the Universe, and the beautiful sex, buried with its charms, everywhere mourned its liberty. (no. 572)

As this epigram from his *Pensées* confirms, Montesquieu considered Islam to be a religion particularly harsh on women. Certainly, his presentation of domestic despotism is in part intended to be just what it seems: an exposé of Islamic polygamy. Polygamy Montesquieu found objectionable not only for its cloistering of women, but for its inhibiting effect on population growth. While polygamy may seem efficient in trying to take advantage of reproductive economies of scale, in fact human reproduction cannot be conducted on the model of animal reproduction. The human male, as we have seen in Usbek's case, is not suited to stud service. Human sexuality is unique, both in certain physical facts (most important is the nonperiodic character of female availability and desire), and in the prominence of psychological factors. According to Montesquieu's psychophysiology of sex, the virtually unlimited responsiveness of women makes it laborious for one man to satisfy many wives. Usbek gives a fair account of the consequences:

I see the good Mussulman as an athlete, destined to compete without letup, but who, overburdened and weakened by his first efforts, languishes even on the field of victory and finds himself, so to speak, buried under his own triumphs. . . . Among us it is common to see a man, in a huge seraglio, with but a very small number of children. Moreover, these children usually are feeble and in poor health and share their father's languor. (#114)

55

In addition to the husband's loss of vigor, the need to assuage his jealousy requires that the reproductive energies of a great number of male and female guardian-slaves be sacrificed. Polygamy necessitates widespread eunuchdom. "So you see how one man employs for his pleasure many subjects of both sexes, making them as good as dead to the State and useless for the propagation of the Species" (#114).

Montesquieu often uses demography to judge the humanity or inhumanity of both divine and human laws. In the sequence of letters on the depopulation of the globe (#113-22)—where the voice of Montesquieu is heard most directly, with essaylike clarity rather than novelistic distance and complication—both the Christian prohibition of divorce and the value placed on celibacy are criticized along with Islamic polygamy for their tendency to produce depopulation. Montesquieu takes such a result as prima facie evidence of the hostility of these religions to human flourishing.

Of the premium that Catholicism places on celibacy, Usbek says:

> This vocation of chastity has annihilated more men than plagues and the bloodiest wars. Each religious house is an eternal family, to which no one is ever born, and which depends upon others for its maintenance. These houses are always open, like so many pits in which to bury future generations.[1] (#117)

"Monasticism spreads death"; and given the rate at which it does so, Usbek predicts the demise of Catholicism within five hundred years.[2] Protestantism, because it tolerates "neither priests nor dervishes," possesses an "infinite advantage" over Catholicism. Nonetheless, Protestant countries continue to suffer population loss, because, unlike the Islamic world, they retain the Catholic prohibition of divorce. Usbek suggests that the first Protestants would have carried their reformation further and instituted divorce—"entirely destroying the barrier which, on this point, separates the Nazarene and Mohammed"—had they not been "constantly accused of intemperance." Perhaps more than other reformers, those recommending sexual latitudinarianism are open to accusations of self-serving motivation.[3] Wishing to avoid the scandals that plagued Martin Luther, Montesquieu is accordingly careful to place his most forthright endorsement of divorce (#116) in the midst of a disquisition on the depopulation of the globe; in other words, his explicit accommodation to the sexual urge appears in a discussion of duty, wherein procreation is treated as an obligation to society and to species. This is not to say that Montesquieu here completely neglects the element of pleasure—far from it; he does, however, subordinate it.

Letter #116 invites closer examination. In it Usbek argues that by so tightening and fixing the marriage knot, Christianity has "removed all sweetness from marriage" and as a result has "put its very purpose under attack." In a remarkable image, Usbek compares the law prohibiting divorce to "those tyrants who used to shackle living men to dead bodies." In a marriage without hope of sunder, quarrels multiply. The partners, Usbek says,

> see only that the disagreements of marriage are lasting or, in a manner of speaking, eternal. Hence arise disgust, discord, scorn, and a loss to posterity. After scarcely three years of marriage the partners neglect to do what is essential to it. Together they pass thirty cold years, privately separated in a way as complete, and perhaps more pernicious, than if it were made public; each lives alone, all to the prejudice of future generations.

Society is harmed not only by the paucity of offspring, but by the rise in prostitution and libertinage, for "a man disgusted by *une femme éternelle* will soon give himself up to *filles de joie.*"

For Christians, marriage is sacramental as well as eternal; the union of man and wife is an earthly likeness of Christ and his bride, the Church. Through the "naive" speculations of his Persian observer, Montesquieu is able to raise some questions about the sacred source of this element of the eternal in Christian marriage. Usbek says:

> It is quite difficult to understand clearly what reason led the Christians to abolish divorce. Marriage, in every nation on earth, is a contract susceptible to all conventions, and from it should be abolished only what could enfeeble its purpose. But the Christians do not regard it from this point of view, and consequently have difficulty in saying what it is. Marriage to them does not consist in sensual pleasure; on the contrary, as I have already told you, it seems they wish to banish that element from it as much as possible. Rather, it is to them an image, a symbol, and something mysterious which I do not understand.

In its attempt to spiritualize a sex-based contract, Christianity introduces a certain hostility toward sexuality into marriage itself. But if the end of marriage—procreation—is to be served, the pleasurability of the means to that end must not be too severely impeded.

According to Usbek, pagan religion was more attentive to such concerns; among the Romans at least, "[n]othing contributed more to mutual attachment than the faculty [or option] of divorce." In explanation of the psychological mechanism at work here, Usbek says: "Husband and wife were encouraged to support domestic troubles patiently,

knowing that it was in their power to end them." Clearly, Usbek's brief
for divorce is based on a particular understanding of the human heart.
David Hume, who took exception both to Montesquieu's endorsement
of voluntary divorce and to his account of European depopulation,
nonetheless gives a succinct presentation of the underlying argument:

> But the liberty of divorces is not only a cure to hatred and domestic
> quarrels: It is also an admirable preservative against them, and the only
> secret for keeping alive that love, which first united the married couple.
> The heart of man delights in liberty: The very image of constraint is
> grievous to it: When you would confine it by violence, to what would
> otherwise have been its choice, the inclination immediately changes, and
> desire is turned into aversion. If the public interest will not allow us to
> enjoy in polygamy that *variety*, which is so agreeable in love; at least,
> deprive us not of that liberty, which is so essentially requisite.[4]

The question arises: can one build an institution on the free motions of the heart, which is, according to Usbek himself, "the most
variable and inconstant thing in nature"? The use made of Rome in
letter #116 seems to indicate that the interests of the individual and
the society can be harmonized, inasmuch as the availability of divorce
serves both affectional freedom and population growth. The family can
be successful as a sexual-economic unit without being indissoluble.
Sparta is also cited by Usbek, although that example (and particularly
Usbek's elaboration of it) points beyond divorce, in the direction of
the abolition of the family altogether: "I hazard to say that in a republic like Sparta, where the citizens were constantly restrained by
singular and subtle laws and where the Republic was the only family,
if it had been decreed that husbands should change wives every year,
an innumerable people would have been born." Apparently, serial monogamy is not afflicted with the same difficulties (with respect to male
performance) as polygamy is.

Are we to understand that Montesquieu finds such "singular" conjugal arrangements perfectly in keeping with the inconstancy of the
human heart? On the basis of this passage, the abbé Gaultier accused
Montesquieu of "desiring that men be metamorphosed into stallions."[5]
There is indeed a palpable shift in tone—a general coarsening—about
midway through letter #116. Initially, the talk is of "the union of hearts"
and what conduces to it; by letter's end, however, if men are regarded
as stallions, women are the brood mares. Usbek laments that "women
no longer successively pass, as they did among the Romans, into the
hands of several husbands, who made the best possible use of them
along the way." Is Montesquieu in fact pointing not to the harmony of

individual and society, but to their being still at odds, or at least moved by very different considerations? Particularly important in this regard is Usbek's harsh reference to the inutility of childless marriages. If procreation is the only purpose of marriage and one in which the state has considerable interest, can the state annul childless marriages, whether happy or not? Hearts may be both more fickle and more intransigent than the conventions that attempt to govern them. Christianity tries to render the heart fixed; Sparta (and Rome to some extent) tried to render it flexible and hence neutral or open to civic determination. Perhaps neither operation can succeed. Liberty of divorce strikes a balance between the Christian attempt to mandate fidelity and the pagan attempt to mandate promiscuity.

Divorce is also alluded to in Rica's letter on the Paris law courts (#86). According to Rica, husbands, fathers, and masters have "only a shadow of authority" in contemporary France. The result of this incipient egalitarianism is an increase in family litigation, as the former subjects seek self-determination. Daughters sue their fathers for permission to marry; wives sue for annulment. They must resort to extraordinarily unseemly measures to establish their rights, however. An annulment, for instance, which declares a marriage invalid and restores the rights of virginity to a woman, differs from divorce, which simply dissolves the marriage contract, in requiring a judicial inquiry into "the hidden mysteries of the marriage night." Annulment is a form of repudiation. In *The Spirit of the Laws*, Montesquieu makes a helpful distinction between divorce and repudiation: "divorce occurs by mutual consent on the occasion of a mutual incompatibility, whereas repudiation is done by the will and for the advantage of one of the two parties, independently of the will and the advantage of the other" (XVI.6); moreover, "by the nature of the thing, there must be causes for repudiation and not for divorce" (XVI.16). Rica's rendition of the breakdown of family governance in France draws attention to the parallelism of women's situation in East and West. In both cases, efforts at reconstituting the domestic sphere require women to abandon their modesty. Rica sketches a comic scene of Aristophanean repulsiveness: one woman documents her own outrages against her husband; another levels an accusation of impotence against her husband, demanding the ordeal *du congrès* to verify her charge—"a proof," Rica says, "as stigmatizing for the wife who holds up as for the husband who sinks." This proof is the obverse of the "chimerical" proofs of virginity talked of in #70. Unlike female virtue, male virtue (since it is synonymous with power) can indeed be put to the test, and its deficiency certified.

Puissance and impotence, however, can be established only at the cost of the dignity of all concerned, judges and participants alike.

Although Rica speaks sarcastically of the "modesty" of these women and is disgusted by the spectacle of intimate complaints being aired in public, his letter in no way favors the restoration of patriarchy. He has little sympathy for "the jealous husband, the vexed father, and the disagreeable master," even as he notes their dispossession. Rica's satire cuts both directions and, I believe, fairly represents Montesquieu's view of the situation. Time and again, on issue after issue, one finds in Montesquieu dissatisfaction both with the old ways and with the destructive manner in which the new ways are being established. His account of a system of justice so overrun by domestic quarrels that "love causes the judgment-seat to reverberate" prompts one to a consideration of judicial reform—a readjustment of public and private that would include something along the lines of no-fault divorce and, for the unwed, an age of marital consent. Interference in the details of private life could be lessened by making divorce hinge on "incompatibilities of temper" (to which Usbek refers in #117) rather than on proofs of impotence. Marriage itself could be made more attractive and sustainable by allowing daughters the freedom to engage themselves.

In *The Spirit of the Laws*, Montesquieu says that "the consent of fathers is founded on their power, that is, on their right of property" (XXIII.7). Montesquieu is very circumspect, in both the *Laws* and the *Letters*, in suggesting that daughters be released from the proprietorship of the father, for the reason that this domestic reform is contingent upon a prior religious reform: the abolition of convents. In France, fathers control their daughters' marriages; the girls, however, always have the religious life to flee to if the father's decision is intolerable. Some choice remains to them, even if it is only the final pick of the prison. In England, where monastic celibacy is not an option, girls are granted more of a say in the choice of a spouse. Because they have no ultimate recourse against marriage, their wishes must be accorded more respect. Significantly, in describing the English situation, Montesquieu does not refer to "the consent of fathers," but rather to girls "consulting their parents" (XXIII.8). It seems that there is a new egalitarianism not only between the generations (as the legal need for approval gives way to the solicitation of advice), but between father and mother as well (parents replace fathers in the new scaled-back position of authority). Perhaps because the man must win the woman's heart, an English marriage begins on a footing of greater equality. He has had, from the first, to submit himself to her judgment. Not surprisingly, English parents pay attention to the education (as much secular as religious) of their daughters; they have every incentive to develop in them the faculties of judgment and discrimination.

Interestingly, the difference that Montesquieu spells out between the two countries continues to be reflected in their novels right through the early part of the twentieth century. Compare Austen's Emma Woodhouse to Flaubert's Emma Bovary. The characteristic English novel concerns courtship, whereas the characteristic French novel concerns adultery. The difference is not to be attributed solely to English prudery. It is as much the result of the differing conditions of women in the two countries, and especially the differing loci of freedom. An English heroine, equipped with wits and charms, exercises her freedom in engaging herself to marry, not in escaping an arranged or otherwise ill-suited marriage.

Montesquieu believes it is best that marriage be regarded as the universal and freely entered into condition of adulthood. Hence he wishes to remove both the refuge of the Holy Father's house and the tyranny of the earthly father. To undermine earthly fathers without also undermining the heavenly father would result only in a truly unpalatable mix of license and celibacy (the situation, according to Montesquieu, in Italy and Spain, where girls do what they like without the requisite education). Montesquieu favors affectional freedom, but within rather close parameters.

Planned Parenthood

As readers of *The Spirit of the Laws* know, Montesquieu is immensely curious about other regimes and ways of life. Montesquieu rivals Aristotle as an analyst of regimes and his masterwork is quite properly regarded as the fountainhead of the modern study of comparative government and sociology. While Montesquieu's investigations are not quite as wide-ranging in the *Persian Letters*, nonetheless China, Africa, India, Egypt, Babylonia, Greece, Rome, Carthage, Circassia, Muscovy, Poland, Germany, Italy, America, England, Switzerland, Portugal, Spain, Turkey, Holland, and Venice, in addition to the two poles of France and Persia, all receive comment in the novel. Often that comment concerns the relationship between domestic and political government. Accordingly, one would not want to deny Montesquieu's genuine interest in the Orient and its practice of polygamy, either here or in *The Spirit of the Laws*, where, for example, we encounter the chapter

"On polygamy in itself" (XVI.6) in the book on domestic slavery. Yet intriguingly, the movement of book XVI as a whole is from polygamy to divorce, thus mirroring the movement of Usbek's letters in the first part of the sequence on population. Indeed, via book XVI's concluding footnote, which refers the reader to XXIII.21, the argument proceeds to an extensive discussion of Roman marriage law, again mirroring Usbek's concluding inquiry into pagan population policy. What are only hints and flashes in Usbek's treatment—state-ordered productive couplings and state-ordered dissolutions upon barrenness, for example—are gone into at greater length in *The Spirit of the Laws*.

According to Montesquieu, the necessity for legal actions to encourage increase was a sure indication of the Roman empire's decline, a decline brought about by the nature of empire itself: "The Romans, by destroying all the peoples, destroyed themselves; constantly active, striving, and violent, they wore themselves out, just as a weapon that is always in use wears out" (XXIII.20). The universal Roman tyranny had depopulated first the periphery (which before being "swallowed" by Rome was "full of small peoples and glutted with inhabitants" [XXIII.19]) and finally the center itself. The development of codes of marital laws and the revival of the old republican office of censor in the time of Caesar and Augustus—an attempt to counter the corruption of mores and overcome the growing distaste for marriage—were, however, repugnant to the populace. As a result, the emperors were forced to modify the laws and otherwise weaken their enforcement, until the harsh system was so riddled with loopholes and favoritism that "the rule became only an exception" (XXIII.21).

Montesquieu first pointed out that the Romans found these laws repugnant at the close of book XVI, when he described how the censors prevailed on Carvilius Ruga to take an oath to repudiate his beloved wife on grounds of her sterility so he could remarry and give children to the republic. For being the first to acquiesce in such demands, Carvilius Ruga became odious to the people. According to Montesquieu, the hatred they conceived for Carvilius is only truly explicable if one understands "the genius of the Roman people" (XVI.16)—"genius" in the sense of a distinctive spirit or character, not creative brilliance. It was not the repudiation of a wife that bothered them, but rather Carvilius's oath-taking, his acknowledgment of an obligation to the state to multiply, for "[t]he people saw that this was a yoke that the censors were going to put on them." In other words, the Roman people's hatred for Carvilius Ruga sprang from their fatalism; it was a form of self-hatred, not haughty scorn. At this point

Montesquieu breaks off, promising to "show later in this work the repugnance they always had for such regulations."

The chapter to which Montesquieu's footnote directs the reader
(XXIII.21) is entitled "On Roman laws concerning the propagation of
the species." Although this chapter looks to be about the laws themselves (including a detailed account of the various provisions and their
evolution), we may say that its real subject is the opposition to those
laws and, beyond that, the source of the opposition in "the genius of
the Roman people." Suddenly, in the last quarter of this chapter, Montesquieu introduces Christianity; it appears that "the genius of the Roman people" has a direct bearing on the receptivity to, if not the advent
of, the new religion.

> Sects of philosophy had already introduced into the empire a spirit of
> distance from public business, . . . From it came an idea of perfection
> attached to all that leads to a speculative life; from it came distance
> from the cares and encumbrance of a family. The Christian religion,
> succeeding philosophy, fixed, so to speak, ideas for which the former
> had only cleared the way.
>   Christianity gave its character to jurisprudence; for empire always
> has some relation to priesthood.

In sum, Christianity is presented not as the antidote to Roman despotism and decadence, but as its culmination.[6] The life-denying other-
worldliness of Christianity was attractive to an enslaved and despairing
people, whose hopes could only be pinned on the next world. Among
the "Romans-become-Christians," all care for the multiplication of
mankind was abandoned. A similar account of the genealogy of Christian morals is available in Montesquieu's *Considerations on the Causes of the Greatness of the Romans and Their Decline*. There, too, when
"the genius of the Roman people" is introduced, it is explained as a
servile fear of harsher servitude and linked to the emergence of Christianity.[7]

Having opened book XXIII of *The Spirit of the Laws* with the lines
of Lucretius in honor of the pagan goddess Venus, Montesquieu concludes his inquiry into population by turning to the vicissitudes of
Christian Europe. With the destruction of Rome, the world was given
over to barbarian depredation—"soon the barbarian peoples had only
barbarian peoples to destroy" (XXIII.23). Depopulation proceeded
apace, until the advent of European feudalism, with its "infinity of
small sovereignties," allowed for a certain resurgence of population
(despite irregular government, ignorance of commerce, and perpetual

wars). Montesquieu implies a very strong inverse relation between the size of government and the fecundity of the people who live under it. Despite the universalistic pretensions of the Holy Roman Empire, Europe was in fact a congeries of independent towns and villages. Now, however, universal monarchy threatens to reappear. Christian France is in the position of imperial Rome: "It is the perpetual unions of many small states that produced this [population] decrease. Formerly, each village in France was a capital; there is only one large one today: each part of the state was a center of power; today everything relates to one center, and this center is, so to speak, the state itself" (XXIII.24). Montesquieu declares that, once again, "laws are needed for the propagation of the human species" (XXIII.26).

Unlike animals, human beings can, and more often than not do, frustrate Venus. The dilemma of human sexuality consists in its being uniquely susceptible to thought, whether in the form of individual caprice and fantasy or in the more entrenched form of religious dogma and political organization. While the constructions of the mind may thwart propagation, so too they may supply incentives that Venus alone cannot. Montesquieu mentions, albeit only to mock, Louis XIV's grant of pensions to those with ten or more children: "rewarding prodigies" is not the same as fostering a "general spirit" conducive to increase (XXIII.27). Montesquieu's own suggestions, while he drapes them with the mantle of the ancient Romans, do not call for bygone republican virtues. Mandating offspring is counterproductive; it is better to create a political climate in which families naturally flourish.

Accordingly, the chapter entitled "How one can remedy depopulation" endorses not a marriage code, but land reform. In "[t]hose countries desolated by despotism or by the excessive advantages of the clergy over the laity," the ill is so deep-seated that it reaches not only human generation, but the soil itself. Just as political centralization leads to depopulation, centralization of property leads to desertification. Such a point is reached that "[w]ith enough lands to nourish a people, one can scarcely nourish a family. . . . The clergy, the prince, the towns, the important men, and some principal citizens have gradually become owners of the whole region; it is uncultivated, . . . and the working man has nothing" (XXIII.28). Montesquieu recommends not only a redistribution of property in the countryside, but welfare provision, particularly for urban artisans. Since an economy dependent on commerce and manufactures is constantly changing, at any particular moment workers in one branch or another may suffer displacement. Montesquieu favors temporary assistance to alleviate such distress. He looks with suspicion, however, on perpetual relief establishments, whether poorhouses or, especially, monasteries. He cites the English example:

> When Henry VIII wanted to reform the Church of England, he destroyed the monks, a nation in itself lazy and one that maintained the laziness of others, because, as they practiced hospitality, an infinity of idle people, gentlemen and bourgeois spent their lives running from monastery to monastery. He also took away the poorhouses where the common people found their sustenance, as the gentlemen found theirs in the monasteries. After these changes, the spirit of commerce and industry became established in England. (XXIII.29)

The thrust of Montesquieu's measures is decidedly anticlerical. While the provision for divorce by mutual consent, with no cause other than incompatibility (XVI.15-16), pertains directly to the Christian marriage bond, his other remedies reach other aspects of Christian repression, namely the Church's lock (via landholdings and monasteries) on the nation's material and human resources.

A New Nativity

What Montesquieu accomplishes in *The Spirit of the Laws* by comparing France to Rome is accomplished in the *Persian Letters* by comparing France to Persia. In the sequence of letters on population (#113-22), Montesquieu begins by establishing a sort of parallelism between Islamic polygamy and the Christian prohibition of divorce. Religiously grounded regulations concerning marriage that look as different as polygamy and unalterable monogamy are shown to have similar effects and, what is more, as another chapter title from *The Spirit of the Laws* has it: "That laws that seem contradictory are sometimes derived from the same spirit" (XXIX.10). Since the birthrate may depend so much on "a certain manner of thinking," sometimes all that is necessary to restore a nation in decline is to give "a new turn to the people's imagination" (#119). The set of political maxims and legislative lessons that emerges from Usbek's treatise on population is similar to, and in some respects more comprehensive than, that of *The Spirit of the Laws*. For instance, the anti-imperial (or foreign policy) element seems to weigh as heavily as the anticlerical (or domestic policy) element. A brief catalog of the sequence of topics may be helpful: after the attack upon the Islamic practice of polygamy (#114) and slavery (#115), and the parallel attack on Christianity's eternal monogamy (#116) and monasticism (#117), Usbek denounces the African slave trade (#118); argues for the abolition of the law of primogeniture (#119); addresses the problem of abortion (#120); opposes all transportations of peoples, whether for purposes of colonization, slavery, or expulsion (#121); finally, and above all, Usbek recommends mild government, characterized by liberty, equality, and prosperity (#122).

Clearly, both primogeniture and abortion relate to domestic life. Although Montesquieu does not emphasize it, the position Usbek takes on these questions is opposed to the position of the Church. Sotto voce, letters #119 and #120 pursue the attack on Christianity's interference with the family. Usbek's condemnation of primogeniture, contained in one paragraph, is as follows:

> It is a spirit of vanity which established in Europe the unjust law of primogeniture, so unfavorable to propagation in that it turns the father's attention to but one of his children and away from all the others, in that it forces him to make a solid fortune for one by forbidding the establishment of several, and, finally, in that it destroys equality, which is the source of wealth, among the citizens. (#119)

Usbek lays stress on the alienation of fatherly affection and the detrimental centralization of property. What he does not mention is that all those younger sons, substantially disinherited, are fodder for the monasteries. Although Hebrew law did allot a double portion to the eldest (Deuteronomy 21:17), the right of primogeniture cannot be said to derive from the Bible; its origins are feudal. Not to be forgotten is the fact that the unity and succession of the French monarchy depend on the right of the eldest (see the penultimate chapter of *The Spirit of the Laws*, XXXI.33). Nonetheless, the Church has come to have a stake in primogeniture's continuance. Alteration of this single provision of the inheritance law, a course Usbek recommends and the founders of the American republic adopted, would have far-reaching effects on family, economy, and polity.

Usbek's statement on abortion is also terse and conceals, to some extent, its real target. It appears at the end of a letter largely devoted to the insalubrious practices of savages:

> Among Savages there is another custom, no less pernicious than the first [aversion to agriculture]: this is the cruel habit the women have of aborting themselves, so that their pregnancy will not make them disagreeable to their husbands.
>
> Here [in France] there are terrible laws against this offense; they reach even to madness. Every unmarried girl who does not declare her preg-

nancy to a Magistrate is punished by death if her offspring dies; neither modesty, shame, nor even accidents excuse her. (#120)

Usbek condemns both the resort to abortion and, in equally strong terms, the French law that punishes abortion. Just as Usbek did not explain the Church's interest in primogeniture, he does not explain its interest in the law requiring French women to register their pregnancies. In fact, this decree of Henry II, dating from 1556 and revived in 1708, had a purpose primarily religious (to ensure that infants did not perish without benefit of baptism), rather than demographic. Souls, not survival, were at stake.

Montesquieu mentions this ordinance in *The Spirit of the Laws* also (XXVI.3), marshaling it as an instance of a civil law contrary to the fundamental natural law of self-defense. Self-defense, in the case of women at least, includes the defense of natural modesty. To punish a woman for protecting her modesty is explicitly compared to punishing a man who kills another in self-defense. In other words, Montesquieu places a woman's defense of her reputation on a par with a man's defense of his life. To what lengths may a woman go in protecting her modesty? When a pregnancy would be a public admission of illicit congress, Montesquieu suggests that a woman may abort herself. Shame-induced abortion is self-defense. Although Montesquieu asserts that female modesty is natural, he does draw attention to the strong element of convention behind such drastic actions: "Education has augmented in her the idea of preserving that modesty, and at such times she can scarcely retain an idea concerning the loss of life" (XXVI.3).

This glimmer of a doubt about the truly natural status and force of female modesty is visible in the *Persian Letters* also. There, in his very brief discussion of abortion, Montesquieu presents us with what seem to be two very different motivations for abortion. Savage women, presumably of untutored natural sentiments, are led to abort by vanity, whereas French girls, perhaps convent educated, are driven to the same action by modesty. However, we cannot help noting that the modesty of the French girls is somewhat defective: it does not secure them from sexual activity; it only seeks to cover or obliterate the publicly visible results of that activity. If that deserves the name of natural modesty, then we must wonder what separates modesty from vanity (see #50, where Usbek explains modesty as socialized vanity—vanity made sensitive to fear of ridicule). Although regular resort to abortion is attributed to savage women, perhaps highly civilized women are even more likely to allow vanity and the quest for unencumbered sexual pleasure to interfere with propagation.[8] It should come as no surprise that the contemporary pro-choice movement employs the language of self-defense (witness the "March to Save Women's Lives") to justify abortions undertaken for the sake of convenience and vanity.

Montesquieu's treatment of abortion in the *Persian Letters* reveals that maternity faces a threat from vanity-inspired shamelessness as well as from religiously inspired shame. Montesquieu seeks to properly domesticate both by making religion less inquisitorial and vanity less cutthroat.

Usbek's condemnation in #121 of any type of forced relocation of peoples is directed, in part, against internal religious persecution and, in part, against external colonization and empire-building. On the religious tally sheet, Usbek alludes both to the Jewish Diaspora and Spain's expulsion of the Moors. What goes unmentioned, but surely not unthought of, is France's treatment of the Huguenots and the Jansenists. Louis XIV's revocation of the Edict of Nantes in 1685 (withdrawing tolerance and rights of worship that the edict accorded Protestants) and the proclamation of the papal bull *Unigenitus* in 1713 (in effect, putting the Jansenists out of the Church) led to widespread exodus and the depopulation of several provinces.[9] France's growing intolerance toward Protestants and those movements within the Church that could be construed to have a "Calvinist" cast is a constant subtext of the *Persian Letters*. Neither the edict nor its revocation is ever mentioned directly. However, the ongoing quarrel over *Unigenitus* (referred to in France as the *Constitution*) is the subject of two letters (#24 and #101). The first of these is particularly significant as it is the first letter written by Rica and the first letter written from Paris.[10] Employing his talent for trenchant caricature, Rica quickly sketches France's most striking features: the constant motion of Paris life; the "great magician" the king (so dubbed for his monetary prestidigitation) and the "even greater magician" the pope ("[s]ometimes he makes the prince believe that three is only one, or that the bread he eats is not bread"); and the revolt against the *Constitution* led, Rica says, by women. Indeed, women were prominent in the Jansenist movement, as were France's Parliamentarians. In sum, women, the *parlements*, and Jansenists are pitted against pope, king, and Jesuits.

After Rica's candid first impressions of the state of the realm, the issue of religious discord in France is alluded to more indirectly, as for instance, through the analogous split in Islam between Sunni and Shi'ite (#6 and #60). In #85, Mohammedan persecution of the Guèbres ("a hard-working people") and the Armenians (comprising "all the merchants and most of the country's artisans") provides another, quite precise, parallel. Shah Abbas, praised for his good will toward the

Armenians, was contemporary with Henry IV, the French king who issued the tolerant Edict of Nantes (1598); Shah Soliman, criticized for his ministers' plan to force conversion or expulsion upon the Armenians, was contemporary with Louis XIV, under whose reign the edict was revoked and the persecution of Protestants reached its height. After coding its criticism of France with Arabic ciphers, letter #85 culminates in Usbek's most forthright endorsement of religious pluralism. He recommends not just toleration, but also the deliberate introduction and multiplication of new sects.

Religious persecution stems from the proselytizing spirit.[11] That spirit is not content to limit its demand for conversion or expulsion to those within national borders; it is universalistic in aspiration. Thus, the proselytizing spirit is closely linked to the imperial spirit. Spain's Jesuits follow hard on the heels of its conquistadors. Usbek's criticism of involuntary human migration in #121 is anticolonial as well as anticlerical. In the sequence on population, Spain serves as Usbek's prime example of regressive imperialism. By expelling the Moors, sending colonists to America, exterminating the natives and then seeking to replace them with enslaved Africans, Spain has managed to depopulate, and otherwise impoverish, three continents: Iberian Europe, Africa, and South America. Although it goes unmentioned for the moment, the ill-fated project of John Law for the French colonization and commercial exploitation of Louisiana forms the background of this denunciation. As always, Montesquieu stresses the self-destructive character of despotism; the conqueror is as ruined as the conquered.

In the simplest of terms—the number and healthfulness of individuals—Nature renders judgment on regimes. "Empires," writes Usbek, "may be compared to a tree in which the overly extended branches deprive the trunk of all its sap and are useful only to make shade" (#121). Usbek had earlier employed a very similar arboreal image to describe monotheism: "The Jewish religion is an old tree-trunk which has produced two branches that now cover the entire earth: I speak of Mohammedanism and Christianity" (#60). Just as surely, these branches too deprive men of life-giving sun. Usbek's final letter in the population sequence—his plea for gentle government, praising the republics of Holland and Switzerland—makes clear that human beings need sun, for "[m]en," according to Usbek, "are like plants and never flourish unless well cultivated" (#122). The great king Cyrus, Usbek's ancestor, was famous for having ruled over men as over domesticated animals.[12] Machiavelli, an admirer of Cyrus, reworked the metaphor, envisioning the ruler himself in animal form—polymorphously feral, not domestic. Montesquieu prefers a gentler simile (though one no less divested of the specifically human): Men are flora rather than fauna. In conceiving of human life in these terms, Montesquieu points to its conditioned quality. Man is formed by and adapted to his environment. Terrain and climate, soil and sun and air, constitute our natural habitat. But we should not forget that Montesquieu made his living from his vineyards. Viticulture is a mode of farming that relies on human intervention and manipulation to an extraordinary degree. It is not simple sowing and reaping, but laborious training of the vines, grafting and pruning to center all development on the fruit-bearing branches. The brambles of nature become the *grands crus de Bordeaux*. Good government is a growth of similar assiduity and complexity.

Chapter Five

Impotence Tyrannus

In addition to the parallelism of Christianity and Islam—"[e]verywhere I see Mohammedanism," Usbek says of France, "though I cannot find Mohammed" (#35)—there is another parallelism, a sexual-religious one, at work in the letters also. One of the remarkable features of Usbek's harem is its fanatical insistence on purity, virtue, and faithful obedience to law. The language spoken by the inhabitants of the harem is full of religious imagery and resonance. The "faithful" eunuchs carry out Usbek's "sacred will." The chief eunuch describes the operation that gains one entry into the master's "ministry" as being "born again." The harem is spoken of as a "holy temple" where women receive a "holy education" in the "mortification of the senses." The eunuchs are directed to "exhort [the women] to cleanliness, the image of the soul's purity." Usbek is a "jealous" master who punishes "sacrilege." Despite the overlay of Oriental sumptuousness and sensuality, the harem is as much convent as bordello. Beneath the perfumed, flowing robes are the hair shirts.

The fact that the harem constitutes a rather elaborate community concerned with the virtuous obedience of its congregants is significant for the ultimate bearing of the harem sequence. If Montesquieu's only object had been to examine the phenomenon of domestic despotism, he could have portrayed the rule of an arbitrary and brutal husband over a much-abused wife, and there is indeed one letter (#51), not to be ignored, that discusses the custom of wife-beating among the Muscovites. Montesquieu instead creates a complex structure comprising an absent lord, his intermediaries the eunuchs, and a community of devoted women. These are conjugal arrangements of a very peculiar sort. Moreover, they deviate, in certain crucial respects, from actual Persian practice (familiar to Montesquieu through his reading

71

of travelogues and early Orientalists).[1] Although eunuchs were customarily employed to guard the living quarters of the women and to run the household, Montesquieu takes liberties with his sources when he speaks of eunuchs dutifully disrobing the women and conducting them to bed and bath.[2] He knowingly exaggerates the intimacy of their relations with one another. What effect, other than titillation of the reader, is gained by this poetic license? We get a clue from the description of the Spaniards in #78: "They are, primarily, devout; and, secondly, jealous. They guard their wives carefully against exposure to the enterprises of a soldier riddled with wounds, or a decrepit magistrate; but they closet them with a fervent novice who lowers his eyes, or with a robust Franciscan who raises his."

Montesquieu redesigns the harem so that it approximates a sexualized model of the divine hierarchy. Put most baldly: God/Church/Men = Usbek/Eunuchs/Women. There are a fair number of nonharem letters that deal explicitly and exclusively with religious issues, for instance, Usbek's correspondence with the mollah (#16-18) or Usbek's letter to Rhédi filled with metaphysical speculations about the nature of God (#69). Most certainly, elements of a critique of revealed religion do emerge from these letters. But one would have to say that the attack upon Christianity in the harem letters—in going beyond questions of dogma and church/state relations to strike at monotheism itself—is more visceral, and more in keeping with the fabulist's preference for the conviction of feeling over argument. Through the harem, Montesquieu can criticize—dramatically rather than analytically—the very notion of an unseen and absolute God, who demands mankind's obedience and love. By his deliberate vulgarization of the love of God to sexual passion, Montesquieu illustrates Christianity's offenses against human nature.

On this reading, the letter from Zachi (#3) relates not simply a beauty contest, but a scene of God's judgment, wherein the believers pursue an extreme ambition to be among the elect. Usbek's gaze is said to penetrate to the most secret places—a sexualized rendition of God's omniscient knowledge of the human soul. Likewise, in Zéphis's letter (#4), the accusation of lesbianism is simultaneously an accusation of idolatry, the worship of false gods. Just as Usbek's judgment and the demand for sexual fidelity define the terms of the women's existence, the prospect of divine judgment and the commandment that "thou shalt have no other gods before me" define the terms of the believer's existence. Right before the final apocalypse, when Usbek's vengeance is about to be wreaked, even the chief eunuch seems to recognize (though not sympathize with) the plight of the women, calling them "everlasting victims of shame and modesty" (#160). The women, of course, are not the only victims of virtue. Indeed, the eunuchs might justly claim precedence in that regard, for repression has rendered them monstrous.

Teratology

The eunuchs are a very curious feature of the *Persian Letters*.[3] Paul Valéry's famous query expresses perfectly the unease they occasion: "But who can explain all those eunuchs? I have no doubt," Valéry wrote, "that there is some secret and profound reason for the . . . presence of these persons, so cruelly cut off from many things and, in a way, from themselves."[4] Eunuchs are present not only in the *Persian Letters*, but in most all of Montesquieu's works, both those published in his lifetime and in his private journals. He had long been occupied with their meaning, and with the similarity between the eunuchs and the priesthood. Priestly eunuchs first appear in "Les Pretres dans le paganisme," a work Montesquieu wrote at the age of twenty-two (*Pensées*, no. 591). In the *Persian Letters*, the analogy between eunuchs and priests is clearly drawn in the letter on the causes of depopulation in Christian countries: Usbek complains of the "great number of eunuchs" in Christian lands, explaining that he is "referring to those priests and dervishes of both sexes who are sworn to perpetual chastity" (#117). In mentioning the vow of silence taken by the Carthusian order, Rica makes the same point, in his own inimitable "modest proposal" fashion: "It is said that the Carthusians cut off their tongues upon entering the convent, and it would be most desirable if all the other dervishes would remove in the same way everything rendered useless by their profession." According to Montesquieu, the eunuchism encouraged by Christianity was made explicit by Origen, one of the early Church fathers, who "castrated himself on account of a verse" (*Pensées*, no. 2162a; the verse he acted upon was Matthew 19:12).

The perniciousness of priestly celibacy is not limited to its external demographic effects, outlined by Usbek in the sequence on population. According to Montesquieu, perpetual continence produces in its practitioners an undesirable modification of the soul. In his *Essay on Causes That Can Affect Spirits and Characters*, Montesquieu speculates on the physical process whereby sexual abstinence communicates itself to the spirit and assimilates the willfully chaste to that "particular genre of men who are usually sad, angry, capricious, weak, vindictive, bizarre, timid: these are the eunuchs" (2:49). In the same passage, Montesquieu likens the relationship of soul and body to a spider in its

web. The spider's motion is communicated to the threads just as motion in the thread is communicated to the spider. The soul, on Montesquieu's metaphor, is not immaterial, since the body itself is spun
from the stuff of the soul. The soul is instead a sort of ganglion—a
sensate entity, a fuzzy, tentacled receiver and transmitter of vibrations.
Montesquieu is famous for explaining human character in terms of the
slackness, extension, and sensitivity of fibers and nerves. The most
notorious instance is in *The Spirit of the Laws* where he backs up his
climatological claims about the difference in temperament between
northern and southern peoples with the record of an experiment he
conducted on the papillae of a sheep's tongue (XIV.2). Crude and
amateurish though they sometimes appear to us, these images of webs
and fibers and reciprocal networks are used by Montesquieu to endow
"matter in motion" with some real-life complexity, certainly greater
complexity than the reductionist, billiard-ball model of kinetics offers.
Montesquieu does on one occasion employ the billiard-ball model, but
significantly it is to describe the motion of obedience in a despotism:
"In despotic states the nature of the government requires extreme obedience, and the prince's will, once known, should produce its effect as
infallibly as does one ball thrown against another" (III.10).

Although the account of the eunuch's character in the *Persian Letters* does not descend to such etiological details as the retention of
semen, it is nevertheless a somatogenic explanation. In *Beyond Good
and Evil*, Nietzsche says, "The degree and kind of a man's sexuality
reach up into the ultimate pinnacle of his spirit" (#75). Montesquieu
would agree. Perhaps the first thing to note about the eunuchs is the
persistence of sexual desire among them despite the loss of sexual
faculties. Zélis relates that "no passion was ever stronger or more violent than that of the white eunuch Cosrou for my slave Zélide" (#53).
Unlike gelded livestock, the eunuchs are far from docile. The disproportion between appetite and ability simply aggravates appetite. Another white eunuch, Nadir, is caught illicitly visiting the apartments
of one of the wives (#20 and #21). In tacit recognition of the guard-
ing-the-guardians problem, only black eunuchs are officially permitted
to wait upon the women. Sexual disability on the part of the guardians must be reinforced by race prejudice on the part of the wives in
order to ensure the fidelity of both. Even so, the temptation to trans-
gress can be overwhelming. In a letter to a younger eunuch in Usbek's
entourage, the chief eunuch finally makes his own confession:

> So I passed a miserable youth. I had no confidant but myself. I alone
> had to consume the regrets and grief that weighed upon me, and I had

to look severely upon the very women I was tempted to gaze at with tender eyes. I would have been lost if they had penetrated me. What advantages would they not have taken then?

I recall one day when, putting a woman into her bath, I felt myself so transported that I entirely lost reason, and dared to move my hand into a fearful place. At first thought I supposed that day would be my last. I was, however, fortunate enough to escape the thousand deaths [i.e., death by torture]. But the beauty to whom I thus confided my weakness sold her silence dearly. I entirely lost my authority over her, and she has since forced me to compliances that have exposed me a thousand times to lose my life. (#9)

The eunuch has manly passions; women act upon him as upon other men. However, because his passions cannot eventuate in manly action, the eunuch must conceal the fact that he suffers passion. His weakness, politically speaking, is not his impotence (of which the women are well aware), but the impassioned state of his impotence. Indeed, for the eunuch, the women's discovery of this vulnerability is tantamount to a reversal of the sexual order: the eunuch fears "penetration" by the women. The one time he reveals his passion, the eunuch loses his reason, his authority, and potentially his life.

The eunuch's defense against the women, his method of power, is indifference, feigned at first, but over time genuine. Believing himself to have overcome the gap between appetite and ability, the chief eunuch, now an old man, can say:

I look at women indifferently and give back to them all the scorn and all the torments they made me suffer. I remember constantly that I was born to command them, and when I do command, I seem to become a man again. I hate them, ever since I have been able to regard them with cold sense, and ever since my reason has been freed to see their weaknesses. Although I keep them for another, making them obey gives me secret joy. When I deprive them of anything, the order is entirely mine, and it always produces indirect satisfaction. The seraglio is a little empire that I rule, and ambition, the only passion left me, is somewhat appeased.

With the standard path of manliness blocked, another has been formulated. A malicious, subterranean hatred circulates through, and eventually dominates the eunuch's being. Sexual passion is not so much expunged as displaced or channeled into the quest for power. In almost Nietzschean manner, Montesquieu links priestly asceticism and the quest for temporal dominion. The same link is made in *The Spirit of the Laws*, where Montesquieu speaks forthrightly of monks, rather than eunuchs:

Why do monks so love their order? Their love comes from the same thing that makes their order intolerable to them. Their rule deprives them of everything upon which ordinary passions rest; what remains, therefore, is the passion for the very rule that afflicts them. The more austere it is, that is, the more it curtails their inclinations, the more force it gives to those that remain. (V.2)[5]

Interestingly, no mention is made of the monks loving God. It is as if their insularity has cut them off from the very source of the rule they live under. Centered on the order itself, their love is ingrown. The surprising placement of this monkish example in a chapter entitled "What virtue is in the political state"—in other words, in a chapter on republics not despotism—is one of Montesquieu's clearest indications of the unnaturalness and undesirability of the ancient city and its brand of patriotism. For both monks and citizens, this inward-looking, politico-religious *esprit de corps* is the product of austerity. Love of the body politic is inspired by punishing the body of the individual. (In today's soft democracies, the only place one still sees the ancient brand of patriotism is in the military. The marines in particular understand that corporal punishment can be the source of *esprit de corps*.)

By careful draftsmanship, Montesquieu directs the eye to the similarity between the French words for "less" (*moins*) and "monks" (*moines*). In English also there is an etymological link between monk and words meaning less or lack. While deriving monk from the Greek *monos* (single), *Webster's Ninth New Collegiate Dictionary* (1981) states that it is "akin" to Old High German *mengen* (to lack) and Greek *manos* (sparse). Priestly power mongering comes not from largeness of soul or spirit, but from its opposite. Theirs is the rule of *ressentiment*—ambitious, but ultimately slavish, for neither monks nor eunuchs can aspire to rule in their own right. Because of this built-in cap on their extreme ambition, the eunuchs are ideally fitted to be the animate instruments of a despot. Their office of mediation between men and women distorts not only their own sexuality but that of others. The eunuchs become the most determined proponents of male supremacy; they are the vehicle of the husband's apotheosis and the wives' subjection. Like the religious orders of the Church, Usbek's eunuchs exercise much of the authority of the lord, but do not share in any of his privileges. Adoration belongs to Usbek alone. The inquisitorial misogyny of Usbek's eunuchs finds its Western analogue in the misanthropy of the ministerial class.

In its attempt to consecrate sexual passion to God's greater glory, Christianity distorts or denies the sexual component of the self. The eunuch is the image and the agent of that self-alienation. Precluded from sexual intimacy, from familial ties, from friendship even, the eunuch becomes inhuman. Zélis speaks of "the black monster" (#4), Roxane and Zachi of "the tiger" (#156 and #157). Usbek also recognizes the eunuch's subhuman status, but from a different perspective; to him eunuchs are as "insects I crush underfoot" (#21). Like a modified version of the legendary manticore, the eunuch has the head of a man, the thorax of a beast of prey, and the tail of an insect—an intelligent, cruel, wretch.

Usbek's only recorded act of mercy is to pardon a black slave, Pharan, who pleads to be spared impressment into eunuchdom (#41, 42, 43). Pharan is a laborer in the "gardens of Fatmé," Usbek's country estate.[6] Pharan writes Usbek, explaining that he regards castration as a descent from and deprivation of humanity. While not an obvious or burlesque retelling of a biblical story such as we find in other letters (e.g., the scatological rendition of Noah's ark in #18 or the makeover of Abraham in #141), this trio of letters, one each from the chief eunuch, Pharan, and Usbek, might be construed as having some reference to the story of man's fall and subsequent eviction from the garden of Eden. Unlike Adam, Pharan declines all inducements to move from the garden to the seraglio. His fall, if it is to happen, will occur under duress, at the hands of other men. By this account, man's fall should be characterized not as original sin, but as a violation of original wholeness. The eunuchs are vicious because unhappy. The modern diagnosis of man's alienation is first made by Montesquieu (of course, second opinions, and more radical courses of treatment, will be given by later thinkers, from Rousseau to Marx to Heidegger).

One might compare Montesquieu's diagnosis with that ascribed to Aristophanes in Plato's *Symposium*. There, too, dismemberment has occurred; men have been cut off from their original well-roundedness. However, for Aristophanes, such is the universal state of mankind. All existing human beings are halves—afflicted by incompleteness. Indeed, that incompleteness is indicated by the possession of sexual organs that allow for a fleeting and inadequate approximation of original union. Erotic desire is a reminder that one lacks self-sufficiency. For Aristophanes, sexuality itself is the sign of incompleteness or alienation. Montesquieu, perhaps betraying his modern optimism, seems to suggest that it is not the nature of sexuality, but rather society's assault on sexuality, the religiously inspired attempt to suppress and extirpate the passions, which produces self-division and unhappiness.

In their correspondence with Usbek, the eunuchs appear only as his factotums; the letters of the wives, showing the ruthless flip side of the cringing servants, complete the picture of consummate bureaucra-

cy. But in the letters where the eunuchs converse with one another
and reflect upon their condition, Montesquieu is able to evoke sympathy for this class of go-betweens who might otherwise emerge as the
villains of the piece. The letters of the eunuchs to one another are
some of the most affecting in the novel. As already mentioned, there
are only four letters that are neither sent to nor written by one of the
two travelers, Usbek and Rica. Three of these four are written by eunuchs to other eunuchs (#9, 15, 22); the last (#39) is from a eunuch
to a Jewish convert to Islam named Joshua. The purpose of this special clutch of letters is to show the eunuchs outside of their official
capacity. The first two (#9 and #15), which provide the dark backdrop
for the idealistic Troglodyte series, are written by the chief eunuch to
two of the eunuchs in Usbek's entourage, Ibbi and Jaron. The first (extensively excerpted above) describes his constant misery and envies
Ibbi his relative freedom. The second, written to a protégé not a peer,
suppresses all talk of regret and instead utters pieties: "I hope that my
master, on his return, will make the pilgrimage to Mecca; in that land
of the angels you can purify yourself." Despite its edifying intention,
this letter is confessional as well, albeit in a different sense than the
letter to Ibbi. The chief eunuch opens his heart to Jaron, making a
confession of love rather than of despair: "Although I have scarcely
known that attachment men call friendship and am entirely wrapped
up in myself. . . . I can tell you now that I loved you as a father
loves his son, if the names of father and son are consistent with our
destiny." In place of outright animosity against androphagous religious
houses ("so many pits in which to bury future generations" [#117]),
here Montesquieu reveals the poignant human longing behind the religious appropriation of the family's structure and language. In #22, Jaron
replies to his mentor, regretfully announcing that he is being sent back
to Persia to reinforce the harem guard: "I would have enjoyed following my master in the Occident, but my will is his property." Jaron
finds the simple slavery of personal attendance upon Usbek far preferable to the complex slavery of being Usbek's intermediary, despite the
chief eunuch's propaganda about "leaving a servitude where you could
only obey, in order to enter a servitude where you would command."

After examining the dimensions of the eunuchs' unhappiness in the
first three intra-eunuch letters, Montesquieu traces that unhappiness to
its origins in #39. We might have expected the fourth intra-eunuch
letter to be Ibbi's response to the chief eunuch. Instead, we have the
letter of "Hagi Ibbi to the Jew Ben Joshua, Mohammedan proselyte."
As a devout believer who has made the pilgrimage to Mecca, Ibbi bears
the title of "hagi." In contrast to Usbek's wives, whose sole worship

is of Usbek and who accordingly make no mention of Islamic belief or practice, the eunuchs are distinguished by their extreme piety and concern with purification. Ibbi's correspondent is a Jewish convert to Islam named Joshua (the Hebrew form of Jesus). I believe that this letter, whose explicit subject is the miraculous nativity of Mohammed (conceived immaculately, and born already circumcised on a night that God put an impassable barrier between men and women), has as its subtext the genesis of the eunuch as a type common to all three revealed religions. The attack on sexuality that begins with God's "covenant in the flesh," the Jewish covenant of circumcision (Genesis 17:1–27), becomes progressively more thoroughgoing in Christian celibacy and Islamic eunuchdom. Joshua is a clever conflation of the three great monotheistic religions; as a Jew named Jesus become a Mohammedan proselyte, he is the equivalent of a eunuch, if not a eunuch three times over.

The assimilation of circumcision to celibacy and castration might seem to overlook, somewhat cavalierly, the fact that circumcision does not preclude procreation. Indeed, according to the Old Testament, Abraham is the "father of a multitude of nations" precisely on account of God's "covenant in the flesh." Circumcision is a pledge of fruitfulness, a sign of God's reversal of a barren marriage. It is nonetheless true that Abraham becomes the progenitor of the twelve tribes of Israel and their offshoots, Christianity and Islam, through his acceptance of a certain sexual mutilation, for himself and his descendants. By taking the knife to every man-child, the Jews give a token of their willingness to surrender their seed to God. Circumcision is a symbolic filiacide. To walk before the Lord and be perfect, a man must consecrate his generative powers to God. That consecration is evident not only in the covenant of circumcision, but in Abraham's binding of his only son, Isaac, and in God's claim on the first-born of the Children of Israel, a sacrifice that is rendered through the creation of an hereditary priestly class, the Levites. Mutilation that is prudently symbolic among the Hebrews becomes zealously literal among the Gentiles.[7]

Despotism's Fundamental Law

In stressing the religious significance of the eunuchs, I do not mean to scant their political meaning. Doubtless, the eunuchs represent ministers of state as well as ministers of the Church; and most especially they represent those in whom the two posts are united, men like Cardinal Richelieu and Cardinal Mazarin, the founders of French absolutism, persecutors of the Huguenots, and suppressors of the Fronde. Montesquieu's choice of the eunuchs, with their bodily mutilation and psychological disfigurement, to represent the bureaucratic *corps* makes clear that order's separation from and hostility to ordinary human life.

However, some of those critics who read the *Persian Letters* as a narrowly political *roman à clef* seem to be forcing the door with a picklock rather than disclosing the interior scene with a real key. In seeking an explanation of the separate functions of black and white eunuchs, J. L. Carr suggests that the black eunuchs symbolize the *noblesse de robe* and the white eunuchs the *noblesse d'épée* (the color scheme derived from the fact that French magistrates wore black robes, while the traditional knightly color was white).[8] Such an allegory seems to me not in keeping with Montesquieu's presentation of the French nobility in the French letters proper. Part of the French nobility is simply decadent, given over to pleasures and negligent of its traditional rights and responsibilities. In the *parlements*, however, the nobility shows itself still capable of mustering in opposition to the king. Rica's letter informing Usbek of the banishment of the Paris *parlement* (#140) honors these pockets of determined resistance.

> These assemblies are always hateful, for they approach kings only to tell them unwelcome truths; and while a crowd of courtiers forever represents to their kings that the people are happy under their government, the *parlements* come to give the lie to flattery and to carry to the foot of the throne the laments and the tears with which they have been entrusted.

It would be more accurate, I believe, to compare the nobility to Usbek's wives, some of whom supinely accept their disfranchisement, others of whom attempt resistance. Indeed, the situation of the women as Roxane describes it in her *cahier de doléances* (#158) is reminiscent of the disbanded *parlements*: "[The chief eunuch] has shut us all into our own apartments, and though we are alone, he insists that we be veiled. We are no longer permitted to talk together; it would be criminal to write; we retain only the freedom to weep." The linkage between the two letters (#140 and #158) becomes even more noticeable when the final batch of harem letters (#147-61), which appear together out of chronological order, are reinserted in their proper place. Roxane's complaint is written on the second of the moon of Maharram (March) 1720 and would have been received by Usbek four to five months later, about the same time that he receives the notice from Rica of the action against the Paris *parlement*, written from Paris the twenty-first of the moon of Gemmadi I (July) 1720 (see appendix, Table A1).

The suspicion that the fate of the wives has a pointed applicability to the fate of the nobility receives some confirmation in one of Montesquieu's *pensées*, where he writes: "Despotic government stifles the talents of subjects and great men, as the power of men stifles the talents of women" (no. 1820). We might say that the French nobility is effeminized, rather than emasculated. Unlike Usbek's eunuchs, for whom emasculation is the condition of an ascent to power, the French nobility is denied any significant political role. The tendency of absolutism is to reduce all subjects to a uniform status, a peerage of nonentities. When the bulwark of the nobility is leveled, however, the king-become-despot is left facing an undifferentiated people and the eventual prospect of a popular revolution. Through the wives, Montesquieu is able to illustrate both developments—the despotic humbling of the mighty and the revolutionary might of the humble. The eunuchs represent not the nobility in general, as Carr claims, but those few, noble or not, who become the king's minions. They constitute a new sort of *corps*, owing their position to favoritism and other special operations, rather than heredity.[9] Since they are made, not born, they might be commoners (Richard II's Bushy, Bagot, and Green) or foreigners (Mazarin, chief minister of Louis XIII and XIV, was born Giulio Mazarini) or, like Usbek's eunuchs, members of a despised race.

The racial division of the eunuchs may well contain some coded comment on the power structure of the French court and the infighting among different factions. For instance, the black eunuchs may represent the inner circle, specifically the Jesuit clerical hierarchy, while the white eunuchs may represent either the Jansenists, or alternatively, the class of nonclerical courtiers. But it seems to me that Montesquieu also intends us to take seriously the surface meaning of the racial polarization in the harem. Montesquieu is inquiring into the operation and curious paradoxes of race prejudice. Certainly, the imprisonment of the wives is made more complete by their hatred for the blackness of their jailers. In lauding Usbek's physical beauty, Fatmé tells her husband, "When I married you I had never seen even the face of a man; and you are still the only man I have been permitted to look upon, since I do not class as men these frightful eunuchs, whose least imperfection is that they are not men. When I compare the beauty of your face with the deformity of theirs, I cannot help deeming myself happy" (#7). Fatmé is repulsed more by the eunuchs' color and facial characteristics than by their condition.

Other wives also experience this seemingly innate racial recoil. In #20, Usbek, in the course of rebuking Zachi for her dalliance with a white eunuch, notes her dissatisfaction with the chief black eunuch:

"His ugliness, you say, is so great that you cannot look at him without pain—as if one should put more beautiful objects in that sort of
post. What really disturbs you is that you have not in his place the
white eunuch who dishonors you." It is Rica—adept at putting himself in the shoes of others—who finds the explanation of this phenomenon:

> It seems to me, Usbek, that we judge things only by a covert reference
> that we make to ourselves. I am not surprised that Negroes paint the
> devil in dazzling white and their gods in carbon black; or that the Ve-
> nus of certain peoples has breasts that hang to her thighs; . . . It is well
> said that if triangles were to create a god, they would describe him with
> three sides. (#59)

Natural aesthetic self-preference leads people of one race to demonize
people of other races, in effect, reading them out of humanity, while
at the same time, projecting themselves into the heavens. Men deny
similarity where it exists (namely, among human beings) and ascribe
similarity where there is none (that is, between humanity and the divine). Just as despotism is a form of politics reduced to elemental
passions, the despotic aesthetic is concerned with surfaces, the simple
(though perhaps deceptive) appearance of things.

The consequences of race pride are examined more closely in the
letter on the Spanish (#78). The anonymous author of this letter-
within-a-letter, forwarded to Usbek by Rica, describes the pride taken
by "these invincible enemies of work" in their mustaches, their swords,
and their white skin—the accoutrements of their masculinity and their
imperialism. He asserts that the pride of the Spaniards living in the
New World hinges entirely on color:

> they consider that they have the sublime merit to be, as they say, *men
> of white flesh*. Never in the seraglio of the Great Prince has there been
> a sultana so proud of her beauty as the oldest and ugliest rascal among
> them is proud of the sallow, olive whiteness of his complexion, as he
> sits, arms crossed, in his doorway in a Mexican town. A man of such
> consequence, a creature so perfect, would not work for all the wealth in
> the world, or persuade himself to compromise the honor and dignity of
> his skin by vile mechanical industry [italics in original].

Race pride of this order produces laziness, poverty, regressive imperialism, and eventually, national destruction.

Montesquieu's best known statement on race appears in *The Spirit
of the Laws*, in a chapter entitled "On the Slavery of Negroes" (XV.5).
There Montesquieu presents all the standard justifications—economic,
political, and religious—for race slavery. He speaks ostensibly in his

own name, saying: "If I had to defend the right we have had of making Negroes slaves, here is what I would say." The conditional form of the opening sentence, however, serves to alert the reader to expect some ironic distance between Montesquieu's own views and the "arguments" offered. For instance:

> Those concerned are black from head to toe, and they have such flat noses that it is almost impossible to feel sorry for them.
> One cannot get into one's mind that god, who is a very wise being, should have put a soul, above all a good soul, in a body that was entirely black.
> It is so natural to think that color constitutes the essence of humanity that the peoples of Asia, who make eunuchs, continue to deprive blacks of their likeness to us in this more distinctive way.

In this string of excuses for slavery, which might at first seem random, Montesquieu traces the progression of race prejudice from an initial perception of physical difference that impairs fellow feeling to an assumption of spiritual and moral difference, and finally to an act, castration, that truly establishes physical (and possibly moral) difference. Concluding that blacks are not men, the Persians have tried to eradicate any attributes that indicate otherwise. Where nature has failed to render supposedly natural differences sufficiently clear, resort has been had to human correction. Rather than sermonize on the injustice of race slavery, Montesquieu mouths the self-incriminating arguments of its proponents. Stripped of all euphemism, these justifications appear for what they are: brutal, prideful, and absurd. In Montesquieu's supremely ironic formulation, "It is impossible for us to assume that these people are men because if we assumed they were men one would begin to believe that we ourselves were not Christians."

In the relationship between the chief black eunuch and Usbek, we see the paradox of despotism at work. The disinclination of the master to labor or even rule means that rule will eventually slip from him. Usbek's power and his fate reside in the hands of those he despises. In *The Spirit of the Laws*, Montesquieu asserts that, in a despotic state, "the establishment of a vizir is a fundamental law" (II.5).[10] By its nature, absolute rule culminates in an abdication of sorts: the devolution of power to the chief minister. This is the only law of an otherwise lawless state. (Accordingly, while acknowledgment is made of the eunuch's role in the household in XVI.14, the more extensive discussion of eunuchs in XV.19 portrays them as magistrates, mandarins, and local governors rather than domestic overseers.) General principles of the different forms of government are not enunciated in the *Persian*

Letters as they are in *The Spirit of the Laws*; instead, the drama of Usbek's household conveys the same teaching.

Overall, the letters exchanged between Usbek and the eunuchs display the same disproportion as the letters between Usbek and the wives: Usbek writes six letters, all very brief, to various eunuchs (four of them are grants of authority, #2, 148, 150, 153; one is a grant of clemency, #43; and one a reproof, #21); the eunuchs write eleven to Usbek, five of them from the pen of the chief black eunuch.[11] Interestingly, the chief eunuch is never given a name. Most of the others bear names indicative of a eunuch's condition (Solim, Narsit, Nadir, and Ishmael: which is to say, solitary, narcissistic, base, and outcast). Leaving the chief eunuch nameless has the effect of concentrating the reader's attention on the office itself. We have already examined the two letters written by the chief eunuch to other eunuchs (#9 and #15). The letters destined for Usbek betray none of the chief eunuch's private regrets and longings; they are instead a manual of despotism written by one who would be its effectual practitioner. From the start, however, the chief eunuch encounters resistance from Usbek, whose initial grant of authority (#2) is far from complete. That is not to say that the eunuch's power is "limited" after the manner of a moderate government; instead, according to Usbek's instructions, the eunuch is to alternate between abasement and imperiousness:

> You command [the women], and you obey them. You execute blindly their every desire, and you make them execute the laws of the seraglio in the same way. You take glory in providing them with the humblest services; you submit with respect and fear to their legitimate orders; you serve them like the slave of their slaves. But resuming your power, you command imperiously, even as I, whenever you fear relaxation of the laws of decency and modesty.

The letters of the chief eunuch to Usbek (#41, 64, 79, 96, 147) are all written with a view to securing a full delegation of power. In #41, the chief eunuch defends his policy of forcibly recruiting new eunuchs; Usbek, however, overrules him, mercifully forbidding impressment (#43). In #64, the chief eunuch complains of the disorder that results from Usbek's tenderness toward his wives. Usbek's preference for gentle remonstration over punishment is most evident in the immediately succeeding general address to his wives (#65), where he seeks to return them to their duty with warm words: "I wish you to forget that I am your master and to remember me only as your husband." The chief eunuch backs up his demand for more authority by telling the story of his apprenticeship to a remarkable chief eunuch from whom he learned "the difficult art of command." This "grand master" taught him how to break women's spirits—through the judicious alternation of severity and compliance, the use of informers, and other Machiavellian techniques—so that the husband might capture their hearts. The chief eunuch promises that all will be well if Usbek will but give him absolute empire over the women. Letters #79 and #96 both concern the acquisition of additional wives. "We have noticed," writes the chief eunuch, "that the more women we have to watch, the less trouble they give us." The chief eunuch explains why numbers are no hindrance to despotic order:

> A greater necessity to please, less opportunity for conspiracy, more examples of submission: all this forges their chains. They are constantly watchful of each other's deportment, and it seems that, in concert with us, they work to make themselves more dependent; they become an accessory to our work and open our eyes when we close them. What do I say? They ceaselessly excite their master against their rivals and do not see how close they put themselves to the punishment they incite against others.

The machinery of fear constructed by the eunuchs functions most smoothly when oiled by hope. In #96, the chief eunuch pleads not for full authority but for Usbek's return. At best, the eunuch can impersonate only half of Usbek; he can menace but not caress. Without Usbek, or at least the promise of Usbek's second coming, the chief eunuch cannot play upon the hopes of the women. The chief eunuch's final letter, #147, relates the full extent of the troubles in the harem and makes a final, desperate plea for a full delegation of authority.

Usbek complies—too late. The chief eunuch is dead before Usbek's letter arrives; there follows the dramatic complication of unopened and misplaced letters. Sovereignty (or scriptural revelation) is temporarily lost in transit. Usbek must extend his grant of authority three times— first to the (now deceased) chief eunuch, then to his incompetent successor Narsit, and finally to the ambitious and sadistic Solim—before it meets with a willing hand. Although Usbek had, before the denouement of the harem intrigue, expressed his intent soon to return to his harem (#155), it seems that, after Solim's punishment of the guilty, return may be impossible. In #160, Solim speaks with joy of "all the blood I am about to spill." However, the novel's final letter, #161, makes clear that the purge did not go as Solim planned. Roxane tells Usbek that before swallowing the poison that will consume her by letter's end, she managed to murder "those sacrilegious guardians who shed the most precious blood in the World" (that of her lover). From Solim's account,

we know that many, perhaps all, of the eunuchs, including Solim himself, were involved in the lover's death. Solim's belated crackdown
seems only to have sparked a civil war, from which neither the government nor the insurgents emerge victorious.

The First Prisoner of the Palace[12]

Video meliora proboque: deteriora sequor. This line from Ovid ("I
see the better way, and approve it; I follow the worse") might serve as
Usbek's epitaph. In his letters on nonharem matters, Usbek shows himself to be a partisan of moderate government. Even in his dealings
with his wives and eunuchs, despite occasional ill-tempered outbursts,
he leans toward mercy. Benevolent despotism, however, proves to be a
contradiction in terms. Unwilling to be cuckolded, Usbek is driven to
grant plenary power to the chief eunuch. He consents to one form of
usurpation in the hope of sparing himself a more humiliating form.
The loyalty of the wives, however, is beyond recovery.

Although the novel appears to close with Roxane's defiant suicide
in #161, in fact letters #140-46 bear dates subsequent to the destruction of the harem (see appendix). Indeed, the last of these postapoca-
lypse letters is written by Usbek when he is already in receipt of
Roxane's blood-drenched missive. Thus, technically, Montesquieu does
give Usbek the last word, although his decision to collect the harem
letters at the end, in striking disregard of chronology, somewhat conceals this fact. Montesquieu's violation of chronology has a double
effect: the drama is intensified by telescoping the final three years
worth of harem letters; at the same time, by abandoning the intercalation of French and Persian letters, the precise parallels between the
harem intrigue and doings in the Palais Royal are somewhat obscured.[13]
Feeling is heightened, but the ultimate object is hidden.

The novel's real conclusion (#146) is a jeremiad against ministers:
"What crime can be greater than that committed by a minister, when
he corrupts the morals of an entire nation, degrades the souls of the
most upright, tarnishes the splendor of rank, obscures virtue itself, and
confounds those of the highest birth with the most despised." Although
Usbek's denunciation is made with ostensible reference to conditions
in India (with no mention of either France or Usbek's own harem), the
letter is pretty clearly a thinly disguised account of John Law's financial mismanagement and the turmoil it brought to France. Whether
speaking of India, France, or Persia, Usbek blames the vizier. When
letter #146 is reread in light of Usbek's investiture of the eunuch Solim

and the collapse of the harem (#147–61), Usbek's assignment of blame cannot but look self-pitying and insufficient. Though a sojourner after truth, Usbek still lacks self-knowledge; he does not realize that the vizier is the essence of despotism and that he who appoints the vizier is at fault. If anything, the explosion of the harem seems to have blinded rather than enlightened Usbek.

While the women, and even the eunuchs, have managed to find satisfactions—both sensual and intellectual—in the seraglio, Usbek has not. Both before and after his departure from Persia, he is made miserable by his attempt to enforce virtue. In the first of three letters that trace his growing despair over his wives (#6, 27, 155), Usbek admits to his friend Nessir that he has no love for his wives, having become insensible to desire even. He explains that "[i]n the numerous seraglio in which I lived, I prevented and destroyed love by the very act of love." While he is present, the enforcement of fidelity is sure. But the very tranquillity of his despotic possession is cloying; it yields not pleasure but disgust. His scorn for his wives, whose virtue is not free, and whose acts of adoration testify only to their self-degradation, is most evident in his words to Zachi: "You must thank me for the manner in which I make you live, since only in that way do you deserve to live at all" (#20).

Tranquillity—according to Montesquieu the object of all despotic government (*The Spirit of the Laws*, V.14)—gives place to tormenting doubts as soon as Usbek leaves Persia. Once across the Persian/Turkish border, Usbek is already convinced that he has "undertaken too much for my peace of mind" (#6). As the journey continues, the women loom ever larger as an obstacle to his pursuit of wisdom. The jealousy that consumes him does not spring from a reawakening of love, however, but as he says, from his *froideur* itself, his indifference or frigidity. This use of the word *froideur* is but the first of many indications that Usbek's situation is similar to that of his eunuchs—where they find themselves unable, he finds himself unwilling. Jealousy is a function of impotence. (Accordingly, Usbek is not jealous over Roxane, the only wife who interests him and whom he has mastered forcibly and recently.)

Montesquieu's *Pensées* contain notes for a projected work to have been entitled *Histoire de la Jalousie*. In one of these passages, he explains jealousy as springing from an incertitude or fear of not being loved (no. 578). Indifferent himself, Usbek yet fears the indifference of others. Another entry from the *Pensées* explains how "the effect becomes itself the cause, and vigilance the greatest motive to vigilance." As a result of this geometric progression of jealousy and impotence, "soon one is persuaded that it would be a calamity worse than the loss of life and goods for another man, a father even, to see the countenance of a wife whom one does not care to see oneself" (no. 580). Although Usbek initially fled Persia out of care for his life (under threat by the flatterers whom he has exposed at the court of the shah), the last of his letters to Nessir shows him contemplating a return to Persia, at the cost of his life if need be, in order to forestall "a blow more cruel . . . than a thousand deaths" (#155). Usbek, who as a subject of the shah had experienced the incompatibility between despotism and virtue and whose self-exile was in part a search for the freedom necessary to virtue, is now ready to submit his head to the agents of the shah's despotism in order to reestablish his own despotism in the harem. Usbek does not see the similarity between his rule and the shah's.

In his failure to see himself aright, Usbek cuts rather a sad figure. Until his flare-up into violence, he is in constant retreat, first from the Persian court, then from Persia itself, and soon from his adopted city, Paris. As he lingers in the French countryside his apathy increases. Usbek writes many more letters in the first five years of his voyage than in the last five (forty-seven versus thirty-two, with only seven written in the last two years). His friendships suffer. Usbek's first three letters to Rustan (#1, 8, 19) all bear the caption "Usbek to his friend Rustan." This appellation is dropped from his last letter to Rustan (#91). He has no communication with his Turkish friend, Ibben, after June 1717 (#104). (As early as #67, Ibben had complained of Usbek's neglect: "Three vessels have arrived here without bringing any news from you. Are you ill? Or does it please you to alarm me?") With increasing frequency, Usbek lapses into prolonged silences, ranging from a few months to upwards of a year. After a letter to Rhédi in August 1719 (#129), Usbek disappears from view altogether while a long string of letters from Rica intervenes. Usbek takes up the pen again in October 1720 (#144). The eclipse of Usbek, it should be noted, actually looks more complete than it is. Usbek writes three letters (#153, 154, 155) during this time (all written on the same day in October 1719), but because of Montesquieu's reshuffling of the letters, our knowledge of them is delayed. Nonetheless, even when these letters are factored in, it emerges that Usbek has been silent for just over a year, dating from his order to "exterminate the guilty" (#153). We might say that Montesquieu's departure from chronological ordering serves to protect Usbek's privacy. Our attention is drawn to his silence; however, the cause of his silence—his anxious suffering as he awaits the implementation of his order—is shrouded from the reader. Montesquieu does what he can to keep the reader unsuspecting of events in the harem, for Montesquieu hopes that the reader will experience an epiphany where Usbek clearly does not.

The example of Usbek suggests that the feasibility of political reform depends on the achievement of self-knowledge. Usbek's failure of self-knowledge is profoundly troubling, for he is, in many respects, a superior man. His persistent inquiry has led him to discover for himself most of the principles of modern science and modern political thought. Moreover, Usbek feels his misery acutely; he claims it is greater than that of either the women or the eunuchs (#155). Yet despite his grasp of jealousy's operation, he remains in its grip. What does the gap between Usbek's theory and his practice say about the prospects of enlightenment, that is, of philosophically guided political reform? The novel's very title may point to the oxymoronic relation of philosophy and politics—*Lettres persanes*: letters in the broad sense being almost synonymous with enlightenment; Persia being the locus of despotism. Are there grounds for thinking the French enlightenment can be more successful than the Persian? For a possible answer to that question, we turn to #67 and #141, two sketches of alternative outcomes in the harem.

Chapter Six

Paradise Regained

Within the *Persian Letters* there are two tales, far and away the longest letters of the book, which serve as counterpoint to the sexual dystopia of Usbek's harem: Ibben's history of the incestuous lovers Aphéridon and Astarté (#67), and Rica's tale of the paradisiacal rule of Anaïs, a philosopher-queen who makes a new covenant with a new Ibrahim (#141). In both tales, the successful reclamation of sexuality depends upon the abandonment of the reigning religious orthodoxy.[1] Religious and sexual revolution are linked. In the first story, natural sexual equality is achieved by a return to natural religion; in the second there is a complete role reversal: the establishment of female rule in heaven. One purports to be a true history; the other is an acknowledged fantasy. Both stories are sent to Usbek by friends who intend Usbek's good; they mean to make him see the overthrow of a harem from a perspective other than the master's.

Letter #141 reaches Usbek at a critical juncture. Unbeknownst to the reader, Usbek has already sent the order to "exterminate the guilty" (#153). Unbeknownst to both Usbek and the reader, the harem has already collapsed. This fictional foreshadowing of his overthrow cannot be pleasant for Usbek, as he awaits word from Ispahan. Rica, however, claims to be sending him this French translation of a Persian tale, which he produced to please a curious French woman, on the chance that Usbek "will be well pleased to see [a Persian tale] travestied." Rica's use of the word *travesty* is suggestive. In its origin, the word is identical to *transvestism*; the root of both is the Latin *trans* + *vestire*, to cross dress. The story Rica presents is indeed a disguised, burlesque version of the tragedy unfolding in Usbek's harem. It is a tale of transvestism, written for a French woman from a woman's point of view.

Rica here reveals something of the technique of the *Persian Letters* as a whole. The *roman* that Montesquieu presents by assuming the guise

of a translator and compiler of letters is itself a travesty; Usbek's seraglio is a fictionalized rendition of the tragedy unfolding, at the time
of Montesquieu's writing, in France. France appears to the reader in
Persian garb, and especially behind the veils of the wives. The need
for a mask is not simply to avoid the censors. In a book that affronts
France's ruling orders openly and at times outrageously, esotericism
for reasons of prudence does not explain much. Rica hints at a deeper
reason when, early on, he casts off his Persian costume, immediately
becoming, as he says, "a frightful nonentity" (#30). In Western dress
he is invisible. Frenchmen look on the exotic with avidity, but take
their own ways for granted. Costume, or the appearance of difference,
is essential to curiosity. Montesquieu seems to believe that we see others better than ourselves; his experiments with literary transvestism are
designed to fool us into seeing ourselves. (It is worth noting that both
of the letters flanking Rica's "travesty" point to elements of the French
tragedy: #140 announces the banishment of the *parlement* of Paris; #142
is an allegory on John Law and the financial ruin of France. Moreover, if the final batch of harem letters [#147-61], which appear together out of chronological order, are reinserted in their proper place,
then Roxane's proclamation of the collapse in Ispahan [#161] would
immediately precede #140-42.) At the conclusion of "Some Reflections
on the *Persian Letters*," Montesquieu, in seeming contravention of his
earlier talk of a secret chain, declares that "[c]ertainly the nature and
the design of the *Persian Letters* are so obvious that they can deceive
only those who wish to deceive themselves." Unfortunately, most people fall into the camp of self-deceivers. Montesquieu uses the fascina-
tion with the other as a route to the self. Through his Persians, we can
come to see ourselves as equally strange and questionable.

Joy of Man's Desiring

Rica's *conte* (#141) begins with Zuléma, a woman learned in the
law and the prophets, but with a playful spirit. This combination of
qualities—this very Montesquieuan combination—makes it difficult for
those who hear her discourses to divine her intention: is it to amuse
or instruct? Questioned as to whether paradise is reserved for men, as
the doctors of divinity claim, she disputes "these injurious opinions,"
whose provenance is "nothing other than the pride of men." Zuléma
particularly faults the Jews, "who maintain on the authority of their
sacred books that we have no souls."
This question of women's share in immortality has been broached

before by Rica. Indeed, his very first letter (#24) describes how women have been the instigators of the revolt against the papal bull *Unigenitus* (and against the king's subscription to it) because it forbade women to read the Bible. Rica, at this point only just launched on his odyssey of enlightenment, says:

> this mufti [that is, the pope] has not reasoned badly: and, by the great Hali, it must be that he has been instructed in the principles of our sacred law: for since women are of a creation inferior to ours, and since our prophets tell us that they cannot enter paradise, why should they trouble themselves to read a book intended only to teach the way to paradise?

As in the case of race slavery, extreme sexual subordination culminates in the attempt to read the inferior out of the human race, to deny a common creation. As Zuléma says, "Nothing has been left undone to degrade our sex." The question of the full humanity of women was debated as part of the seventeenth century's *querelle des femmes*; Montesquieu would have been familiar with the controversy over the proposition "mulieres non esse homines" through the writings of Bayle.[2] In their religiously sanctioned humiliation of women, both Christianity and Islam are seen, once again, to follow Judaism's lead.

In his letter on sexual equality (#38), Rica, already moving away from his tradition, shows that the ascendancy of men, despite the teaching of Genesis (2:18-24 and 3:16), is by no means universal. He cites as examples the ancient, highly developed peoples contemporaneous with the early Hebrews and the early Christians: "It must be admitted, however it shocks our customs, that among the most civilized nations women have always had authority over their husbands. This was established by a law among the Egyptians, in honor of Isis, and among the Babylonians, in honor of Semiramis. It is said of the Romans that they commanded all nations but obeyed their wives." Montesquieu here indicates a connection between the worship of female divinities and the establishment of matriarchy. As we shall see, both of the utopias sketched in the *Persian Letters* have female characters named after fertility goddesses.

The *Pensées* further illustrates Montesquieu's interest in the matriarchal alternative. Along with a number of selections about the goddess Isis, the religious source of the matriarchal order of Egyptian life, the *Pensées* contains this striking passage:

> Is it not true that if Mohammedanism had subdued the entire earth women would have been everywhere confined? This manner of govern-

ing them would have been regarded as natural, and it would have been difficult to imagine that there could be another. If the Scythian women had continued their conquests, if the Egyptians had continued theirs, the human race would live subject to women, and it would be necessary to be a philosopher to say that another government would be more conformable to nature. (no. 579)

According to Montesquieu, the spread of chauvinistic "prejudices" (whether of the male or female variety) via the route of empire "can be so great that it changes, so to speak, the whole genius of human nature. This is the reason that man is so difficult to define." Human life is malleable even in its most elemental character. The political meaning of the sexual division is neither obvious nor fixed; it is open to new determinations. But despite the pliability of our natures, Montesquieu suggests that there is something wrong with the ascendancy of either sex. Interestingly, Montesquieu implies that the injustice of male ascendancy is more recognizable than its opposite: although "difficult," it is not an insight reserved for philosophers alone, as the injustice of universal female ascendancy would be. The explanation of this is perhaps supplied in #38, where the "gallant philosopher" says that "the authority men hold over women is nothing but tyranny. They permit it only because they are gentler than we, and consequently more humane and reasonable; these advantages, which would give superiority to them if we were reasonable, make them instead lose it, because we are not." The rule of men, founded as it is on superior strength, is both more common, more perdurable, and more intensely felt by its subjects than the gentler rule of women would be.

As a woman who has not only read the sacred books but memorized them, Zuléma does not call into question "the empire that men have over us here below." She claims only that God will reward virtue in women just as He does virtue in men. For both sexes, the delights of heaven will be sensual; each man will be surrounded by celestial beauties and each woman by divine beaux. These divine seraglios will come complete with faithful eunuchs as well. Zuléma's description of the separate but equal accommodations in paradise brings to mind another letter of Rica's, #125, the general topic of which is the difficulty of conceiving of eternal paradise, inasmuch as "the nature of pleasures is to be of short duration." Whether filled with higher or lower pleasures, the paradise promised by most religions is a horrifyingly tedious prospect. To judge by Rica's account, even Nietzsche's doctrine of the eternal return of the same would be preferable, for it at least offers a changing spectacle, even if as part of a recurring cycle. By contrast, heaven is usually conceived as unvarying. (The importance Montesquieu attaches to the need for variety cannot be underestimated: variety is the aesthetic principle guiding his manner of composition and it is a moral/political conviction of sorts as well, guiding his appreciation of regimes.)

Rica illustrates the paltriness of the priestly imagination with a story about an Indian woman who refuses to practice *suttee* when she learns from a Hindu priest what the afterlife holds for her, namely, reunion with her earthly husband. She refuses to be a "good woman" (the word *suttee* is the feminine form of the Sanskrit word for good) for that reward. Her previous willingness to immolate herself was simply an acceptance of tradition—"[m]y mother, my aunt, and my sister were all properly burned"—and had nothing to do with attachment to her husband, who was, she says, "jealous, irritable, and also so old that, unless the god Brahma has somehow improved him, he surely has no need of me."

To illustrate her own opinion of what awaits women in the beyond, Zuléma also tells a story (drawn from an Arab book) of an "insupportably jealous" husband and a woman's stance toward death. These two stories, the Indian and the Arab, are like mirror images of one another. In the Indian case, the woman is reconciled to life since it ensures separation from her dead husband; in the Arab case, the woman embraces death rather than continue living with her husband. In each case, the divide between life and death is the woman's only hope of salvation. Zuléma's story concerns Ibrahim and his twelve enslaved wives. Ibrahim is, of course, an Islamicized Abraham, the biblical patriarch non pareil; his twelve wives evoke both the twelve tribes of Israel and the twelve apostles of Jesus. One of Ibrahim's wives, Anaïs (the name is that of an ancient Persian goddess), denounces his rule. Speaking on behalf of the assembled women, Anaïs tells Ibrahim:

> When one searches so hard for means to make himself feared, . . . he always finds means to make himself hated first. We are so unhappy that we cannot be prevented from wanting change. Others in my place might wish for your death; I desire nothing but my own. Since in this way only can I hope to be separated from you, death will be the sweeter for that reason.

Before Anaïs can, like Roxane, make good on her aspiration to tyranny-defying suicide, she is murdered by Ibrahim with a dagger to the breast. According to Zuléma, she receives the reward of her virtue in heaven: not the spiritualized heaven of religious tradition, but a sensual heaven filled with natural beauty (meadows, flowers, brooks, birds) and celestial men—numerous and tireless in their dedication to her pleasure.

In contrast to the sexual violence present in the erotic letters of Zachi and Usbek (#3 and #26), where pleasure was derivative of triumph, the eroticism in this letter is more purely physical: there is Anaïs's favorite *ménage à trois* and the night she successively visits all fifty of her men. Here (since paraphrase just won't do) is Montesquieu's description of Anaïs's first encounter with her divine duo:

> By then in utter ecstasy, she was carried even beyond her desires. "I am totally transported," she told them, "I would believe I were dying, were I not so certain of my immortality. It is too much! Leave me; I succumb to the violence of pleasure. Yes, now a little calm returns to my senses; I breathe again and come back to myself. Why have the torches been taken away? Why can't I still see your divine beauty? Why can't I see? . . . But why see? You bring me back to my first raptures. O Gods! How lovely this darkness is! What! Am I to be immortal, and immortal with you? I shall be? . . . No, I beg for mercy; for I see you are such men as never ask it for yourselves."

The ellipses, present in the original, convey well the self-annihilation of intense pleasure. Anaïs is lost to herself, in utter darkness. It is as if the pleasures of touch extinguish the pleasures of sight—the prehensile snuffs out the contemplative. We also note that, although this is supposedly an Islamic tale, Anaïs invokes the "gods."

Aristotle, more decorous than Montesquieu, says that "no one is capable of rational insight while enjoying sexual relations" (*Ethics* 7.11.4); Montesquieu however manages to raise serious questions about the nature of pleasure and the ontological foundations of hedonism through the exclamations of a woman in the throes of passion. Few erotic novels have similar merit. Because pleasure is not a state but a process tied to a cycle of depletion and repletion, Anaïs is forever alternating between the various pleasures of the bed—sleep and sex— and the various pleasures of the table—not only food, but all that accompanies it, music and games and dancing. Even unmixed sensory pleasures, such as the pleasures of sight, which do not operate on the emptiness-fullness model and are not preceded by want or pain, flow in a Heraclitean stream—Anaïs "appeared to her idolatrous court first in the charm of simple undress and then clothed in the most sumptuous raiment." Moreover, pleasure cannot succeed pleasure endlessly; there must be at least an instant of intervening pain. Pleasure it seems is unavoidably contaminated with its opposite. Following the first night of love, after "two moments of sleep repaired her lassitude," Anaïs wakes to the pain of doubt: "I am disturbed," she tells her partners, "for I fear you no longer love me." No sooner is doubt assuaged than new dilemmas arise:

> Yes, yes, I confess, no one has ever loved so much. But what is this? You quarrel over the honor of persuading me! Ah, if you contend with each other, if you join ambition to the pleasure of my defeat, then I am lost; you will both be conquerors, and I the only one vanquished. But I will sell the victory dearly to you!

Apparently, the battle of the sexes is not resolved even in paradise. In this bedroom banter, the language, if not the reality, of triumph and despair is preserved.

For more than a week, Anaïs gives herself up to such self-forgetting ecstasies.

> [I]n that blissful place, always outside of herself, she had not had a single reflection; she had enjoyed her happiness without contemplating it, without one of those tranquil moments when the soul, so to speak, takes account and listens to itself in the silence of the passions.
> The blessed have such vivid pleasures that they seldom enjoy this liberty of spirit.

There are certain similarities between the heavenly harem in which Anaïs now finds herself and the hellish harem she so recently escaped. In both, the din of the passions threatens to squelch the spirit. Anaïs's harem is an ideal despotism; although fear and jealousy still exist, those passions now conduce to pleasure. The doubt she momentarily experiences turns out to be a part of delight. Her subjects, being angelic, may be treated as means to her pleasure without offense to them. Likewise, they cannot offend her. Nonetheless, in the heavenly harem as in the earthly harem, an order founded entirely on passion is despotic. At issue is not rule by fear over other human beings, but the unrestrained rule of nature. Anaïs is pleasure's captive.

In a chapter of *The Spirit of the Laws* entitled "The idea of despotism" (V.13), Montesquieu similarly links despotism to the unthinking pursuit of immediate gratification. This two-sentence chapter, one of the work's shortest, declares that "[w]hen the savages of Louisiana want fruit, they cut down the tree and gather the fruit. There you have despotic government."[3] Despotism exists in the moment, oblivious of time and of history. (Usbek's harem, for instance, does not really live "in history" until his voyage begins. The regime of the immediate cannot survive the mediation of letters—presumably not even if the scriptures are holy. A gap inevitably emerges between the communication of the despot's wants and compliance with them.) In its pure, unprotracted form, despotism is not a regime at all. Any order a particular despotism possesses comes from adventitious factors; according to Montesquieu, a despotism "can maintain itself only when circumstances, which arise from the climate, the religion, and the situation or the genius of the people, force it to follow some order and to suffer some rule" (VIII.10). However, in Anaïs's despotic paradise, living in the moment may be endlessly indulged because regeneration is miraculously assured. No human effort is necessary to secure the future or preserve the past.

Montesquieu's implicit censure of this unproblematic life of delight makes it clear that his opposition to despotism is not simply in the service of expanded pleasure-seeking (although the stress he places on the sexual dissatisfaction of the women living under despotism could lead one to that conclusion); rather, his opposition to despotism is ultimately grounded in concern for the human spirit. The aspiration toward heaven is misplaced if the blessed themselves are debarred from *liberté d'esprit*.

Esprit is one of the most significant words in Montesquieu's political vocabulary. What Machiavelli does for *virtù*, radically terrestrializing it, Montesquieu does for *esprit*. The spirit he is intent on elucidating is neither holy nor immortal; it is the spirit of laws and the general spirit of nations. Spirit is a capacious word, and in no language more so than French. Indeed, in his *Pensées*, Montesquieu complained of the ambiguity of *esprit*, saying "[t]he French are wrong in confounding what the English designate *wit, humour, sense, understanding*" (no. 784). Nonetheless, as his manner of composition shows, Montesquieu knew how to capitalize on the confusion. More important for Montesquieu than the peculiarly Gallic conflation of wit and wisdom is another pair of overlapping meanings present in *esprit*: that of spiritedness and mind. We can see the linkage very clearly in Anaïs, who eventually rejects the enslavement of the blessed because she is possessed of a "truly philosophic spirit." It was this same "force of spirit" that led her, unlike her companions in the harem, to despise both fear and death, and so break the bonds of earthly despotism. Anaïs proves herself superior to both pleasure and pain.

When her spirit, first developed in the enforced isolation of the harem, reasserts itself in her new surroundings, Anaïs again seeks solitude—not the "solitary pleasures" of the gardens where "delights crowded to present themselves to her," but true solitude. Throughout the *Persian Letters*, enclosure has been an essential part of despotism;

here, in a sudden reversal, enclosure is associated with the life of the mind and political freedom. Voluntarily enclosing herself in a cell, insulated from the seductions of the present, Anaïs recovers both the memory of the past and a concern for the future. In recollecting her former life, Anaïs is moved to pity for those she left behind. According to Zuléma, "Anaïs did not remain within the mere limits of compassion; more tenderly inclined toward her unfortunate friends, she resolved to aid them." The passage suggests that pity, taken by itself, is passive; something more is necessary to spur Anaïs's action, something we might well call spirit. Aristotle says of spiritedness (*thumos*) that it is "the capacity of soul by which we feel affection" and also that "[b]oth the element of ruling and the element of freedom stem from this capacity" (*Politics* 1327b41, 1328a5-6). In her last moments on earth, Anaïs had held out to women the pious hope of divine retribution: "My dear companions . . . if Heaven pities my virtue, you will be avenged." Pity and piety, however, effected nothing. Now Anaïs herself, under the impulse of her loving and indomitable spirit, assumes the lawgiver's task.

She directs one of her celestial cohorts to impersonate and evict Ibrahim. In the space of an hour, while Ibrahim is away from home, the "false Ibrahim" proves his superiority in husbandly duties: "Entering, he first surprised the wives by his gentle and agreeable manner; immediately thereafter, he surprised them even more by his eagerness and by the rapidity of his enterprises. All of them had a part in the astonishment." Upon the reappearance of the old Ibrahim, with the eunuchs unable to distinguish the true lord from the false, it falls to the wives to choose between them. They make known their election of the "new Ibrahim" by a maenadic assault upon the old Ibrahim, who barely escapes with his life. The wives are fully aware that they have installed a usurper. They explain to the "triumphant Ibrahim": "If you are not Ibrahim, it is enough for us that you have so well deserved to be; you are more Ibrahim in one day than he has been in ten years." This "divine man" then establishes a new covenant with the women, declaring "I will not be jealous." However, a brief absence by the "beloved Ibrahim" (undertaken in order to convey the cuckolded Ibrahim to a distant land), during which the eunuchs immediately reinstitute harsh measures, reveals that a simple substitution of a love master for "*le jaloux*" (as the old Ibrahim is now called) is not sufficient. The movement from the old to the new order has been derailed by those who act in the master's name in his absence. Upon the return of the "celestial Ibrahim"—his second coming, so to speak—he enacts the structural reforms that will secure the women's happiness: dismissing the eunuchs, opening the house, forbidding the veil, and introducing mixed company. Three years later, "Ibrahim" (now sans qualifier) has fathered thirty-six children and lavishly distributed the hoarded wealth of his predecessor.

The course of the imposter's reception by the women is traceable in the succession of names: from the "false" Ibrahim to the "new," the "triumphant," the "beloved," the "celestial," until he is Ibrahim simply. Zuléma's story of Ibrahim reads like a burlesque version of the establishment of a new religion. It is the story of the advent of Christianity rewritten as a tale of cuckoldry. The new dispensation to replace the old Ibrahimic one is brought to earth by a "divine man" with a three-year mission of love who "signalized himself with miracles unknown until then."

Behind Montesquieu's ridicule is a serious correction of Christianity, on the subjects of family and property. As has been noted already, Montesquieu was an opponent of the Church's vast holdings and accumulated wealth. In one of the letters on depopulation (#117), Usbek explains how in Catholic countries, "dervishes hold in their hands most of the state's wealth; and they are an avaricious lot, always taking and never giving. . . . All this wealth becomes paralyzed, so to speak, thus putting an end to the flow of currency, to commerce, the arts, and industry." Ibrahim's dispersal of his predecessor's goods may thus be understood as an auspicious economic consequence of the new sexual/religious order. It may be the first step toward a revitalized economy. In contravention of this interpretation, however, is the inescapable suspicion that Ibrahim's reforms end badly and abruptly. The story concludes with the obsession-driven return of the first Ibrahim who "found nothing left but his wives and thirty-six children." The whereabouts of the substitute Ibrahim are unclear; it seems as if he has disappeared, perhaps recalled by Anaïs. We do not learn whether the first Ibrahim reassumes his place. Alternatively then, it seems as if the new Ibrahim's prodigality eventuated in bankruptcy. The ending, inconclusive though it is, suggests perhaps a certain insufficiency or political limitation in Anaïs's solution: the radical reconstitution of an individual household is not enough. The story's penultimate sentence reads: "Ibrahim believed, with reason, that the customs of the country were not made for citizens like him." The conduct of his household remains "a singular thing." Wider reform is necessary to guarantee the connection between propagation and prosperity, between the domestic/religious and the economic/political order. Far from being a denial of the linkage between the household and the state, the story's conclusion is an indication of the pervasiveness, and the resulting intractability, of the linkage, which can only be addressed societally, not individually. Even if Usbek, as the recipient of this cautionary tale, were to take heed of the fate of the jealous Ibrahim, what course of action would be open to him? He might face ruin whatever he does.

Of course, when the lone reformer happens to be a king rather than a householder, the prospects for success are greater. In *The Spirit of the Laws*, Montesquieu cites the example of Peter the Great of Russia who was able to lay the foundation for his far-reaching program of Westernization simply by summoning the heretofore sequestered wives of the nobility to court and issuing them bolts of sumptuous fabric. Montesquieu explains that the women "immediately appreciated a way of life that so flattered their taste, their vanity, and their passions, and they made the men appreciate it" (XIX.14). Montesquieu concludes that Peter should have relied exclusively on the gentle reformation of manners by manners; it was not necessary for him to turn to despotic measures (i.e., laws) to achieve liberalization. Montesquieu faults the Russian reformer for interfering directly with religiously based customs. For example, the law obliging men to shorten their beards was an affront to the orthodox. According to Montesquieu, it is best not to beard the Christian lion.

Since Machiavelli, modern philosophers have followed the vocation of religion taming, each after his own style. Neither Hobbes, Spinoza, nor Locke shies from the encounter with Scripture. In *Leviathan*, Hobbes scrutinizes the authorship, and hence the authority, of the Pentateuch and other books of holy writ. His aim is to leave the canon at the disposal of the temporal sovereign, thereby subjecting religion to political determination. In *A Theologico-Political Treatise*, Spinoza performs new feats of biblical interpretation, on the one hand finding scriptural mandate for the independence of philosophy from theology and on the other debunking the foundations of Scripture altogether. In such works as *The Reasonableness of Christianity* and *A Discourse of Miracles*, Locke conducts his own two-pronged fundamentalist/rationalist biblical critique, inquiring into the content of the fundamental articles of Christianity as well as into their soundness. His biblical studies culminate in his *Paraphrase and Notes on the Epistles of St. Paul*, a work of biblical exegesis by means of restatement.[4]

Although Hobbes, Spinoza, and Locke show varying degrees of caution in their textual criticism, all address themselves explicitly to the Bible. Montesquieu, by contrast, rarely meets revelation head-on. There are only seven citations to the Bible in *The Spirit of the Laws*, all to the Old Testament, most of them to the laws of Moses regarding particular issues such as slavery and treason. Judaic laws are discussed impartially and compared with the laws of other peoples.[5] In his general avoidance of Scripture (as well as in the interest he nevertheless betrays in the princely example of Moses), Montesquieu might appear to be more like Machiavelli. Machiavelli does not expend much effort on the imaginary regimes he rejects. His method is not disputation (the definitions of Hobbes, the Bible science of Spinoza, the commentaries of Locke), but rather extermination and expropriation. On those few occasions when Machiavelli does acknowledge holy writ, he simply annexes it to his purposes. For instance, in his *virtùous* retelling of the David and Goliath story, Machiavelli equips David with a knife as well as a sling: one's own good arms replace divine favor.[6]

However, Montesquieu's indisposition to quote chapter and verse is somewhat different from Machiavelli's. He makes more of a concession, on the surface at least, to the Christianity of his audience. Thus, he does not hesitate to offer this apology for the *Persian Letters*:

> Some people have found certain remarks excessively bold; but they are advised to regard the nature of the work itself. The Persians who play such a large part in it found themselves suddenly transplanted in Europe—which is to say, in another world. For a time, therefore, it was necessary to represent them as full of ignorance and prejudice; the author's purpose was to show the formation and development of their ideas. . . . Far from intending to touch upon any principle of our religion, he did not even suspect himself of imprudence. The remarks in question are always found joined to sentiments of surprise and astonishment, never to a sense of inquiry, and much less to one of criticism. In speaking of our religion, these Persians could not be made to appear better instructed than when they spoke of our customs and manners; and if they sometimes find our dogmas strange, their observations are always marked by a complete ignorance of the links between these dogmas and our other truths.[7] ("Reflections")

The literary device of the Persian visitors allows for, at the same time that it antagonizes, Christian sensibilities. If the *Persian Letters* can be described as Montesquieu's theological-political treatise, it is one that crafts a new rhetorical strategy for the problems posed by "our religion" (or as Machiavelli likes to put it, "the present religion").[8] Instead of engaging his readers directly in biblical controversy, Montesquieu relies on comparative scriptural allusion. We have seen the technique most clearly in the story of Anaïs and Ibrahim, where Montesquieu rewrites Scripture from a woman's perspective. When today's feminists propose to purge the Bible of male bias, their edit is largely a matter of substituting gender-neutral pronouns. Montesquieu's redaction is more radical. His new fable inverts the Christian conception of virtue. In place of Christianity's emphasis on the control of the individual's passions, he presents us with an alternative conception of virtue: spiritedness in defense of political liberty. However, because Montesquieu's use of the Bible is both nonspecific and elaborately distanced from himself, he gives disputatious believers nothing firm to fix upon. Christianity is not without its own form of spiritedness, which Montesquieu does not want to provoke. The *Persian Letters* is an insinuating book.

The modern assault upon revelation has relied extensively on the power of ridicule. In the *Persian Letters*, where direct argumentation is so largely avoided, Montesquieu makes ingenious use of this auxiliary to criticism. Indeed, he deploys it much more ambitiously and subtly than his predecessors had. Montesquieu makes the reader complicit in ridicule, the object of which is the reader's own beliefs and behavior. Usbek and Rica do not write with the intent to mock Christianity; it is the reader who supplies the irony, in both the simple instances and the complex, from Usbek's calling the priests "dervishes" to Rica's translation of Zuléma's story of Anaïs and Ibrahim. Contrast the famous passage in the *Leviathan* where Hobbes cleverly but crudely compares the papacy to the kingdom of fairies (IV.47). Hobbes uses ridicule in order to effect a change in public opinion; if argument is not sufficient to gain the day, the ecclesiastical commonwealth can always be laughed out of court. Montesquieu uses ridicule in a much more thought-provoking way that relies for its efficacy on the epistolary form. When he explains the provenance of the present collection of letters in the preface, Montesquieu draws attention to the violation of the Persians' privacy: "The Persians who write here were lodged in my home, and we spent our time together. . . . They would show me most of their letters; I copied them. I even fell upon several which they would surely have kept from me, so mortifying were they to Persian vanity and jealousy." The epistolary form compromises readers by casting them in the role of voyeurs. What we are promised is the spectacle of another's humiliation. We participate in exposing Usbek's pretensions. However, to the degree that we have understood the chain linking Usbek to ourselves, we uncover our own pretensions as well. Self-understanding requires the administration of a check to our pride. Ridicule can accomplish this, but individuals generally do not welcome ridicule of themselves. Montesquieu contrives his book in such a way that readers turn the power of ridicule inward upon themselves. Ridicule becomes a goad to self-examination, rather than an instrument of scorn and separation. In Montesquieu's hands, ridicule becomes more than a substitute for criticism, it becomes a mode of criticism.

Brotherly Love

Montesquieu goes to great lengths to distance himself from the story of Ibrahim's supplanting. The story of Anaïs and Ibrahim comes from an Arab book; Zuléma repeats this story verbally to a gathering of female companions; Rica discovers a written account of this conversation in a Persian book and translates a fragment of it for his French female friend, sending a duplicate to Usbek. Montesquieu may intend not only to place as many removes as possible between himself and this "feminist" reinterpretation of Scripture, but also to indicate the tortured transmission of all such stories, as they move from oral to written status, from one language to another, fragmenting and augmenting along the way.[9]

The novel's other story of paradise regained (#67) comes to Usbek through his Turkish friend Ibben. Like Rica, Ibben serves as a conduit conveying a text ("The History of Aphéridon and Astarté") that he believes will be of interest to Usbek. However, the enclosure in Ibben's letter, unlike that sent by Rica, has a straightforward genealogy. The document is penned by Aphéridon himself at the request of Ibben who wishes to forward a friendship between his two dearest friends, Usbek and Aphéridon. Ibben has already been sharing Usbek's letters to him with Aphéridon; and Aphéridon in turn consents to have his autobiography sent to Usbek. This letter, in addition to being, as we shall see, one of the most radical of the book, has a special status as the most generous. Through the medium of the written word, Ibben attempts to forge a new friendship between men unknown to one another. Like the "editor" Montesquieu, Ibben violates the confidentiality of Usbek's correspondence. Ibben does so for Usbek's advantage, Montesquieu for the reader's. Whether Usbek appreciates Ibben's matchmaking is open to doubt, however, for Aphéridon is a man who has successfully stolen a woman away from an Islamic harem. One imagines that the history of Aphéridon's adventures is about as pleasing to Usbek as the story of Ibrahim's overthrow. In subsequent letters to Ibben, Usbek makes no reference to Aphéridon.

In his autobiography, Aphéridon relates the story of his passionate love for his sister, Astarté. The two were born Guèbres—Guèbres being the derogatory name given by the Mohammedan conquerors to the followers of Zoroaster, or Zarathustra. Montesquieu is not the only modern thinker to display an interest in Zoroastrianism, but he is the first. In 1769 Voltaire would write a play *Les Guèbres* about their persecution, and Nietzsche would rediscover Zarathustra with a vengeance—his Zarathustra proclaims the death of God and teaches the overman. Montesquieu's Zoroastrian, while less inflammatory in his rhetoric than Nietzsche's, does effect a sort of transvaluation of values, replacing the principles and practices of Islam with those ordained by natural religion—primary among them: incest.

In the ancient religion of Persia, which is perhaps the oldest religion altogether, brother/sister pairings are regarded as holy, "naive images of a union already formed by nature," according to Aphéridon. (Despite Aphéridon's claim about the naturalness of incestuous unions, he does acknowledge, albeit indirectly, that such unions were not always permitted among Zoroastrians; the custom was introduced by a particular ruler, Cambyses.) Since the advent and rapid establishment of Islam, the Guèbres have had to abandon their ancient ways. Thus, Aphéridon and Astarté's father, fearful of Muslim persecution, separates his overly loving children, devoted to one another from before the age of reason, sending the boy out of the country and the girl to be a maidservant in the king's harem, an act that renders her a Moslem. She is eventually married off by the sultana, who is jealous of her beauty, to a eunuch who is "the most jealous of men." Because such sham husbands have not the same absolute authority as other husbands, Aphéridon at last manages to obtain an interview with his sister, conducted through a *jalousie* or *persienne* window. Aphéridon's voice pierces through the blind of Persian jealousy to tell Astarté that "[i]n losing your religion you have also lost your liberty, your happiness, and that precious equality which forms the honor of your sex." Since the fate of their love depends on Astarté's reconversion to her ancient faith, Aphéridon's love-pleadings must take a theological direction. He strives to weaken his sister's subscription to Islam. He points approvingly to the autochthonous character of Zoroastrianism, contrasting it with the alien imposition of Islam. Astarté concedes the fact, but quarrels with the supposition that the oldest is the best. She contends that Islam, being monotheistic, is more pure than its pantheistic predecessor. Aphéridon dismisses the charge of pantheism as a Muslim calumny; Zoroastrians, he says, revere the heavenly bodies and the elements not in their own right, but as works of the deity. By Aphéridon's account, Zoroastrianism is an enlightened religion in which the sacred law affirms the inclination of nature.

It seems as if Montesquieu is presenting even the sun and fire worship of the Guèbres as but the outward sign of their enlightenment, in contrast to the *jalousie*-cast shadows in which the Mohammedans live. In *The Spirit of the Laws*, in a chapter on the dangers of overly contemplative religions, Montesquieu confirms this positive view of Zoroastrianism in his own name, saying: "The religion of the Guèbres formerly caused the kingdom of Persia to flourish; it corrected the bad effects of despotism: today the Mohammedan religion destroys that same empire" (XXIV.11). Elsewhere he praises Zoroastrianism's encouragement of population growth—it is no accident that the name Montesquieu chooses for Aphéridon's sister/wife originally belonged to a Babylonian fertility goddess. The interview concludes with Aphéridon giving Astarté the text of the *Avesta*—the Zoroastrians are people of the book as well. By the time Aphéridon next visits, Astarté's reconversion has been accomplished; broken are "the chains that my spirit had forged for itself." Physical freedom follows upon that spiritual release. Effecting her escape in the most symbolically powerful manner, by sawing through the shuttered windows, Astarté flees Persia with her brother.

Before establishing themselves happily and comfortably by the aid of an Armenian merchant, the couple undergo some further tribulations at the hands of slave-holding Jews and indifferent Turkish and Christian priests. Interestingly, the story of Aphéridon and Astarté, like that of Anaïs and Ibrahim, begins with the sexual and religious and ends with the economic, as the pair undergo poverty, governmental expropriation, the depredations of marauders, and slavery. The Armenian merchant to whom they owe their freedom is a member of another despised race and, as Aphéridon says, "a gentle man." Unobtrusively, this letter suggests a connection between commerce and the softening of manners, a connection Montesquieu makes explicit in *The Spirit of the Laws*: "Commerce cures destructive prejudices, and it is an almost general rule that everywhere there are gentle mores, there is commerce and that everywhere there is commerce, there are gentle mores" (XX.1).

Aphéridon himself becomes some sort of negotiant in the Turkish city of Smyrna. The fact that Aphéridon and Astarté settle in Turkey is significant. Usbek had passed through Turkish lands on his westward route; in letter #19, he offers a devastating assessment of Turkish decline. Turkey is a despotism on the verge of anarchy: "Impunity rules in this severe government." Usbek predicts that the Ottoman Empire "will be the scene of some conqueror's triumphs in less than two hundred years" (199 years after the publication of the *Persian Letters*, the liquidation of the Ottoman Empire would be ratified in the Treaty of Sèvres). Although Turkey may be the sick man of Europe, Smyrna at least is a place of refuge. The two most admirable figures in the *Persian Letters*, Ibben and Aphéridon, both reside in this cosmopolitan trading port, a city sustained by the enterprise of foreigners. Here, the outcast Aphéridon and Astarté can live undisturbed as husband and wife. According to Ibben's testimonial: "[Aphéridon] lives peacefully upon the income from an honest trade, and with a wife he loves. His life is marked by many generous acts, and although he seeks obscurity he has more heroism in his heart than the greatest of monarchs."

What are we to make of the fact that the only happy marriage depicted in the *Persian Letters* is an incestuous one? While I do not want to depreciate the significance of Montesquieu's serious reconsideration of the incest taboo, I believe that a large part of the reason for portraying the erotic love of a brother and a sister is to stress the fundamental equality of the partners. In *The Spirit of the Laws*, Montesquieu examines the question of incest in greater detail in a chapter entitled, "In which cases of marriages between relatives must one be ruled by the laws of nature, and in which cases should one be ruled by civil laws" (XXVI.14).[10] There we are informed that "the Persians married their mothers . . . because the religion of Zoroaster gave preference to these marriages." This practice is not mentioned in letter #67. Montesquieu has instead substituted the practice of brother/sister incest, not I think to be less shocking, but because that particular form of incest is illustrative of other points he wants to make. Flattery and jealousy—the fear-based manifestations of a relationship in which power is lodged in the hands of one—are absent from this relationship. At one point in their adventures, Aphéridon sells himself into slavery to purchase Astarté's liberty, and she in turn is ready to do the same. Each refuses to accept freedom at the cost of the other's slavery. It is not slavery that is most disagreeable to them but the introduction of disparity. Each declines his or her own aggrandizement. On Astarté's suggestion, they finally arrange for mutual enslavement, to be followed by mutual freedom.

Interestingly, it is the woman who is responsible for the two decisions that secure their life together: the rejection of Islam and the deal struck with the Armenian merchant. Clearly, there is some modification of the traditional division of labor in this model marriage. Just as Astarté enters into theological disputes and business agreements, Aphéridon takes more of a hand in the household. For instance, he claims that during the time they were both enslaved, he delighted to do the work that was his sister's lot. Aphéridon also assumes womanly duties when, for a brief period, he has the sole care of their daughter. Each partner is driven outside his or her usual sphere by extraordinary circumstances, and there is no suggestion that the role reversals are permanent. Nonetheless, Montesquieu has given us a glimpse of marital equality based not on complementarity but on likeness—a more androgynous vision. We might say that in the relation of Aphéridon and Astarté, the sexual distinction of the partners is overwhelmed by their family likeness. Thus, long after their marriage, they continue to address one another, at least when speaking privately, as brother and sister.

Some clues about the political significance of the history of Aphéridon and Astarté can be gotten by recurring to Aristotle, an author who, like Montesquieu, favors household analogues. When Aristotle discusses the multiplicity of regimes in the *Nicomachean Ethics* (8.10), he proceeds by finding household equivalents of each political order. It is as if the elemental relations of the household—parental, conjugal, fraternal—present under one roof all the constitutional alternatives. The association of father and son has as its political likeness, kingship; that of husband and wife, aristocracy; that of brothers, timocracy. Similarly, degenerate regimes are modeled on degenerate households: democracy has its prototype in the radically egalitarian household, oligarchy in excessive male (or female) dominance, and tyranny in the Persian father's enslavement of the son. The household is a microcosm not of the *polis*, but of the *politeíai*, the political universe. In the story of Aphéridon and Astarté, Montesquieu intentionally blurs categories that Aristotle keeps separate. In presenting us with a brother and sister who are also husband and wife, he unifies the conjugal and the fraternal (or sibling) relation. Of course, Montesquieu similarly confounds Aristotle's categorization of regimes. In place of Aristotle's three good regimes and their corresponding perversions, Montesquieu speaks of republics, monarchies, and despotisms. According to Montesquieu, both aristocracy/oligarchy and timocracy/democracy (remember, the virtue or vice of the rulers is not the issue for Montesquieu) are republican governments. The distinction between the few and the many, so crucial to the conduct of ancient politics, is simply elided by Montesquieu. Just as he conjoins the conjugal and the fraternal in the marriage of Aphéridon and Astarté, so he conjoins the aristocratic and the democratic in the form of the republic.

Is incest—that is, some sort of republicanism—Montesquieu's prescription for good politics? To be sure, republics are not very visible in the *Persian Letters*, where despotism and monarchy dominate. But in this prospectus for a model marriage, Montesquieu hints at a republican alternative. It is most significant that this letter is sent by Ibben, whose nephew, Rhédi, is at this moment in Venice instructing himself in "the secrets of commerce" as well as the sciences and the arts (#31) in preparation for writing his own disquisition on the history and origin of republics (#131). We may say that Ibben and Rhédi are the republican counterparts of Usbek and Rica.

Chapter Seven

The Parliament
of Women

Those of Usbek's correspondents whom we have examined thus far seem to speak for, or in some way represent, markedly different political outcomes. Usbek's wives range from the accommodationist to the reformist to the revolutionary. Usbek's chief eunuch counsels him on the maintenance of despotic rule. Usbek's companion Rica pictures for him a thoroughgoing transformation: a husband and master remade after a woman's heart. Usbek's Turkish friend, Ibben, indicates the possibility of a new liberal commercial order emerging phoenix-like out of despotism's collapse. Of these correspondents, it is Rica who is Usbek's most persistent advisor. More than a quarter of the letters received by Usbek are from Rica;[1] and Rica is the only nonharem connection who remains in contact with Usbek in the novel's final two years. It is necessary to look more closely at Rica's character and his relations with Usbek.

The most important thing about Rica may be his unattached status. He has no harem to plague him during his travels. He does, however, have a mother who worries about him. We learn from Rustan that "Rica's mother is inconsolable; she asks you [Usbek] to return her son, whom she says you have taken from her" (#5). Rica's evident lack of homesickness and his decision to remain permanently in the West suggest that, whether through Usbek's influence or not, so far as he is concerned the filial tie has been broken. Although Usbek's first letter asserted that he and Rica had gone abroad in quest of wisdom, a subsequent letter emends that account: "the real reason for my journey" (#8), Usbek reveals, is self-preservation. Usbek's difficulties were not shared by Rica, however. So far as we know, Rica's motive in leaving Persia was unmixed.

Not surprisingly, Rica has adjusted much more readily than Usbek to Western ways. The variance in their attachment has become a source of some friction between the two travelers. With unconcealed bitterness, Usbek complains to Nessir (#155) about Rica's Francophilia: "I have urged Rica a thousand times to leave this alien land, but he is opposed to all my resolutions and keeps me here with a thousand excuses. It seems he has forgotten his country, or rather, he seems to have forgotten me, so insensible is he to my displeasures." We may well question whether Rica's attempts to thwart Usbek's return are as selfish and thoughtless as Usbek judges them to be. Throughout the letters, Rica has been much occupied with "the woman question"— not, like Usbek, as the possessor of a tumultuous harem, but rather as a theoretical issue. In the tale of Anaïs and Ibrahim, his incipient feminism was very much in evidence. By contriving to keep the "old" Usbek in France, Rica may be doing what he can to favor the emergence of a "new" Usbek. Moreover, Rica would prefer that Usbek remain with him in Paris rather than take up residence in the provinces as Usbek is inclined to do. In #63, Rica reproves Usbek for rusticating: "I do believe that you intend to spend your entire life in the country. At first I lost you for only two or three days, but here it is fifteen since I last saw you." Of course, Usbek's temperamental choice of country over city is most convenient in allowing for a correspondence to spring up between the novel's two main characters. However, that correspondence is strikingly lopsided. Whereas Rica sends Usbek fourteen letters, Usbek sends only two to Rica.[2] Neglect and avoidance would seem to be chargeable to Usbek not Rica. Usbek much prefers to lavish his pedagogical attention on Rhédi, the nephew of his friend Ibben, to whom he writes twenty-nine letters.[3]

In #67, before presenting the history of Aphéridon and Astarté, Ibben gives his own traveler's credo:

> In whatever lands I have visited, I have lived as if I had to spend my life there. I have felt the same attraction to virtuous people, the same compassion, or rather love, for the unfortunate, the same esteem for those whose prosperity has not blinded them. Such is my character, Usbek; wherever I find men I choose friends.

Usbek's conduct in a strange land has been far different. In his last letter to Nessir (#155), Usbek declares, "I live in a barbarous country, surrounded by everything offensive to me, absent from all my interests." As Anne Cohler has suggested, "Usbek may well . . . be a model for how not to travel."[4] By comparison, the open and curious Rica seems distinctly more worthy of emulation. That is not to say that Rica's assimilation meets the standard set forth by Ibben. For one thing, Rica does not have friends. Instead, he has acquaintances—the blind man, the gallant philosopher, the alchemist, the Capuchin, the magistrate, the geometer, the librarian—whom he uses as fodder for his satiric sallies. Rica is the consummate observer—amused and detached. He roams the city of Paris, compiling a survey of its institutions—the opera, the Academy, the Invalides, the salons, the law courts, the University of Paris, and the Tuileries—as well as its human types. The reportorial coldness of Rica's letters may account for the tendency of commentators to slight their importance.

Judith Shklar is something of an exception in this regard. Recognizing similarities in the ironic stance of Montesquieu and Rica, she goes so far as to say that, throughout Montesquieu's works, "Rica remained his model." Nonetheless, elsewhere she says of Rica that "[h]e does not, however, deal with any serious moral questions, only with surface foibles."[5] Presumably Shklar does not mean this characterization to apply to Montesquieu himself; but even with respect to Rica it is mistaken. It is true that Rica's letters dwell on the surface: fashion, gossip, costume, and all the elaborate trappings of vanity. His mode is the critical examination of *la Mode*. "It makes for lively reading," according to Shklar, "but it also raises the question of how much criticism one should direct at minor flaws, considering the suffering inflicted by oppression and violence."[6] In other words, because Persia is so horrible, one shouldn't bad-mouth France. This is to miss not only the seriousness of Rica's contributions (concerned as they are with the relationship between the manners of a people and the form of government) but indeed to miss the point of the *Persian Letters* as a whole (premised as it is on the analogy of despotism and monarchy).

As previously noted, Rica and Paris make their debut together: #24 is the first letter written by Rica and the first letter written from Paris. Rica is our guide to Paris specifically. His aim, by his own account, is to "go about in society and try to understand it" (#63). Usbek, by contrast, tends to use his observations about France only as points of departure for more wide-ranging speculations and pronouncements on general themes. Indeed, in many of Usbek's most important disquisitions, France does not figure at all. Although Rica lays claim, so to speak, to Paris, Usbek had been the first to write from European soil (#23). After forty days upon the water (a good biblical number for a journey), the travelers reach Livorno, which Usbek describes as a "new city" carved out of the marshes by the ingenious Tuscans. The reader may—I believe without straining credulity—be reminded of the "new modes and orders" entailing the conquest of nature mapped by that greater Columbus, Machiavelli. The second thing Usbek notes is the liberty of the women of Italy—a phenomenon that he must see as yet another reversal of nature.[7] Altogether, Christian Europe presents itself to Usbek as "a great spectacle."

These two themes of flux and the feminine are continued in Rica's first letter from Paris. Rica speaks of being in "constant motion." He also remarks that "the houses are so tall you would suppose them inhabited only by astrologers." While Livorno reclaims land from the waters below, Paris attempts to establish solid ground in the firmament itself. The fundamental distinctions between the seas, the dry land, and the heavens—made by God at the time of the Creation—are confounded by human builders. In Paris we see the aspiration represented by the Tower of Babel carried out on a mass scale, for it is not astrologers but ordinary men and women who live in these skyscrapers. Since the inhabitants cannot spend all their time stacked one atop another in the air, conditions on the streets are understandably crowded. Here is how Rica describes his daily constitutional: "One man, passing me from behind, shoves me half around; another, passing on the opposite side, pushes me back to my original position, and I am more weary after a hundred paces than if I had gone ten leagues." Like a scene from Charlie Chaplin's *Modern Times*, all the frenetic motion of Paris produces a stasis of its own as competing motions cancel one another out. When we speak of Persia as an analogue for France, we must not lose sight of certain massive differences between the two nations, differences to which Montesquieu's Persians immediately draw our attention. If France is on the verge of despotism, it may well be a new sort of despotism, a despotism at the other pole from Asiatic tranquillity.

In the second half of #24, Rica shows that the really interesting motions of Paris are not physical but psychological. Unlike Persia, where despotism exists on the plane of the body, in Paris despotism takes a step up. According to Rica's summary, the king of France moves the minds of his subjects (making them believe, for example, that a piece of paper is money); the pope moves the mind of the king (among other things, making him believe that bread is not bread). Opinion triumphs over matter. The propagation of opinion is not always successful however.

> Two years ago he [the pope] sent him [the king] a large document which he called the *Constitution*, and with threat of heavy punishment he insisted that the prince and his subjects believe every thing contained in it. He succeeded with the prince, who submitted immediately and gave the example to his subjects; some of them, however, revolted and said that they would not believe anything in the document. Women have been the prime movers in this rebellion, which divides the court, the entire

kingdom, and every family, because this *Constitution* forbids their reading a book which all the Christians claim has come down from heaven;
it is, in fact, their Koran. Indignant over this outrage to their sex, the
women rose as a body against the *Constitution*, and have brought over
to their side all the men, who are not anxious about their superiority in
this affair.

In Paris we encounter motion and, above all, the motion of women
with respect to opinion. Women are the "motrices," the motors—or in
an interesting variant reading, the "matrices," that is, the wombs—of
rebellion. Certainly, this rebellion furthers female equality and enlightenment. And yet this rebellion against religious strictures emanating
from the pope presents itself as in the service of female piety—the
women fight for their right to read the Bible. (One is reminded of
Aristophanes and the "conservative" or nonimpious character of his
plays of female insurrection.)

In both his Parisian and Persian women, Montesquieu offers an alternative conception of female virtue—one that emphasizes female
spiritedness. To arrive at Montesquieu's final position on "the woman
question," it is necessary to balance the harem letters with Rica's letters discussing women in France. While the harem letters might be said
to elaborate the natural law with respect to human sexuality, and to
support women's claim to liberty and equality, the French letters address the more complicated question of the possible political and conventional embodiment of those claims. Beginning in #24, Montesquieu
begins to examine the tangle of nature and convention.

All Is Vanity

Unlike the Persian women, the French women do not speak for themselves in the novel.[8] It is Rica who speaks about them and, on occasion, for them. Fittingly, "Rica" is a woman's name; presumably it was
not by accident that Montesquieu chose this name. Nor is it accidental
that Rica writes sixteen letters on the subject of women, thus equaling
the number of letters that pass between Usbek and his wives.[9]

After charting the tidal motions of Paris, so heavily influenced by
women (creatures, after all, of the moon), Rica in his next letter (#28)
reports on his first foray into Parisian high society. Spending an evening
at the theater, Rica is unable to distinguish the actors from the audience; he mistakes the varied social and romantic encounters enacted
in the loges and the pit for the play itself. To the philosopher as to
the naif, the true comedy of manners is visible not on the stage, but

in the conventions of social life. In the French case, those conventions are highly theatrical. The actress whose acquaintance Rica makes and who writes him a letter, which he appends to his own, reveals something of what goes on out of the public eye, behind closed doors. This star of the stage relates how a young abbé took advantage of her as she dressed for her role as a priestess of Diana. In other words, a modern woman playing a classical virgin is ravished by a Christian clergyman. She complains that he was "without respect" for her veil—an accessory he doubtless saw as nothing more than a stage prop. While the Persian women wear four veils and the Italian women one, the French women, actresses all, only pretend to the veil. Although her virtue has been lost, she claims still to be in possession of her modesty (a dubious claim in light of the circumstances under which Rica was introduced to her, namely, as she undressed after a show). She beseeches Rica to take her to Persia, where she believes she can make her fortune as a dancer. Presumably she also believes that the veil is still respected in Persia, even when worn by an exhibitionist.

What are we to make of the fact that the only French woman to speak on her own behalf expresses a longing for Persia? Is the situation of women in France so false and so compromised that Persian despotism is to be preferred? Interestingly, the only other letter written by a non-Persian woman expresses a similar regard for domestic despotism. Nargum, the Persian ambassador in Muscovy, writes Usbek on the subject of Russian mores and includes a letter from a Muscovite wife to her mother as evidence of "how much Muscovite women like to be beaten." Like the letter of the actress, this letter is enclosed within a male correspondence. The point of presenting them in this fashion is, I believe, to indicate that these two women are no less enclosed by despotic conventions than the women of Ispahan in their seraglios. Indeed, the confinement of the mind can be more complete than the confinement of the body. Whereas most of the Persian women see and feel the prison bars, the Muscovite wife is able to reinterpret even physical abuse as "marks of affection."

As her letter demonstrates, her desire to be beaten is not a privately conceived, masochistic one—that is, she cannot properly be said to have a taste for suffering. Rather, she desires preeminence; and since custom decrees that her standing vis-à-vis other women is proportionate to her husband's severity, she will do what she can to provoke such ill-treatment. In particular, she wishes to worst her sister:

My sister is treated much better: her husband thrashes her every day, and if she but looks at another man he instantly knocks her down. . . .

This is what makes her so proud, but I will not give her the chance to scorn me much longer. I have determined at all costs to make my husband love me, and I will make him so angry that he will be forced to give me some marks of affection. No one shall say that I have not been beaten, and that I live in a house where no one thinks of me.

This pitiably comic letter, exposing women's complicity in their subjection, is the only instance in the book where one woman writes to another. As the saying goes: "Like mother, like daughter." The daughter, however, had not always been a party to the mother's peculiar view and peculiar desires. In the course of enlisting her mother in her campaign to be beaten, the daughter unconsciously reveals her original and natural reaction to domestic despotism: "Dear Mother, I beg you to point out to my husband how unworthily he is treating me. My father, who is an excellent man, did not act this way. In fact, I recall thinking as a little girl that sometimes he loved you too much." Whereas the girl instinctively sensed the falsity, or at least the limits, of the equation of love and punishment, the grown woman fully accepts that equation. Her acceptance is not rooted in some sort of natural, womanly predilection for the whip. Nor is her acceptance simply coerced by men (according to Nargum, the Russian patriarchs—whatever treatment they accord their wives—in fact try to prevent the worst abuse of their daughters, actually stipulating in the marriage contract that they are not to be whipped); rather, her acceptance is conventional, sustained by women's emulation of one another.

In his account of the Russian way of life, Nargum stresses its insularity: "The Muscovites cannot leave their country even to travel; so, separated from other nations by their own laws, they have become even more attached to their old customs and cannot believe it possible for there to be others." The subjection of women is only an instance of the larger confinement of the nation. According to Nargum, "excepting four families, the people are all slaves." And yet, reform, even rapid reform, is possible. One of Montesquieu's few footnotes as editor of the letters (note 12 of 21) has reference to the Muscovite practice of wife-beating. The footnote says simply: "These customs have changed." In other words, in the space of eight years (from 1713, the date of Nargum's letter, to 1721, the date of the letter's publication and Montesquieu's footnote), the relations between men and women in Russia have been revised. What is the source of this remarkable transformation? And what bearing does it have on the political order in Russia? Nargum does inform us that "the presently reigning prince [Peter the Great] wants to change everything." He briefly hints at Peter's methods (attacks upon religious orthodoxy, introduction of the arts, and imperial expansion), but gives no indication of their relative merit or success. From what we already know of Montesquieu's views, the middle course—the introduction of the arts—is the only one that operates nondespotically.

After living in Paris little more than a year, Rica raises the question of women's liberation (#38). This letter is unique in being Rica's only explicitly theoretical inquiry. He first views the question from a man's perspective, casting it as a matter of policy: "is it more advantageous to allow women liberty or to take it from them?" His formulation and prosecution of the question assume male superiority and authority to be by nature. The status of woman is for man to determine. The only question is what serves male pleasure better: Asiatic confinement or European license. Rica gives the arguments on both sides, but professes himself nonplussed, adding that "[p]robably a wiser man than I would be embarrassed to decide." Chauvinism proves insufficient even to the calculation of self-interest.

The inquiry must be begun again. This time the question, purged of bias, is "whether the natural law subjects women to men." The answer is supplied not by contending spokesmen for Asiatic and European custom, but by "*un philosophe très galant.*" While the appearance of a philosopher on the scene is most promising, we must of course wonder how much the conclusions of a philosopher partial to the ladies would diverge from the conclusions of a philosopher simply. Does a gallant philosopher flatter women or do them justice? According to Rica's new interlocutor, the empire of men is "a veritable tyranny." Gentleness and its ancillaries, humanity and reason, are all on the side of women. These superiorities, however, work against their possessors because masculine unreasonableness permits them no scope. It seems that the virtue of women is unarmed, and thus incompetent to secure the condition of its own exercise.

In *The Spirit of the Laws*, Montesquieu devotes a chapter to the question of "administration by women" (VII.17), wherein he concludes that women are perfectly able to govern nations. Their very weakness inclines them toward the gentleness and moderation of good government.[10] It does not seem that women aspire to rule however; instead, in certain countries, it may fall to them by the laws of monarchic succession. (It is interesting to note how many of the world's recent female rulers have been impressed into politics and have won democratic elections in effect by inheritance from a slain husband or father. Aquino, Chamorro, and Bhutto were all legacy candidates, in whom the hope was vested that a female hand could better salve a battered nation.) Elsewhere in *The Spirit of the Laws*, Montesquieu expresses his disapproval of French subscription to the Salic law, which forbids the crown, and estates in general, from passing either to or through the distaff side (XXVIII.22, also XXXI.33-34).

Despite their political dispossession, women still have resources at their command. According to the gallant philosopher, there is a natural empire of beauty that, unlike the regime-specific empire of men, is universal. Moreover, even respecting the seemingly greater male allotment of strength and courage, the gallant philosopher avers that "power would be equal if education were equal." By his account, it would appear that the manly virtues are the product of nurture, while the feminine virtues are a natural endowment. Thus, women might be both equal to men in manliness and superior to them in beauty and sweet reason. (The gallant philosopher does not link women's milder disposition to bodily weakness, as Montesquieu does in *The Spirit of the Laws*.) While the gallant philosopher is ready to cede supremacy to women, Rica remains undecided at letter's end.

Montesquieu himself seconds some of the assertions of the gallant philosopher, although not the latter's practical program of reform. In the *Pensées*, Montesquieu declares that "women have scarcely ever pretended to equality: for they already have so many other natural advantages, that equal power ever constitutes empire for them" (no. 581). Unlike Rousseau, who thought the agitation for equality would entail the loss of women's actual, albeit indirect, empire in the realm of morals, Montesquieu sees social and political equality as augmenting their already considerable position.[11]

The gallant philosopher had spoken of the empire of beauty. In Rica's next letter on the subject of women (#52), we see behind the operation of this empire. A pretty picture it is not. Beauty, though imperial, is also fleeting. Rica's encounter with the four society ladies, evenly spaced in age from twenty to eighty, documents the deceits of age and ugliness. Such deceits are practiced even by women in their prime. Beauty is so fragile that its loss is always incipient.

This letter on the deceptions and self-deceptions practiced by women appears in the center of a string of letters by Rica, all detailing illusions and conceits of various kinds. Rica writes eleven letters from the date of his physical assimilation (casting off his Persian garb in #30) until the date of his mental assimilation (in #63 he announces, "my mind is gradually losing its Asiatic cast"). A brief summary brings out the common theme: Rica's costume conversion (#30); Rica's meeting with a man who guides him adeptly through Paris, and who turns out to be blind (#32); Rica's questioning of male supremacy under the aegis of a gallant philosopher (#38); Rica's meeting with the alchemist who thinks he has converted dross into gold (#45); Rica's meeting with the Capuchin who has a project for the conversion of Persian souls (#49); Rica's meeting with the four ladies of convertible generations (#52); Rica's overhearing of the two dullards as they plot their conversion into wits (#54); Rica's account of French marriage as licensed adultery—that is, the convertibility of partners (#55); Rica's survey of the charlatanry of Parisian tradesmen and his description of the city itself as "the mother of invention" (#58); finally, Rica's insights into the phenomena of nostalgia and religion: the one being memory's falsification of the past, the other being men's habit of "proposing themselves as the exact model for providence"—in other words, the conversion of man into God (#59).

Behind each of these attempted conversions is an aspiration to be free of particular bodily givens or natural limitations: to cast off the parochialism of national custom (Rica's Persian dress), to overcome physical defects (blindness), to overcome gender chauvinism (the gallant philosopher), to alter the essential constitution of matter (alchemy), to render faith catholic or universal (the proselytizing Capuchin), to deny the effects of age and the inevitability of human mortality (the society women), to obscure the differences in native intelligence (the planned witticisms), to evade the constraint implicit in choice (open marriage), to skirt necessity (via invention), to manipulate the past and the significance of man (through selective history and anthropocentric religion).

The question for the reader is which of these can indeed be accomplished? and which should be accomplished? In two of the first three conversion letters, Rica is himself a participant in the transformation; he adopts Western dress and takes seriously the question of female emancipation. Rica, however, mocks the remainder of these attempted conversions. He angrily dismisses the pseudoscientist and the priest; the doctrine of a single substance or a single truth is repulsive to him. He is less outraged by the evasions and deceits practiced in society. On the whole, he views the vanity of ordinary men and women with ironic amusement. Is it possible to take part of the package, as Rica does—to move toward liberal egalitarianism, lessening the differences between the sexes and the nations, while rejecting other transformations that seem absurd, disgusting, or tyrannical?

The culminating letter in this transmogrification series (#63) returns to the subject of Rica's own conversion to French ways, now complete. Rica describes it in sexual terms: "I am no longer surprised to find five or six women together in a house with five or six men; in fact, I have decided it is not a bad idea." He now looks favorably on the public and social mixing of the sexes for the reason that this contrivance has enabled him to "know" women for the first time: "I have learned more about them in a month here than I would in thirty years in the seraglio." Rica's sentimental education awakens him to the variety of female character and destroys the mystery of the "eternal feminine": "Among us [Persians] character is uniform because it is forced; one never sees people as they are but as they have been obliged to be. In that servitude of heart and mind, only the monotonous language of fear is heard, and not nature, which expresses itself so differently, and assumes so many forms." Taking some etymological liberties, we might say that it is Paris that is truly polygamous, characterized as it is by female multiformity. It is interesting that "*la nature*" is lowercase in the French context, whereas in the immediately preceding letter (#62, written from the harem), the same noun is capitalized. In the one case, "nature" is conceived as flexible and manifold; in the other, "Nature" is conceived as fixed and unitary. Despotism, it seems, exaggerates or absolutizes sexual differentiation; liberty, by its encouragement of individuality, erodes it. The facts of nature doubtless remain, but their social bearing is far from ossified.[12]

Remarkably, after having exposed all the poseurs of Paris, Rica yet maintains that "[d]issimulation is unknown here; everything is said, and seen, and heard. Hearts are as open as faces, and in manners, in virtue, even in vice one always perceives something naive." In his attempt to sharpen the contrast between Paris and Persia, it seems that Rica loses sight of the many dissimulations (induced by vanity rather than fear) that he has already documented and that he will continue to document. Yet, there is a sense in which Rica speaks the truth. Hypocrisy is indeed a rarity in Paris. Vice no longer pays its homage to virtue, as we can see from the frankness of the French of both sexes about their infidelities—infidelities tolerated by society and by their partners (#55). Even when there is a concern to preserve appearance or make an appearance, Parisians allow the gap between appearance and reality to be glimpsed. Men, for instance, call upon women in their dressing rooms as they prepare their faces—the application of the concealer is open to public view. In Paris, there is much simulation, but perhaps not dissimulation.

The opening up of the private to the public is the defining feature of French life. Indeed, Rica credits this open house policy with forming "the general character of the nation" (an early rendition of "the general spirit"—Montesquieu's famous coinage). Here is how Rica describes the metamorphosis:

> To please women, one must have a certain talent rather different from what pleases them even more. It consists in a species of badinage, which amuses them because it seems to promise them at every instant what can be performed only very occasionally.
> This badinage, naturally appropriate to the boudoir, gradually seems to be forming the general character of the Nation: they banter in the council room, they banter at the head of an army, they banter with an ambassador.

Far from the public realm intruding upon the private and violating its sanctity, the private realm is enlarging itself, engrossing the public. When what had been private becomes a publicly traded stock, it is soon the only game in town. The manners of private life become the manners of social life; and the manners of social life become the manners of political life. Flirtatiousness—really a sort of verbal simulation of sexual relations—reigns.

In *The Spirit of the Laws* as well, Montesquieu discusses the political ramifications of the French desire to please women. He begins one such discussion by propounding the following tripartite theory of love:

> Our connection with women is founded on the happiness attached to the pleasures of the senses, on the charm of loving and being loved, and also on the desire to please them because they are quite enlightened judges of a part of the things that constitute personal merit. This general desire to please produces a gallantry which is not love, but the delicate, flimsy, and perpetual illusion of love.
> According to the different circumstances of each nation and each century, love is inclined more to one of these three things than to the other two.[13] (XXVIII.22)

Not surprisingly, this tripartite division of eros (pleasure, love, gallantry) correlates with Montesquieu's tripartite division of regimes. The quest for physical pleasure predominates in despotisms (Montesquieu cites the example of imperial Rome). The gentleness of reciprocal love, epitomized in the pastoral romance, is linked to republicanism; Montesquieu points to the Greek literary origin of this ideal. Arcadian love is a feature of modern republicanism as well. Pastoral romances are reborn in the Italian Renaissance and, of course, the pastoral ranks as one of the favored English forms. In monarchies, gallantry and the desire to please women flourishes. Book XIX on "the general spirit" contains a lovely paean (chapters 5-9) to the results of this desire:

> If there were in the world a nation which had a sociable humor, an openness of heart; a joy in life, a taste, an ease in communicating its thoughts; which was lively, pleasant, playful, sometimes imprudent, often indiscreet; and which had with all that, courage, generosity, frankness, and a certain point of honor, one should avoid disturbing its manners by laws, in order not to disturb its virtues. If the character is generally good, what difference do a few faults make?
>
> One could constrain its women, make laws to correct their mores, and limit their luxury, but who knows whether one would not lose a certain taste that would be the source of the nation's wealth and a politeness that attracts foreigners to it?

For Montesquieu, the extent and character of women's influence is linked to the form of the regime. Through Usbek's harem, we have seen how closely despotism confines women. That confinement, however, does not negate their influence; instead it produces a noxious concentrate of it. "Women's quarrels, their indiscretions, their aversions, their inclinations, their jealousies, their spiteful remarks, in short that art by which narrow souls affect generous ones, cannot be without consequence there [in despotic states]" (VII.9). In monarchies, where women move from being the objects of luxury to being the orderers of luxury, women's influence is equally great, but potentially more salutary. It is not that women are more virtuous under monarchy, only that their vices are put to better use. Instead of being distilled, they are dispersed, and in the process of dispersion undergo a transformation, the familiar shorthand formula for which is "private vices, public benefits."

The emancipation of women—their entry into the public sphere—is also the emancipation of female vanity. Montesquieu demonstrates how vanity, which had traditionally been regarded by moralists as a female weakness or vice, can become an engine of reform—economic, social, and political reform. In Usbek's letter in defense of the arts and sciences (#106), he gives an example of vanity's operation:

> A woman takes it into her head that she should appear at a gathering in a certain dress, and from that moment fifty artisans can sleep no more nor find the leisure to drink and eat; she commands and is more promptly obeyed than our monarch would be, because self-interest is the greatest monarch on earth.

Women are consummate consumers. In Montesquieu's view (that is, in the view of a thinker who had much to do with their original formulation) feminism and capitalism are naturally linked; they are elements of the self-same project of human liberation.

As so often, confirmation of assertions made on the basis of the *Persian Letters* can be found in *The Spirit of the Laws*. Here is how Montesquieu, a quarter-century later, describes the link between commerce proper and commerce with women:

> The society of women spoils mores and forms taste; the desire to please more than others establishes ornamentation, and the desire to please more than oneself establishes fashions. Fashions are an important subject; as one allows one's spirit to become frivolous, one constantly increases the branches of commerce. (XIX.8).

Montesquieu cites *The Fable of the Bees* at this point—Mandeville being the originator of the pithy saying: "private vices, public benefits." Three pages (and three chapters) later, Montesquieu completes his rehabilitation of vanity with this marvelous one-paragraph chapter entitled simply "Reflection":

> I have not said this to diminish in any way the infinite distance there is between vices and virtues: God forbid! I have only wanted to make it understood that not all political vices are moral vices and that not all moral vices are political vices, and those who make laws that run counter to the general spirit should not be ignorant of this.[14] (XIX.11)

Just as the women energize the artisan class with their demands, the success of the artisan class energizes the nobility. Usbek says that "[t]his ardor for work, this passion for gain, passes from one class to another, from artisans to nobles. No one likes to be poorer than those he sees immediately below him." We might dub this Montesquieu's theory of "trickle-up economics." The indirect effect of the unleashing of female acquisitiveness is the advent of social mobility and a consequent lessening of hereditary class distinctions. Inequality of wealth of course remains (as a natural accompaniment of economic liberty), but the distribution of wealth is now in better accord with certain standards of individual merit. Moreover, in *The Spirit of the Laws*, Montesquieu points out that the "usage that permitted commerce to the nobility of England is one of the things that most contributed to weakening monarchical government there" (XX.21). Remember that England is already "a republic under the guise of a monarchy." Under threat of impoverishment (in his letter on fashion, #99, Rica says, "one cannot believe the cost to a husband of maintaining his wife in fashion"), the French nobility may be driven to adopt similar measures. Thus, through the vanity of its women, France is set on a course of economic, social, and political change.

Interestingly, it is Usbek, not Rica, who lays out the case for the political utility of *amour-propre*. He does so in response to Rhédi's "virtuous republican" doubts about the value of progress in the arts and sciences. (The exchange between Rhédi and Usbek, #105-6, reads like a prefiguration and refutation of Rousseau's argument in the *First Discourse*.) Rica, despite his approval of the social integration of the sexes, seems to have some reservations about the decidedly feminine tone of French life. At least, he continues his merciless spoofs: #82 on the art of smiling; #86 on female immodesty; #99 on the caprices of fashion; #110 on the role of a pretty woman and the ennui lurking behind the gaiety of social life; and especially #107 on "the republic of women." In this last, Rica is favorably impressed with the person of the young monarch ("his physiognomy is majestic, but charming"); however, he holds off on a final judgment pending two great tests: the king's selection of his mistress and his confessor. At the time of this letter, His Majesty Louis XV is all of seven years old. Rica goes on to describe the late king as "absolutely governed by women, although at his age I think no monarch on earth had less need of them." Even in their nonage and their dotage, the kings of France give themselves up to women. What is true of the king is equally true of all subordinate officeholders and office seekers. According to Rica, whatever the motives of the men involved in these affairs, the women of France have business, both public and private, in mind:

> Do you think, Ibben, that a woman decides to become a minister's mistress so she may sleep with him? What a thought! Her purpose is to be able to submit five or six petitions to him every morning; and the natural goodness of women shows itself in their eagerness to do favors for a host of unfortunate people who procure for them incomes of one hundred thousand livres.

Rather in the mode of our own Congress, these women, moved by pecuniary self-interest, prostitute themselves on behalf of a handful of constituents before the appropriate executive bodies. The women, moreover, do not operate independently. According to Rica,

> [t]hese women are all in contact with each other; they form a *species of republic*, whose members are continually active in mutual aid and service. It is like *a new Estate within the State*; and anyone at court, in Paris, or in the provinces who observes the action of the ministers,

magistrates, and prelates, unless he knows the women who govern them, is like a man watching a machine work without knowing about the springs that drive it. [Emphasis added.]

It would seem that France, too, after its own fashion, is "a republic under the guise of a monarchy." As for Rica, he is repulsed by his glimpse of the real internal mechanism. His letter concludes: "In Persia we complain that the kingdom is governed by two or three women. It is much worse in France, where women in general govern, not only taking over wholesale, but also dividing up piecemeal all authority."

Regardless of Rica's negative judgment, the situation he describes is highly interesting. There is not a separation of powers in any functional or structural sense, but there is a diffusion or decentralization of power. Might hopes for the amelioration of absolutism be lodged in this "new Estate within the State"? Certainly, the traditional estates no longer act as counterweights to the king. Usbek's letter announcing the death of Louis XIV is really an elegy for Louis' victims, the *parlements*:

> The *parlements* resemble those ruins which are trampled underfoot but are reminiscent always of the idea of some temple famed in the antique religion of the people. They now interest themselves only in judicial questions, and their authority will continue to weaken unless something unforeseen rejuvenates them. These great bodies have followed the destiny of all things human: they have yielded to time, which destroys everything, to moral corruption, which has enfeebled everything, and to supreme authority, which has overthrown everything. (#92)

The best portrait of the moral bankruptcy of the nobility is given in #74, where we make the acquaintance of a "grand seigneur" of the realm—"who took snuff with such haughtiness, who blew his nose so pitilessly and spat so phlegmatically, and who caressed his dogs in a manner so offensive to mankind." Montesquieu dwells on the physical repulsiveness of this "little man," the manner of whose expectorations shows a lack of even the merest civility towards his fellows. Whereas he holds himself superior (and indifferent) to mankind, he stoops low indeed in his unseemly attachment to his pets. We may speak figuratively of the "bestiality" of the nobility when their social standing is no longer accompanied by any real human excellence.

We learn something of how the nobility reached this pass through Usbek's discussion of the "point of honor" in #90. The most characteristic outcome of the point of honor is the tradition of judicial combat, better known to us as dueling. The crown, however, had set itself against what Usbek (seconded by Montesquieu himself in *The Spirit of the Laws*, XXVIII.23) calls a "badly conceived" method of decision. A 1679 edict of Louis XIV punished dueling with death. This attempt to outlaw dueling was itself badly conceived, however, succeeding only in creating an unbridgeable gulf between the laws of honor and the laws of justice. As Usbek summarizes the predicament of the nobleman: "There is, then, only this harsh alternative: to die or to be unworthy of life." Despite the king's attack upon the honor code of the French nobility, he is greatly interested in maintaining French military valor. In #84, Rica visits *l'hotel des Invalides*, the veteran's home erected by Louis XIV in the 1670s, and has this to say: "What a spectacle it is to see assembled in this one place all these victims of the fatherland, who breathed only to defend it, and who now, having the same heart but without the same strength, complain only that their impotence prohibits their again sacrificing themselves for it."

Taken together, the king's two innovations—the edict against duelling and the provision of a military shrine for common soldiers—point toward the replacement of the chivalric *point d'honneur* by the patriotism of the masses, a movement from feudal loyalties to nationalistic ones. When honor loses its political efficacy, so do the men who used to live by its dictates. No longer important in securing the liberty of the constitution, the nobility is rendered a superfluous and vain body.

It is difficult to know how much Montesquieu's criticism of the current state of the French monarchy is a criticism of the role of women in it. We have seen how despotic the confinement of women is, yet it seems that giving them free rein can eventuate in despotism as well. At times the ascendancy of women seems to be the root of the French problem. But there are also hints that they may provide the solution. So while women appear as one of the sources of the corruption of the monarchic principle (that is, the degeneration of honor into vanity), that very unleashing of vanity might well open up the route to a new order—one in which commerce and the arts of peace will prevail.

In a chapter of *The Spirit of the Laws* entitled "On the vanity and the pride of nations" (XIX.9), Montesquieu contrasts the effects of two passions, *vanité* and *orgueil*, on the public weal. Vanity, he says, is productive of "innumerable goods": luxury, the arts, fashions, politeness, taste, and above all industry and commerce. The salutary effects of vanity stand in contrast to the "infinite evils" born of the spirit of pride: laziness, poverty, and the devastation of nations. According to Montesquieu, the Spanish are a people characterized by such arrogance, which we might today call *machismo*.

The letter of the Frenchman visiting the Iberian peninsula, which

Rica passes on to Usbek (#78), expands brilliantly on this same assessment of the Spanish.[15] In contrast to the vivacity and vanity of the French, the Spanish are grave, prideful, devout, and jealous. Their gravity is worn upon their faces in the form of spectacles (a proof of profundity) and mustaches. The letter writer tells the story of the colonial viceroy who "finding himself in need of money, cut off part of his mustache and demanded from the inhabitants of Goa a loan of twenty thousand pistoles on this collateral; the money was lent at once, and he later recovered his mustache honorably." Among the Spanish, this secondary sex characteristic of the male is "intrinsically respectable." One can even bank on it. Interestingly, the same prominence is accorded the secondary sex characteristics of the female—"[t]hey permit their wives to appear with exposed bosoms, but they let no one see their heels or be surprised by the sight of their toes." The Spaniards make a sort of fetish of sexual difference: "They are the foremost men in the world in dying of languor beneath the window of their mistresses, and no Spaniard without a head cold can pass for a gallant."

There are more serious health risks for those successful in their suits, for "often there remains with them a long and disagreeable souvenir of an extinct passion." The letter writer alludes here to the syphilis epidemic that greatly afflicted Spain in the two centuries following the discovery of the New World. Elsewhere Montesquieu surmises that syphilis had been brought by the conquistadors as they returned from the Americas to Europe.[16] In his *Pensées*, Montesquieu reflects on the meaning of venereal disease: "The pleasures and health have become almost incompatible. The pains of love, so much chanted by the ancient poets, are no longer the rigors or inconstancy of a mistress. The times have caused other dangers to be born, and the Apollo of our day is less the God of verse than that of medicine" (no. 447). Despite their decimation, the Spanish have not turned to modern science. Their two polestars remain romance and religion. The letter writer describes the contents of a Spanish library, with "romances on one side and scholastics on the other; you would say the parts have been made and the whole assembled by some secret enemy of human reason."

Perhaps not surprisingly, the Spanish are being consumed by religious, as well as sexual, maladies. The Inquisition ravages the population. Under the cover of a discussion of different standards of courtesy in France and Spain, Montesquieu delivers one of the most bitter lines of the *Persian Letters*: "the Inquisition never burns a Jew without making its apology to him"—an example of a "petty politeness" the French would regard as "badly placed." The same ironic tone characterizes Montesquieu's much more extensive denunciation of the Inquisition in *The Spirit of the Laws* (XXV.13). On both occasions, Montesquieu somewhat obscures the degree to which he is speaking on behalf of the Jews. In the *Persian Letters*, he arrives at his point tangentially, from the rather absurd angle of courtesy. In *The Spirit of the Laws*, instead of speaking in his own name, Montesquieu presents a "very humble remonstrance to the inquisitors of Spain and Portugal" written by a Jew present at the burning of a young Jewess. The appeal is rendered more powerful by giving it in the voice of the victims; at the same time, it allows Montesquieu himself to feign piety with a theological footnote on "the source of the Jews' blindness."

Montesquieu's treatment of Judaism and the Jews is illustrative of his unsentimental *humanité*. Montesquieu is often harsh toward Judaism, but unfailingly gentle toward Jews. In the *Persian Letters*, we have seen Montesquieu frequently refer objectionable elements in both Christianity and Islam back to Judaism (see especially #17–18 on the origin of the notions of purity and impurity). At the same time, Montesquieu welcomes and seeks to foster religious tolerance toward Jews. Done as Montesquieu does it, the impugning of Judaism is part of an attempt to moderate Christian fanaticism, thereby making religious pluralism and the civic equality of Jews possible. Moreover, it should be noted that if Montesquieu blames Judaism for a dispensation hostile to humanity, he praises the Jews for their role in the emergence of a new, more friendly dispensation. Long before Marx began fulminating about "the emancipation of mankind from Judaism" (Judaism understood as synonymous with huckstering, i.e., capitalism),[17] Montesquieu had acknowledged—and in his understated way, celebrated— the Jewish role in the advent of modern capitalism. In a chapter of *The Spirit of the Laws* entitled "How commerce broke through the barbarism of Europe" (XXI.20), Montesquieu credits the Jews with the resuscitation of commerce in its revolutionary modern form. As a result of the proscription of lending upon interest, common to both classical political philosophy and medieval Christianity, commercial activity became the despised province of the Jews. Such wealth, in hands unsecured by the privileges of citizenship, was too much for the greed of princes to resist. Throughout Christendom, the Jews were plundered, tortured, killed, and exiled. Earthly salvation came in the form of letters of exchange, for by this Jewish invention "commerce . . . became capable of eluding violence, and of maintaining everywhere its ground." (Marx's version of this—"the bill of exchange is the real god of the Jew"[18]—may be a twisted rendering of Montesquieu's account.)

According to Montesquieu, the independence of commerce from theological-political control produces more than prosperity and material goods; it fosters tolerance and peace and humanity. "The Theologians," Montesquieu explains, "were obliged to limit their principles," by introducing, for example, a distinction between lending upon interest and usury. Apparently, once the bill of exchange had rendered commerce safe for the Jews who engaged in it, the Church found it difficult to maintain the ban on Christian involvement. It was certainly easier to convince believers of the choice-worthiness of poverty when the possessions and persons of wealthy outsiders were insecure, exposed to expropriation and violence. Montesquieu approves of the mitigation of Christian reservations against commerce and property: he describes commerce as having "re-entered, so to speak, the bosom of probity." Again, Marx's lament that Christianity "has now been re-absorbed into Judaism"[19] reads like a vicious inversion of Montesquieu. The despair-driven ingenuity of the Jewish merchants not only forced the Church to soften its proscriptions; it imposed new restraints upon the avarice of the secular rulers as well. Montesquieu concludes this chapter on the Jewish origins of capitalism with one of his most famous pronouncements:

> We begin to be cured of Machiavellism, and recover from it every day. More moderation has become necessary in the councils of princes. What would formerly have been called a master-stroke of politics would be now, independent of the horror it might occasion, the greatest imprudence.[20]

Letter #78 concludes that the anti-Semitic Spanish are "so devout that they are hardly Christian." Although those who seek to introduce some moderation into Christianity might deny them the name, the Spaniards take an inordinate pride not simply in being Christian, but in being what they call "Old Christians," that is, not descended from individuals forcibly converted by the Inquisition. Thus, even the supreme practitioners of coerced virtue hold such virtue in disesteem (echoing Usbek's scorn for his wives—"You boast about a virtue that is not free" [#20]). For those Spaniards living in the colonies, it is racial, rather than religious, ancestry that matters. Sexism, racism, religious fanaticism, elitism, colonialism: although these words were unknown to Montesquieu, his portrait of the Spanish is compounded out of today's most castigated -isms. In his parting shot, the letter writer even casts aspersions on the renown of the Iberians as explorers and mapmakers:

They have made enormous discoveries in the New World, and yet they do not know their own country; their rivers are not yet entirely explored, and their mountains hold nations unknown to them.

They say that the sun rises and sets within their lands, but it must also be said that, in making its course, the sun encounters only a wasted and deserted countryside.

Without doubt, Montesquieu prefers the feminine vanity of France to the masculine arrogance of Spain. The French tone is superior not simply in aesthetic terms, but in muscular terms as well. According to Montesquieu, "the arrogance of a Spaniard will incline him not to work; the vanity of a Frenchman will incline him to try to work better than the others" (XIX.9). French society, with its powerful feminine influence, is more elastic, more responsive, more vigorous, in sum, healthier.

The Charms of Modernity

The comparison with Spain puts France in its best light. Viewed more objectively, France is greatly troubled. Rica's final string of letters (#132-43) undertakes to diagnose the patient and propose a cure. The primarily diagnostic letters are the three dealing with the economic crisis (#132 and #138 explicitly so, #142 allegorically) and the one on the fate of the Paris *parlement*, banished for its refusal to register a financial decree (#140). Sandwiched between Rica's first two accounts of the reversals of economic fortune is his library series (#133-37), which surveys the present state of human knowledge. The library is located in a convent, but its guardians are "required to admit the public at certain hours" (#133). Thus do we see learning, which had been under the exclusive control of the Church, gradually becoming accessible to people at large. While conducting Rica on a tour of the library, the librarian (not himself a member of the convent) passes judgment on the worth of the various divisions, dismissing all religious writing (#134), much scientific writing (#135), and most poetry, excepting dramatic poetry and those "most dangerous" authors who "give point to epigrams" (#137); only modern history comes through largely unexpurgated (#136). This clearing away of intellectual baggage is continued in #142, where Montesquieu once again utilizes the letter-within-a-letter frame. While the "Fragment of an Ancient Mythologist" is an allegory on John Law's swindle of the French, the letter of the savant that encloses it (and that is in turn enclosed in Rica's letter) shows us "a useless member of the Republic of Letters," an antiquarian blind to the contemporary import of his researches.

In between the final two economic letters (#138 and #142) are three letters concerned with the question of regime change. Letter #140 on the exiling of the Paris *parlement* is flanked by two letters documenting female rule—both the assumption of such rule and its abdication. In #139, Rica comments favorably on the abdication of two Swedish queens, one abdicating in favor of her husband, the other abdicating to pursue the philosophic life. Letter #141, Zuléma's utopian tale of Anaïs and Ibrahim, reverses the situation, picturing a philosophic woman's assumption of rule and overthrow of her husband. I don't know quite what to make of this neat pair of letters, other than to note that in the three examples given (Queen Ulrika Eleonora, Queen Christina, and Anaïs), the women reject "the post in which Nature has placed them" and by dint of "greatness of soul" prove themselves "superior to their fortune." Man or woman, one's lot in life is far from fixed if Nature can be transformed into a humanly masterable fortune.

The culmination of this series and the book's final letter by Rica is #143, written to Nathaniel Levi, a Jewish doctor in Italy. Rica is replying to the doctor's inquiry about "the virtue of amulets." Rica is greatly angered by this inquiry. In response he mocks both his own practice of wearing phylacteries and the cabalism of the Jew:

> What result do you expect from the arrangement of certain letters? What is it that their arrangement can disturb? What relation have they with the winds, that they should calm the storm; with gunpowder, that they should overcome its effects; with what doctors call peccant humors and the morbific cause of disease, that they should be cured?

Here, Montesquieu has most cleverly and disarmingly posed what must be the question in the mind of every reader of the *Persian Letters*: what result do you, Président Montesquieu, expect from the arrangement of certain letters? Rica goes on to show how the attachment to occult explanations obstructs the search for real causes. Essentially, Rica makes the case for the unknowability or unrecognizability of miracles: "to be certain that an effect, which can be produced by a hundred thousand natural causes, is really supernatural, one must first have determined that none of these causes has acted—and that is impossible to do." Of course, to say that a miracle cannot be known because of the limits upon our knowledge of nature is not to say that miracles are impossible. But Rica declares that he will say nothing further "for it seems to me that the matter does not deserve such serious treatment."

After thus dismissing the talismanic power of words, Rica, in a postscript, appends a broadsheet circulating on the streets of Paris entitled "Letter from a physician in the provinces to a physician in Paris." This bagatelle has just come to his attention and he sends it along "since it has some relation to our subject." Perhaps the word has some mysterious power after all. The broadsheet tells the story of a chronic insomniac cured by a bookseller who prescribed the reading of Father Caussin's *The Holy Court.* The provincial physician who compares the efficacy of Father Caussin to that of opium,

> being a subtle man, versed in the mysteries of the cabala and in the power of words and spirits . . . resolved to change his practice entirely. "This is a very singular fact," he said. "I must push the experiment further. Why shouldn't a mind [*un esprit*] be able to transmit to his work the same qualities he has himself? Don't we see this happening every day? At least, it is worth the trouble of a trial. I am tired of apothecaries; their syrups, potions, and Galenic drugs ruin patients and their health as well. Let us change the method; let us test the virtue of minds." On this idea he set up a new pharmacy.

I believe that Montesquieu has done something similar in the *Persian Letters.* He acts upon the minds of his readers through a book which is a distillate of his own mind. In the fanciful pharmacopoeia of #143, Montesquieu makes oblique reference to his own writing when he mentions certain "rare remedies" like "a dedicatory letter which made no one yawn" and "an excessively short preface." Remember that Montesquieu had made quite a point in the preface of his refusal to write a dedicatory letter, as well as his refusal to lengthen his preface with the usual panegyrics. A dose of Montesquieu should act as a stimulant rather than a soporific. Throughout the *Persian Letters*, Montesquieu seeks to charm the reader, substituting new spells and new spectacles for the old ones of superstition and cruelty. The chain of despotism, composed of three tightly braided strands (domestic, political, and religious)—the "secret, and in some manner unknown, chain" that unifies the *Persian Letters*—is reworked by Montesquieu into a bracelet of charms. Montesquieu, the great provincial doctor of law, replaces the Levitical doctor of law, and, like his analogue in #143, offers the letter(s) containing his new pharmacy for sale in the streets of Paris. The remedy of the *Persian Letters*, acting as it does upon minds and through manners, is fully in accord with *l'esprit des lois.*

Chapter Eight

Continuation of
the Same Subject

Montesquieu has no greater liking for conclusions than he has for beginnings. *The Spirit of the Laws* virtually ends with an ellipsis (in a chapter entitled "Continuation of the same subject"): "Italiam, Italiam, . . . I close the treatise on fiefs where most authors have begun it" (XXXI.34). Similarly, the *Considerations* ends in a trickle: "I have not the courage to speak of the miseries which followed: I will say only that, under the last emperors, the empire, reduced to the outskirts of Constantinople, ended like the Rhine, which is no more than a rivulet when it loses itself in the Ocean" (XXIII). The end of the *Persian Letters* is also fluid. When the eunuchs pour out the blood of Roxane's lover, she retaliates by envenoming the blood of the eunuchs and herself. As her own life ebbs away, she manages to drown Usbek in a final, violent flow of ink (#161):

> Yes, I deceived you; I corrupted your eunuchs, made sport of your jealousy, and learned how to make your frightful seraglio into a place of delight and pleasure. . . . No doubt this language seems new to you. Is it possible that after crushing you with sorrow, I may yet force you to admire my courage? But all this is done now: the poison is consuming me; my strength is departing; the pen is falling from my hands; I feel even my hatred growing weaker; I am dying.

We know what Usbek's response to the revolutionary deluge is. In letter #146 (written shortly after receiving Roxane's letter, but placed by Montesquieu out of chronological order), Usbek says nothing of his harem's collapse. Instead, he speaks of the ruin of princes and peoples at the hands of false ministers: "the evil [of a minister's bad example] is communicable and does not spare even the healthiest members; the most virtuous men do unworthy things and violate the first principles of justice, on the vain pretext that they had been first violated." Usbek remains to the end utterly uncomprehending of the real source of opposition to his rule. In blaming his ministers (the eunuchs), he refuses to believe that the virtuous Roxane acted on her own initiative and that she regarded her marriage to him as a violation. Broken and dispirited, Usbek, in his final lines, relegates the current generation to "the frightful oblivion into which it has sunk."

Are we to conclude that Montesquieu's message is similarly pessimistic? Most recently, Dena Goodman has argued that in demonstrating the interdependence of so many factors, "Montesquieu has stymied any possibility of reform arising out of his criticism. . . . Not only Usbek but Montesquieu as well has failed to bridge the gap between knowledge and action, criticism and change." Further, Goodman finds that the helplessness of author, character, and readers is attributable to the epistolary form of the work: "The overriding static effect of the polyphonic form results from an emphasis on the relationships displayed in and created by the correspondence as a whole, rather than on the dynamics of the action narrated from letter to letter."[1] On her reading, the epistles of Montesquieu, while not aporetic, are impotent. Goodman, as her epigraph from Marx reveals, desires the coincidence of wisdom and power: "Philosophers have only interpreted the world in various ways. The point, however, is to change it." I believe that Montesquieu comes as close to that wished-for consummation as possible without recourse to despotism (whether in the form of philosopher-kings or the reason of History) and moreover, that the epistolary form, through its enticement to a new state, plays matchmaker to that consummation. In *The Spirit of the Laws*, in a chapter titled "What are the natural means of changing the mores and manners of a nation" (XIX.14), Montesquieu says, "In general, peoples are very attached to their customs; taking their customs from them violently makes them unhappy: therefore, one must not change their customs, but engage the peoples to change them themselves." And again in the preface to *The Spirit of the Laws*: "I would consider myself the happiest of mortals if I could make it so that men were able to cure themselves of their prejudices. Here I call prejudices not what makes one unaware of certain things but what makes one unaware of oneself." Self-knowledge is the remedy.

The very structure of the *Persian Letters*—the departure from strict chronology, which delays for the readers the spectacle of the harem's collapse until after we have had the benefit of Rica's metaphorical warnings of collapse—provides the opportunity for that self-knowledge. If the owl of Minerva takes its flight at dusk, it is too late. For his readers (but not for his characters) Montesquieu arrests time, so that insight might precede rather than accompany the end. By rearranging the letters as he does, Montesquieu has performed something of a miracle, suspending the course of the sun. Moreover, his rearrangement deprives Usbek of the last word. Usbek's reaction is not permitted to serve as a model for the reader. Montesquieu allows the reader to take the warning but scorn the despair. Indeed, he even encourages us to sympathize with and admire Roxane's courage, while perhaps learning how to avert the need for such suicidal measures. In the future, the ending might be rewritten.

Like Thucydides who breaks off his account of the Peloponnesian War midsentence, Montesquieu spares us. We know what awaits, and we know that for the Greeks, for the empire of Constantinople, and for the Persian harem it is too late. But perhaps France is salvageable. The Virgilian ". . ." from the closing lines of *The Spirit of the Laws* offers ground for hope. Similarly, while the Rhine (in the *Considerations* a metaphor for the Byzantine Empire) may dissipate into the ocean, just before it does so it is largely diverted into the westward-flowing Waal.[2] Could Western Christianity achieve a nondespotic (perhaps even Protestant) culmination? In the *Persian Letters*, the despotisms of the East, from the Turkish empire to the Persian harem, are on the verge of anarchic collapse. Can France reverse its own Orientalization?

In a chapter of *The Spirit of the Laws* entitled "Distinctive properties of monarchy" (VIII.17), Montesquieu says that "Rivers run together into the sea; monarchies are lost in despotism." Flux is the problem, recognized as such by both ancients and moderns. The enraged Achilles does epic battle with an equally enraged river (*Iliad* 21.211-382). In a famous passage of the *Prince* (XXV), Machiavelli likens Fortune to rampaging rivers, noting however that "it is not as if men, when times are quiet, could not provide for them with dikes and dams so that when they rise later, either they go by a canal or their impetus is neither so wanton nor so damaging." Montesquieu also hopes that the floodwaters can be contained, that the natural tendency toward despotism can be impeded.

While all monarchic rivers may terminate in the despotic ocean, Montesquieu suggests that it is possible for men to reclaim land directly from the ocean itself. Both of the Italian republics that appear in the *Persian Letters* are striking examples of such reclamation. So while monarchy may be inherently unstable, partaking of the indefiniteness of the fluid element, republics—at least if they are of a certain sort—might be more humanly habitable. Of Livorno, Usbek says, "It is a new city and a testament to the genius of the dukes of Tuscany, who have made a swampy village into the most flourishing city in Italy" (#23). Livorno was founded by the Medici in the sixteenth century as a free port, open to religious and political refugees. Immediately upon his uncle Ibben's receipt of this letter, Rhédi resolves to set out for Italy, his sole aim being self-instruction. Rhédi takes up residence in Venice, which while not a new city like Livorno is marked by the same singularity. Rhédi writes: "One may have seen every city in the world and yet be surprised on arriving in Venice: it will always be amazing to see a city whose towers and mosques spring out of the water, and to find an innumerable people in a place where there should be only fish" (#31).

Thus, the real contest is between dry land and ocean, between republicanism and despotism. If monarchy is, as Usbek asserts (#102), "a violent state, invariably degenerating into either despotism or a republic," then the question for Montesquieu is how to cause moderate republics to emerge out of the wreckage of monarchy. Does monarchy yield an alluvial delta that can serve as the ground of republicanism?

The original principle of monarchy is honor. The *Persian Letters* shows the corruption of French honor into vanity, the disintegration of corporate identity into self-interest. Self-interest, however, is an amphibious passion able to live both in water and on land. In other words, self-interest can serve as the principle of either despotism or republicanism. Fear, the principle of despotism, is the primordial incarnation of self-interest. Despotism is the first and easiest and most pervasive of regimes: "since only passions are needed to establish it, everyone is good enough for that" (V.14). Montesquieu searches for another, more civilized incarnation of self-interest. I believe he finds it in vanity. Vanity is a kind of socialized fear—not the natural, dissociative, Hobbesian fear that culminates in despotism, but a man-made, communicative, opinion-based fear that renders human beings interdependent. Modern republicanism shares with despotism a reliance on the passions; however, in a republic those passions can be given institutional form. Instead of being unlimited and oceanic, they are bounded, separated, and linked. So vanity may be the detritus of monarchy, but it is also the fertile ground from which the commercial republic springs.

The Structure of the Spirit

The essential lines of Montesquieu's thought can be seen by a quick survey of the structure of *The Spirit of the Laws*. Part 1, books I-VIII, lays out Montesquieu's tripartite scheme of governments (republics, monarchies, despotisms). Beneath the scientific veneer, Montesquieu dissects all three regimes, but particularly the ancient republic, the regime dedicated to virtue. Very gently, he uncovers the impossibility and the undesireability (indeed the inhumanity) of the ancient conception of virtue. The fundamental problem of the ancient republic is the contradiction between its nature and its principle.[3] Its nature is to be governed by the will of the people; its principle is virtue understood as self-renunciation. As Montesquieu presents it, there is no lasting equilibrium possible between republican willfullness and republican austerity. The classical republic self-destructs.[4] In part 2, books IX-XIII, we learn of a new standard—liberty—and of a regime explicitly devoted to liberty—England—a regime that we might call a modern commercial republic. According to Montesquieu, modern republicanism differs from the ancient (and Christian) variety in being based on liberty rather than virtue, commerce rather than constraint. In part 3, books XIV-XIX, Montesquieu seems to turn away from the consideration of political liberty. He inquires instead into the despotism of nature itself. He details the ways in which climate and terrain shape human character and laws, virtually mandating domestic, civil, and political slavery. He tempers our liberal universalism by showing us the natural obstacles to its realization. In part 4, Montesquieu at last arrives at the subject of commerce. He takes up the human art whereby men can transform the determinism and despotism of nature. Commerce is the art which remedies "both the defect of nature and the defects of art itself" (XXI.6). Just as liberty replaces virtue, commerce corrects necessity.

The two books on commerce are, in large part, an epic of navigation and maritime empire. After his "Invocation to the Muses," asking for their assistance in making reason sing, Montesquieu begins his modern Odyssey by saying, "The following material would require more extensive treatment, but the nature of this work does not permit it. I should like to glide on a tranquil river; I am dragged along by a torrent." Unlike the monarchic flood, however, the commercial flood is a salutary one, and the outlet into the sea bespeaks not despotism, but the possible advance of civilization, for "[t]he history of commerce is that of communication among peoples" (XXI.5). Montesquieu disparages certain barbarian nations who have actually closed off access to the ocean: "This communication no longer exists. All these countries have been laid waste by the Tartars, and this destructive nation still lives there and infects them. The Oxus no longer runs to the Caspian

Sea; the Tartars have diverted it for particular reasons; it disappears
into arid sands." Those nations that traverse the oceans best are most
often republics in originally straitened circumstances:

> It has been seen everywhere that violence and harassment have brought
> forth economic commerce among men who are constrained to hide in
> marshes, on islands, on the shoals, and even among dangerous reefs.
> Thus were Tyre, Venice, and the Dutch towns founded; fugitives found
> security there. They had to live; they drew their livelihood from the
> whole universe. (XX.5)

Perched precariously at water's edge, these nations learn how to move
upon the surface of the deep as upon land. With the invention of the
compass, the universe becomes their oyster: "The compass opened the
universe, so to speak" (XXI.21).

Book XIX occupies a very crucial position in *The Spirit of the Laws*.
Coming at the end of part 3, it serves as the link or the fulcrum between nature and commerce. Somehow the subject of book XIX, the
general spirit, is the key to the successful movement from despotism
to liberty. Montesquieu's discovery of the general spirit represents an
epoch in the art of legislation. It is a legislative compass, making it
possible freely to navigate the political universe, no longer hugging
the coastline in the manner of ancient mariners. Given that Montesquieu presents the general spirit as the resultant of a variety of influences—climate, history, law, custom, religion, and so on—we might
have expected him to discuss the general spirit after having discussed
each of the contributing factors. However, Montesquieu discusses commerce and religion subsequent to his discussion of the general spirit.
Why is it that the discussion of the general spirit is placed between
parts 3 and 4 rather than at their end?[5] I believe that Montesquieu
intends to show how the end product, the general spirit, can itself
become a means, a means whereby a philosophic legislator introduces
new manners and mores.

Book XIX presents itself as more frankly devoted to teaching legislators than any earlier book. Those who aspire to give laws must understand the character of the people for whom they are legislating, since
that character sets the boundaries of reform. As Montesquieu says, "The
legislator is to follow the spirit of the nation when doing so is not
contrary to the principle of the government, for we do nothing better
than what we do freely and by following our natural genius" (XIX.5).
In chapters 5–9, Montesquieu delivers his tacit encomium of the French
spirit (though the nation goes unnamed, nothing could be more clear
than that France is meant). He describes a nation marked above all by

its "sociable humor": a nation gay and gallant, in which the feminine tone predominates, establishing politeness and taste. In tracing the effects of this sociable humor, Montesquieu stresses the link between commerce with women and commerce simply, concluding with his express preference for vanity over pride and his criticism of the Spanish character. Just in case the message has not sunk in yet, Montesquieu gives us the central chapter (14) of book XIX, entitled "What are the natural means of changing the mores and manners of a nation." Here, after criticizing Peter the Great for his violence toward the orthodox in banning customary religious attire, Montesquieu praises Peter for certain more gentle sartorial ventures:

> The women had been enclosed and in a way enslaved; he called them to court, he had them dress in the German way, and he sent them fabrics. They immediately appreciated a way of life that so flattered their taste, their vanity, and their passions, and they made the men appreciate it.

The court as couturier achieved what the court as censor could not.

The brief chapter that follows the story of Peter the Great, entitled "Influence of domestic government on political government," states forthrightly the intrinsic connection between the conditions of domestic life and the prospects for political freedom: "This change in the mores of women will no doubt affect the government of Muscovy very much. Everything is closely linked together." Despotism begins at home, and that is where the amelioration of despotism should begin also.

Note how Montesquieu describes Peter's task: he sought to "give the mores and manners of Europe to a European nation." The implication is that Eastern mores and manners had been introduced into Russia through the Christian Church. Just as Russia had been Orientalized by means of Eastern Orthodoxy, the other nations of Europe, France included, had been Orientalized by Roman Catholicism. Although book XIX does not deal explicitly with religion, Montesquieu discreetly broaches the subject through his example of a new Peter—the rock of a new dispensation.

There are other hints that the reform of mores through the unleashing of female vanity is really a reform of religion. For instance, Montesquieu says that "[l]aws are established, mores are inspired" (XIX.12), and he goes on to discuss those legislators who have mistakenly made a single code for laws, mores, and manners. In their "singular" institutions, they have united things that ought to be separate—closely related, but separate (XIX.21). In the body of the text, he mentions China and Sparta as examples, but the footnote refers to Moses: "Moses made a single code of laws and religion" (XIX.16.n.16).

I believe that the series of chapters on China (beginning with 13, interrupted for the story of Peter in 14 and 15, continued in 16-21) is meant to be read as a disguised critique of the laws of Moses and the principle of biblical morality. According to Montesquieu, "[t]his [Chinese] empire is formed on the idea of family government." The community appears to be bound together by relations of love between fathers (or father figures) and the subjects of fatherly rule. This sublime principle of love for the father gives rise to an infinite variety of detailed rites and ceremonies. Despite the Christian missionaries who have expressed admiration (seconded by Bayle and Voltaire) for the Chinese system, Montesquieu makes his own disapproval perfectly clear, both here and throughout *The Spirit of the Laws*. Back in book VIII, at the conclusion of part 1, he stated unambiguously, "China is a despotic state whose principle is fear" (VIII.21). The same combination of fear and love is at the heart of the biblical order. The love of the heavenly father masks the fear of the heavenly father. The relation between man and God is despotic.

We see how politically questionable Chinese morality is in chapter 20, entitled "Explanation of a paradox about the Chinese." Montesquieu informs us that the Chinese are "the most unscrupulous people on earth. This appears chiefly in commerce, which has never been able to inspire in them the good faith natural to it" (XIX.20). According to Montesquieu, it is commerce not religion that effectively inspires good faith. The good faith that matters is the observance of contracts, rather than the covenant with God. Fittingly, the section on China concludes, as it began, with a critical reference to Moses: "When the divine wisdom said to the Jewish people, 'I have given you precepts that are not good,' this meant that the precepts were only relatively good, which sponges away all the difficulties one can propose about the Mosaic laws" (XIX.21).

This chapter, "Explanation of a paradox about the Chinese" (XIX.20), must be paired with an earlier chapter "Explanation of a paradox of the ancients in relation to mores" (IV.8). The paradox he there refers to is the significance that the ancients attached to education in music. Montesquieu says that this "is one of the principles of their politics." Moreover, it is a principle that draws its breath from hostility to commerce. Montesquieu explains that "in the Greek towns . . . all work and all professions that could lead to earning silver were regarded as unworthy of a free man." Because of the way in which the ancients understood freedom (leisure over labor, public business over private business), they were led to disapprove of commerce and glorify war: "In the Greek republics, one was, therefore, in a very awkward position. One did not want the citizens to work in commerce, agriculture, or the arts; nor did one want them to be idle. They found an occupation in the exercises derived from gymnastics and those related to war. The institutions gave them no others."

The problem is that gymnastics does not just harden the body, it hardens the soul as well, rendering men "harsh and savage." Music was introduced as a kind of antidote: "music curbed the effect of the ferocity of the institution." Music offered a means of restoring fullness and humanity to the soul: "In short, the exercises practiced by the Greeks aroused in them only one type of passion: roughness, anger, and cruelty. Music arouses them all and can make the soul feel softness, pity, tenderness, and sweet pleasure." In this debunking treatment of the education of a gentleman, Montesquieu explains the origin of the education in music as essentially medicinal, a hedonistic purgative for anger. In the final paragraph, Montesquieu raises the question "why should music be preferred?" Why not some other form of pleasure, for instance, sexual pleasure? Montesquieu continues: "We blush to read in Plutarch that the Thebans, in order to soften the mores of their young people, established by their laws a love that ought to be proscribed by all nations in the world."

I believe Montesquieu's point is that the real paradox of the ancients was their reliance on homosexuality. Romance can indeed accomplish the same ends as music. Love of the collective, being a spirited form of love, hardens men. By contrast, the erotic love of a particular individual softens men. In this passage, Montesquieu mentions only the Thebans, but elsewhere he makes it clear that homoeroticism was the Greek ideal. In a chapter entitled "On the condition of women in the various governments" (VII.9), he says, "in the Greek towns where a blind vice reigned unbridled, where love took only a form one dare not mention while only friendship was to be found within marriages, women's virtue, simplicity, and chastity were such that one has scarcely ever seen a people who had a better police in this regard." Montesquieu's footnote to this passage reads: "'As for true love,' says Plutarch in the *Moralia, Amatorius*, p. 600, 'women have no part in it.' He spoke as did his age. See Xenophon, in the dialogue entitled *Hiero*." So women were virtuous among the Greeks because they were not the primary object of male desire. Marriage was for the utilitarian purpose of procreation. The prevalence of homosexuality among the Greeks, and particularly its pedophilic character, followed from the Greek understanding of freedom. It would be as disgraceful for a free man to love a woman as a slave, so long as women are little more than slaves; much better to love a boy who is destined for public affairs and is with respect to beardless beauty the equivalent of a woman. Quietly Montesquieu indicates that homosexuality is one of the "singular" institutions of the Greeks—an institution intimately connected with hostility to commerce and the inequality of women.

After thus illustrating the origin and character of biblical mores through the discussion of China (and reminding us of the origin and character of ancient virtue as well via the similarity of chapter heads), Montesquieu turns to the Romans to trace "How the laws follow mores" (chapters 23-26). He discusses Roman law on such economic and household topics as embezzlement, female guardianship, dowries, and divorce. The final chapter on the Romans explains that in the later Roman empire, which is to say the Christian Roman empire, "the usages of the East had taken the place of those of Europe" (XIX.26). Chief among those customs was the servitude and, indeed, the infantilization of women: "The first eunuch of the empress, wife of Justinian II, threatened her, history says, with the chastisement used to punish children in schools." There is no more striking instance of the connection between religious, political, and sexual despotism than this ministerial spanking of a queen.[6] We note also that there is perhaps no more striking instance of the connection between *The Spirit of the Laws* and the *Persian Letters*. Usbek's despotic rule culminates in the very same act as that of Justinian II. Roxane, Zachi, and Zélis each write to protest the eunuch's resort to "that most humiliating of all punishments" (#156-58).

A discussion of the English character abruptly reverses book XIX's focus on the mores of the unfree. This extended survey of English life (the complement to the survey of English institutions in XI.6) completes book XIX and serves as the segue to parts 4, 5, and 6. As with the previous description of the French, no names are used. It is an extremely nuanced presentation, appreciative of much, but also highly critical. Among those things of which Montesquieu is critical are the conduct of English imperialism, particularly as manifested toward Scotland and Ireland; the religious intolerance shown toward Catholics; and the isolation, misanthropy, and unhappiness of individuals, particularly of the best and most intelligent individuals. (On this latter subject, Montesquieu sounds like a harbinger of Tocqueville in his treatment of the deleterious effects of individualism.)

Of the position of women in English society, Montesquieu says:

> In a nation where each man in his own way would take part in the administration of the state, the women should scarcely live among men. Therefore, women would be modest, that is, timid; this timidity would

be their virtue, whereas the men, lacking gallantry, would throw themselves into a debauchery that would leave them their liberty as well as their leisure.

In England men have less to do with women, and to the extent that they are involved with them, it is likely to be in a more sordid fashion.[7] Prostitution and pornography replace *liaisons dangereuses*. The exclusively male pub and club replace the female-centered salon. The "debauchery" characteristic of the English is a function, at least in part, of their radical individualism. Because of their proud belief in their own self-sufficiency, they are led to deny human interconnectedness. They deny the sympathy between men and women, and they deny as well the sympathy between fellow citizens. Montesquieu says that "the men in this nation would be confederates more than fellow citizens." Among the English, even commerce—whose natural tendency is to render men softer and more peace-loving—has a hard and haughty aspect. Montesquieu says that the English laws respecting commerce and navigation are "so rigid" that the English "seem to negotiate only with enemies."

Comparing this criticism of the English spirit with the earlier praise of the "sociable humor" of the French, I believe the suggestion would be that while the English government is far superior to the French, the French character has the edge over the English. In one of the chapters on the French (XIX.7), Montesquieu had compared the French character to that of the Athenians. He had mentioned the Spartan character as well ("grave, serious, dry, taciturn"), although he had not said what modern nation might resemble the Spartans. After reading this final chapter of book XIX, I think it is fair to say that the Englishmen bear a certain resemblance to the Lacedaemonians: gloomy, practical, deficient in taste and beauty, and averse to the society of women. If the French could reform their government and reverse the slide toward despotism, then the resulting liberal order might be superior to that of the English, for in France a new commercial order would have an erotic rather than a prideful foundation. If France is like Athens in being an erotic polity, its superiority over Athens would be attributable to the orientation of its eros—summed up in the slogan for which the French are renowned: "Vive la différence!"[8]

Whether in fact superior or not, the French spirit is different than the English, and that difference must be taken into account by legislators: "If one gives a pedantic spirit to a nation naturally full of gaiety, the state will gain nothing, either at home or abroad. Let it do frivolous things seriously and serious things gaily" (XIX.5). An interpretation of book XIX along these lines is able to account for the remarkable introduction to the books on commerce (XX-XXII), where Montesquieu summons the Muses in a prose poem: "Charming Muses, if you cast me but a single glance, everyone will read my works, and what was not intended as an amusement will be a pleasure. . . . You are never as divine as when you lead to wisdom and truth through pleasure."

Montesquieu is at one with his fellow moderns in recognizing the importance of economics. But unlike them, he seeks to transform the dismal science into something pleasing, even something noble. In Hobbes, reason basely panders to the passions; in Montesquieu, passion is the divine consort of reason: "Divine Muses, I sense that you inspire me, not with what is sung in Tempe with the pipes or what is repeated at Delos on the lyre. You want me to make reason speak. It is the most perfect, the noblest, and the most exquisite of our senses."

Book XX has an epigraph from the *Aeneid*—"That which great Atlas taught"—as well as an "Invocation to the Muses." The world-bearer Atlas taught Iopas how to play on a cithern of gold for Dido, princess of Tyre and founder of Carthage, who swears by Juno and Bacchus (*Aeneid* 1.723-47). In his epic on commerce, Montesquieu likewise teaches how to make gold musical, how to fashion commerce and finance so that human life is bettered and beautified, and at the same time how to avoid the fate of Croesus (imperial Spain being the most recent example of death by riches). Through the independence of economics from the proscriptions of theologians and the depredations of princes, "[o]ne has begun" Montesquieu says, "to be cured of Machiavellism" (XXI.20). On the basis of this discovery, the remainder of *The Spirit of the Laws* unfolds. After commerce (books XXI–XXII) comes population (book XXIII), religion (books XXIV and XXV), and political evolution (books XXVI–XXXI), particularly the evolution of the French monarchy. Thus, the overall metamorphosis is from domestic and economic reform to religious and political reform.

Erotic Liberalism

Just as the teaching of *The Spirit of the Laws* must be pieced together by the reader out of the welter of the details, so too the task of assembling and reassembling the *Persian Letters* falls to the reader. Montesquieu's writings are mosaic with a small "m"—enigmatic rather than lapidary. We get one explanation for Montesquieu's allusive style and his eschewal of conclusions in a chapter of *The Spirit of the*

Laws with the unique and promising title "End of this book" (XI.20). There Montesquieu says:

> I should like to seek out in all the moderate governments we know the distribution of the three powers and calculate thereupon the degrees of liberty each one of them can enjoy. But one must not always so exhaust a subject that one leaves nothing for the reader to do. It is not a question of making him read but of making him think.

So, Montesquieu himself proceeds nondespotically. The completion of his project to assess and extend constitutional liberty depends decisively upon the deliberative powers of his readers. The disjointed and open-ended quality of Montesquieu's writing is a call to self-government.

Moderate alternatives to despotism are much more visible in *The Spirit of the Laws* than in the *Persian Letters*. In his first work, Montesquieu seems more concerned to explore all the interlocking gears of despotism and to trace its psychological as well as its political effects. The seraglio of Usbek, which provides the frame for the novel, allows for an examination of three aspects of despotism: sexual, religious, political. The most fundamental of despotisms, the sexual, is treated at the level of the literal, while political and especially religious despotism are treated figuratively (through the equation of eunuchs to ministers of church and state, with Usbek as Lord and master). In the attempts, both at the time of publication and since, to read the novel as a *roman à clef*, the literal text has often been overlooked. Like the legendary purloined letter, it has been too visible to attract critical attention. Just as an object or an argument may be obvious by its absence, so too it may be concealed by its presence. I believe that Montesquieu means for the theme of sexual despotism to be taken seriously. It is certainly true that the parallelism of the various forms of despotism allows Montesquieu the luxury of couching his political and religious criticism in sexual terms. However, he focuses on sexual despotism not just as an analogue, but because it is truly fundamental. Despotism makes its first appearance in the relationship of men to women and the relationship between men in regard to women.

Throughout the novel, religion, both Islamic and Christian, is presented as a tool and justification of sexual domination. In Rica's letter considering the question of female equality (#38), the philogynist position of the gallant philosopher is juxtaposed to that of the religiously orthodox: "The Prophet has decided this question, and ordained the rights of the sexes. 'Wives,' he said, 'ought to honor their husbands, and husbands ought to honor their wives; but men have the advantage of being created one degree superior to women.'"

As Rica surmises, the same point underlies the pope's recent attempt (*Unigenitus* 1713) to forbid women to read the Bible (#24): "since women are of a creation inferior to ours, and since our prophets tell us that they cannot enter paradise, why then should they trouble themselves to read a book intended only to teach the way to paradise?" The religious attitude toward women is summed up by Zuléma: "Nothing has been left undone to degrade our sex"; there are even those "who on the authority of their sacred books maintain that we have no souls" (#141). Thus, a despotism that begins in superior strength, a despotism over the body alone, takes on the trappings of ontological right and is transformed into a despotism over the mind and spirit.

Aristotle gives a similar genealogy of male supremacy through his marvelously subversive use of the story of Amasis.[9] After repeated assertion that the relationship between husband and wife ought to be political rather than despotic, Aristotle must account for the fact that we do not see husbands and wives ruling and being ruled in turn:

> In most political offices, it is true, there is an alternation of ruler and ruled, since they tend by their nature to be on an equal footing and to differ in nothing; all the same, when one rules and the other is ruled, [the ruler] seeks to establish differences in external appearance, forms of address, and prerogatives, as in the story Amasis told about his footpan. The male always stands thus in relation to the female. (*Politics* 1259b1-10)

Amasis was a lowborn individual who upon seizing the kingship of Egypt had his golden footpan fashioned into the image of a god for his subjects to worship. According to Herodotus, Amasis then informed his people that

> the image had been made out of a footbath in which formerly the Egyptians used to vomit and piss and wash their feet, and now they reverenced it mightily. So now, he said to them, he himself was just like that footbath. For if he had been formerly a man of the people, he was now and in the present their king, and so he bade them honor and respect him. That was how Amasis conciliated the Egyptians to the justice of their slavery to himself.[10]

To describe male ascendancy in footpan-to-idol terms is to deprive it of any natural justice. According to Montesquieu, religious despotism culminates in a denaturing of men and women alike. All are enslaved, including the master himself. "*Per servir sempre, o vincitrice, o vin-*

ta" ("to be enslaved always, victorious or vanquished"): this was the epigraph Montesquieu chose for the *Persian Letters*.[11]

So long as politics remains in the vise-grip of the subpolitical and the suprapolitical, it will be despotic. In the *Persian Letters*, Montesquieu seeks to understand and address this theological-sexual problem.[12] Through Montesquieu's use of comparative religion, we come to understand the degenerative tendency of Western Christianity, and particularly Roman Catholicism. Of course, Machiavelli had already blamed Christianity for an effeminization of political life; and in a certain sense, Montesquieu could be said to agree with him. Christianity does indeed make men eunuchs. But paradoxically, that emasculation is attributed by Montesquieu to a depreciation of the feminine. Whereas Machiavelli sought to counter Christianity's bad effects by reviving the virile impulses of impetuous young men who might conquer the lady Fortuna, Montesquieu prefers the gentler mode of homeopathic treatment. A real dose of the feminine is his cure for Christianity's effeminization. Whereas Machiavelli forwards a politics of virility, Montesquieu favors a politics of fecundity.

Throughout the *Persian Letters*, women are instrumental in breaking the chains of despotism, in disrupting the lines of mutually reinforcing causality. The first letter from Paris (#24) shows French women in the vanguard of a rebellion against sexual/religious strictures emanating from the pope. However, the protests of the Parisian women pale before the insurrectionary doings of the Persian women. Upon penning her declaration of independence, Roxane offers up her life in plighted troth to her dead lover. Zélis, who has repeatedly shown her interest in law and rule, engages in a more measured, but also more public and potentially far-reaching act: the dropping of her veil. The two utopian tales also present models of female revolution: the philosophic legislator Anaïs and the revisionist storyteller Zuléma together transvalue the teachings of Islam, giving us a new scripture of a new covenant; Astarté abandons Islam entirely and returns to the natural religion, based on marital equality, of her forebears.

In each case, while justifiably struck by the boldness of the act, we ought also to note the presence of certain moderating, even conservative, elements in the rebellion. Roxane, though unfaithful to Usbek, is not a wanton woman; her fidelity is engaged to another. Zélis's care is bestowed upon the education and worldly prospects of her daughter; that motherly concern may well inform her decision to seek a modicum of social freedom and significance for herself. Although Anaïs is depicted in the enjoyment of orgiastic polyandry, those pleasures do not content her. Even in heaven, she turns to the activity of thought and legislation. Moreoever, in her solicitude for her sisters below, she does not seek to replicate her own experience; far from instituting polyandry, her reforms do not fully abolish polygamy. As for Astarté, that most devoted daughter, sister, wife, and mother (the only woman in the *Persian Letters* who illustrates the full panoply of female roles), her rebellion can best be described as reactionary. It is her incestuous love of family that leads her back to the ancient ways. Unlike Sophocles' insurrectionary female, Antigone, against whom she might best be compared, Astarté's family-based rebellion issues in peace and prosperity. Whereas the Greek tale emphasizes the polarity of *oikia* and *polis*, Montesquieu illustrates how the domestic and political realms might be harmonized. The strict separation of public and private central to both ancient and modern republicanism is not desirable.

We might describe Montesquieu's feminism as Astartic rather than Antigonic—a feminism rooted in the biological (Astarté's namesake is the Babylonian goddess of fertility) rather than hostile to it (Antigone means "against reproduction"). While Montesquieu's preference for the liberty of women is clear, he regards the social incorporation of women as far more important than their (rights-based) political participation. Indeed, it may even be that socialization averts politicization.[13] Montesquieu does not regard natural right as a source of universal public law; accordingly, although Montesquieu emphatically defends a woman's ability to govern a nation, he nowhere recommends female suffrage (of course, he is not insistent on male suffrage either).

The emancipation of womanliness achieved on the basis of Montesquieu's correction of Christianity is recommended not just for its own sake, but for its political benefits. According to Montesquieu, a revision of the relationship between the sexes would foster both population growth and commerce. Population and commerce constitute the links between domestic and political government. What we see of economic vibrancy in France begins in the acquisitive and coquettish desires of women, fanning out to embrace all walks of life in productive endeavor, and even introducing merit-based social mobility. What we see of economic disaster in France begins in the centrally planned policies of the minister of finance. The schemes of the bureaucrats result in the revolution-breeding social upheavals of speculative bubbles, runaway inflation, a devalued currency, and both private and public bankruptcy.[14]

Usbek, in his enlightened rather than despotic incarnation, is our guide to the constitution of moderate government. In place of repressive political and religious absolutism, Usbek maintains that the best government is that which works in accordance with self-interest and the promptings of nature: "I have often asked myself what kind of government most conformed to reason. It has seemed to me that the most perfect is that which attains its goal with the least friction; thus that government is most perfect which leads men along paths most agreeable to their interests and inclinations" (#80).

Following upon his religious doubts, Usbek suggests that the precepts of any and all true religion are reducible to "the obligations of charity and humanity" (#46). If God loves mankind, then the way for us to please God is by emulating His philanthropy. For Montesquieu, the imitation of God ought to redirect human sight earthward. Montesquieu transmutes religion, and Christianity specifically, into socially useful morality. Montesquieu does not aim, as Hobbes does, to subject matters of belief to political determination; nor does he, like Bayle, recommend a society of atheists; but Montesquieu does strive to constrict the sphere of universalistic religion. Just as the economic solution is a multiplicity of interests and the avoidance of monopoly, the religious solution is multiplicity. Montesquieu recommends religious pluralism, even to the point of introducing new sects. Such a solution lessens the virulence of religion and fosters toleration, without depriving belief of the sense of its independence. Montesquieu uses the schismatic tendency of religion to advantage. And in the political realm itself, the solution is the multiplication and separation of powers.

Montesquieu's teaching on the separation of powers, so familiar from *The Spirit of the Laws*, can be seen in the *Persian Letters* as well. Institutionally, the independence of the judiciary is the key to moderate government. Remember that the French *parlements*, whose fate is recounted with such sadness, are judicial bodies rather than legislative bodies. According to Montesquieu, an independent judiciary, by dividing decision from execution, preserves both the separation of powers (or the liberty of the constitution) and the security of the individual (or the liberty of the citizen). This distinction between the liberty of the constitution and the liberty of the citizen (books XI and XII of *The Spirit of the Laws*) is roughly analogous to the distinction Americans often draw between the Constitution as originally adopted and the Bill of Rights—the first laying out the structure of the government, the second largely concerned with creating a preserve of personal liberty, and seeing to the security of the individual by setting the boundaries of a decent penal law. Usbek's letter recommending gentleness and proportionality in punishment (#80) is written midway through his travels and appears midway through the novel; it is a peak from which Usbek steeply descends until the eunuch Solim, in obedience to his command, declares "we are going to exterminate crime and make innocence itself grow pale" (#160).

From Rica we learn how one might conjoin Usbek's sense with the sensibility of Usbek's wives, in other words, how the despotic disjunction between his wisdom and his women might be overcome. Whereas Usbek soon feels that he is in a state of unendurable exile "in a barbarous country, surrounded by everything offensive to me" (#155), Rica is open to the flirtatious spirit of the French nation; he responds to its charm, although he is also aware of its dangerous excesses. What is needed is a way to transform libertinage into liberty, to combine the feminine spirit of the French monarchy with the laws and institutions of a new sort of republic, a commercial republic of balanced powers. Such a combination might be called erotic liberalism, a liberalism that goes beyond the asocial and sterile formulations of rights, sovereignty, and legitimacy. For Montesquieu, man is not a solitary being, but a coupling being. Montesquieu's new modes and orders try to find the middle ground between the despotic communitarian republicanism of the ancients and the "frenzy of liberty" (XIX.27) brought about by modern individualist republicanism.

In his epigraph to *The Spirit of the Laws*, Montesquieu characterizes his achievement for us: "*Prolem sine matre creatum.*" Now, to describe one's writings as "an offspring born without a mother" does not sound like the words of a man interested in giving the female her due, indeed it sounds like usurpation. However, the first impression is misleading. The line is from Ovid (2.553) and refers to the siring of Erichthonius. Hephaestus, the god of the forge, desired to marry Athena, the goddess of the city. We note that Athena had sprung forth, fully armed, from the brow of Zeus and that Hephaestus was created by Hera alone in retaliation for Zeus's solitary conception. Thus, the fatherless god Hephaestus sought union with the motherless goddess Athena. Although Zeus consented to the marriage, he gave Athena liberty to refuse, and refuse she did. In the ensuing struggle between Hephaestus and Athena, "his seed fell on the earth, which thus became fertile and in due season produced a boy. Athena took charge of the infant. . . . The child was called Erichthonius and remained a favourite of Athena."[15] Despite being a bit unorthodox, the birth of Erichthonius is a result of sexual desire, quite unlike the births of Athena and Hephaestus. Moreoever, while Athena found Hephaestus repulsive, she lovingly embraced his earthly offspring—the virgin warrior turns out to have maternal instincts. We see once again the curious humor-tinged hubris of Montesquieu in equating himself with Hephaestus, the only deformed immortal.

Unlike his modern predecessors, Montesquieu shows his awareness of the Hephaestian character of modern thought: Hephaestus, the divine artisan, the laboring, peace-loving god, but also Hephaestus, the half-bred, fatherless, ugly, lame, and ridiculous god. Montesquieu acknowledges his erotic longing for the beautiful and wise Athena. While he does not achieve the consummation he desires, his lifelong pursuit of her is far from fruitless. Like Hephaestus, Montesquieu has spilled his philosophic seed liberally; his quest was for wisdom but his congress was with the earth. His philosophic offspring are not sprung from the mind of man alone; he has not aimed to imitate Zeus's act of autogenesis. His philosophic creations are instead like Erichthonius (*eris* [struggle] + *chthonios* [earth]), emerging and growing from ground he has sown in the course of erotic struggle—the matter of political life animated by the spirit of Montesquieu. Athena entrusted Erichthonius to the daughters of King Cecrops; the writings of Montesquieu likewise were delivered up to the care of the daughters (and sons) of monarchy.

Appendix

Table A1 shows what the order of the final third of the letters (#108-61) would be if the harem letters (#147-61) were intercalated with the nonharem letters (#108-46, in bold) according to Usbek's perspective, that is according to when he either writes or receives each harem letter. It usually takes about five months for a letter to arrive in Paris from Ispahan. For instance, #147, which the chief eunuch writes on 9/1/17, has been received by Usbek on or before 2/11/18 since Usbek writes #148 in reply on that date. To aid in understanding the chronology, I have given the dates in number form; thus, "the 1st of the moon of Rhegeb 1717" becomes 9/1/17.

Table A1 Reshuffling the deck

#	Written	Received	From/To	Subjects
108	**1/5/18**	**n/a**	**Usbek/ —**	**Journals and journalists**
147	9/1/17	2/11/18	Chief eunuch/ Usbek	Troubles in the harem
148	2/11/18	Unopened	Usbek/chief eunuch	First grant of authority
109 to 126	**2/25/18 to 12/3/18**	**n/a**	**Rica, Usbek, Rhédi/various correspondents**	**Women, *Fronde*, series on population (112-22), Turkey, misrule, suttee**
149	8/5/18	12/25/18	Narsit/Usbek	Death of chief eunuch; #148 was not opened
150	12/25/18	Unopened	Usbek/Narsit	Second grant of authority
127 to 131	**4/25/19 to 9/20/19**	**n/a**	**Rica, Usbek, Rhédi/various correspondents**	**Misrule, geometer, art of legislation, newsmongers, republics**
151	5/6/19	10/4/19	Solim/Usbek	Solim denounces Narsit; claims #150 was intercepted
152	5/6/19	10/4/19	Narsit/Usbek	Narsit reports all is well; regrets #150 was lost
153	10/4/19	3/2/20	Usbek/Solim	Third grant of authority
154	10/4/19	3/2/20	Usbek/wives	Letter of rebuke
155	10/4/19	3/2/20	Usbek/Nessir	Letter of despair
132 to 141	**11/17/19 to 7/26/20**	**n/a**	**Rica/various correspondents**	**Economics, library series (133-37), queens abdicate, *parlement* banished, Anaïs**
156	3/2/20	8/2/20	Roxane/Usbek	Letter of protest
157	3/2/20	8/2/20	Zachi/Usbek	Letter of protest
158	3/2/20	8/2/20	Zélis/Usbek	Letter of protest
159	5/8/20	10/8/20	Solim/Usbek	Roxane's treachery
160	5/8/20	10/8/20	Solim/Usbek	Day of Judgment
161	5/8/20	10/8/20	Roxane/Usbek	Suicide letter
142 to 146	**10/9/20 to 11/11/20**	**n/a**	**Rica and Usbek/various correspondents**	**Economics, amulets, scholars, ministers**

In figure A1, a smaller set of the final letters is diagrammed to show the succession of crises and rule in East and West. The harem letters (#156-61) are incorporated twice, both when sent and when received.

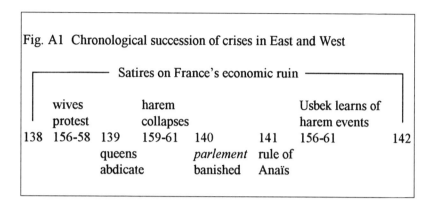

Fig. A1 Chronological succession of crises in East and West

Notes

Preface

1. Montesquieu, *The Spirit of the Laws*, trans. and ed. Anne M. Cohler, Basia Carolyn Miller, and Harold Samuel Stone (Cambridge: Cambridge University Press, 1989), xlv.

2. Joseph Cropsey, *Political Philosophy and the Issues of Politics* (Chicago: The University of Chicago Press, 1977), 15.

Chapter One

1. Montesquieu, *Lettres persanes*, ed. Jean Starobinski (Paris: Éditions Gallimard, 1973), 420. (Hereafter referred to as *LP*.)

2. *LP*, 421.

3. Henry James, *Literary Criticism: Essays on Literature, American Writers, English Writers* (New York: Library of America, 1984), 307.

4. In the preface to *Le Temple de Gnide*, Montesquieu similarly mocks the gravamen of "*les gens graves.*" "If [they] desire of me some work less frivolous," Montesquieu says, "I am in a position to satisfy them. For thirty years I have been working on a book of twelve pages which is to contain all that we know of metaphysics, politics, and morals, and all that the great authors have forgotten in the volumes that they have produced on these sciences" (1: 388).

5. Montesquieu here pretends to cultivate anonymity, yet simultaneously compromises it, for he alludes to his wife who was known for her slight limp.

6. *LP*, 421.

7. In his discussion of Montesquieu's allegiances, Robert Shackleton, *Montesquieu: A Critical Biography* ([London: Oxford University Press, 1961], 386-92), unambiguously classes Montesquieu as a *philosophe*. However, Roger Laufer, "La Réussite romanesque et la signification des *Lettres persanes* de Montesquieu" (*Revue d'histoire littéraire de la France* 61 [Avril-Juin 1961]:

192), points out that the Encyclopedist Helvétius saw the "Reflections" as "an attempt to mitigate the philosophic bearing of a work which had made a date in the history of 'enlightenment.'" Regardless of such measures, the enlightening influence of the *Persian Letters* was not impaired for all readers, nor was it limited to France. Beccaria, the Italian jurist responsible for introducing Montesquieuan penal reform throughout Europe, made plain his intellectual debt: "I date from five years ago the epoch of my conversion to philosophy, and I owe it to the reading of the *Persian Letters.*" (Beccaria to Morellet, 26 Jan. 1766, cited by Shackleton, 386.)

    8. Montesquieu did contribute an essay on "taste." Interestingly, it was on the issue of public taste that Rousseau chose to confront the Encyclopedists in his *Letter to D'Alembert on the Theatre.* The self-deprecating response of Montesquieu to the polemicization of philosophy should be compared with the self-aggrandizing tactics of Rousseau. Rousseau himself asks that the comparison be made in his *Confessions* (*Pléiade*, 1:497-98).

    9. Shackleton, 27n.3.

    10. Robert Francis O'Reilly, "The Artistry of Montesquieu's Narrative Tales" (Ph.D. diss., University of Wisconsin, 1967), 181.

    11. George Saintsbury, "Montesquieu," *French Literature and Its Masters*, ed. Huntington Cairns (New York: Knopf, 1946), 85.

    12. Jean-François de La Harpe, *Philosophie du dix-huitième siècle* (Paris: Chez Deterville, Libraire, 1818), 1: 42.

    13. C. A. Sainte-Beuve, "Montesquieu," in *Portraits of the Eighteenth Century: Historic and Literary*, trans. Katherine P. Wormeley (New York: Frederick Ungar Publishing, 1964), 1: 128.

    14. Albert Sorel, *Montesquieu*, trans. Melville B. Anderson and Edward Playfair Anderson (Port Washington, NY: Kennikat Press, 1969), 34.

    15. F. C. Green, "Montesquieu the Novelist and Some Imitations of the *Lettres persanes*," *Modern Language Review* 20 (Jan. 1925): 37. See also Alan M. Boase, "The Interpretation of *Les Lettres persanes*," in *The French Mind*, ed. Will G. Moore (London: Oxford University Press, 1952): 152-69.

    16. Green, 32.

    17. Roger B. Oake, "Polygamy in the *Lettres persanes*," *Romanic Review* 32 (Feb. 1941): 62.

    18. Gustave Lanson, *Histoire de la littérature française*, 3d ed. (Paris: Hachette, 1895), 702.

    19. Green, 34.

    20. Oake, 61.

    21. Pierre Testud, "Les *Lettres persanes*, roman épistolaire," *Revue d'histoire littéraire de la France* 66 (Oct.-Dec. 1966): 651.

    22. Franz Neumann, "Montesquieu," introduction to *The Spirit of the Laws* (New York: Hafner Press, 1949), xiii.

    23. Jean Starobinski, *Montesquieu par lui-meme* (Paris: Éditions du Seuil, 1953), 68; Pierre Barrière, "Les Éléments personnels et les éléments bordelais dans les *Lettres persanes*," *Revue d'histoire littéraire de la France* 51 (1951): 17-36; Anton Vantuch, "Les éléments personnels dans les *Lettres persanes*,"

Annales de la Faculté des lettres et sciences humaines de Nice 8 (1969): 127-42.

24. Aram Vartanian, "Eroticism and Politics in the *Lettres persanes*," *Romanic Review* 60 (Feb. 1969): 23.

25. Kate Millett, *Sexual Politics* (Garden City, NY: Doubleday, 1970), 65.

26. Cf. Simone de Beauvoir, *The Second Sex*, trans. H. M. Parshley (New York: Knopf, 1953), 121, 584.

27. Susan Moller Okin, *Women in Western Political Thought* (Princeton: Princeton University Press, 1979), 103.

28. The citations are beginning to accumulate: Robert F. O'Reilly, "Montesquieu: anti-feminist," *Studies on Voltaire and the 18th Century* 102 (1973): 143-56; Claude Dauphiné, "Pourquoi un roman de sérail?" *Europe* 55 (Février 1977): 89-96; Jeannette Geffriaud-Rosso, *Montesquieu et la féminité* (Pise: Libreria Goliardica Editrice, 1977); M. J. Pollock, "Montesquieu on the Patriarchal Family: A Discussion and Critique," *Nottingham French Studies* 18 (1979): 9-21; Sheila Mason, "The Riddle of Roxane," in *Woman and Society in Eighteenth-Century France: Essays in Honour of John Stephenson Spink*, ed. Eva Jacobs, W. H. Barber, Jean H. Bloch, F. W. Leakey, Eileen LeBreton (London: The Athlone Press, 1979): 28-41; Mary Shanley and Peter Stillman, "Political and Marital Despotism: Montesquieu's *Persian Letters*," in *The Family in Political Thought*, ed. Jean Bethke Elshtain (Amherst: University of Massachusetts Press, 1982): 67-79; Susan Tenenbaum, "Woman Through the Prism of Political Thought," *Polity* 15 (Fall 1982): 90-102; Pauline Kra, "Montesquieu and Women," in *French Women and the Age of Enlightenment*, ed. Samia I. Spencer (Bloomington: Indiana University Press, 1984), 272-84; Katherine M. Rogers, "Subversion of Patriarchy in *Les Lettres Persanes*," *Philological Quarterly* 65 (Winter 1986): 61-78.

The first four scholars, O'Reilly, Dauphiné, Geffriaud-Rosso, and Pollock, all writing in the 1970s, castigate Montesquieu for misogyny and patriarchalism. The others, Mason, Shanley and Stillman, Tenenbaum, Kra, and Rogers, in all but one case writing in the 1980s, present Montesquieu, in varying degrees, as sympathetic to the cause of women's liberation. This line of interpretation picked up the thread of scattered earlier suggestions: Kra cites Léon Abensour, *La Femme et le féminisme avant la révolution* (Paris: Leroux, 1923) and one might add Oake who in 1941 described Montesquieu as "a pioneer feminist" (60).

29. See Suzanne L. Pucci, "Orientalism and Representations of Exteriority in Montesquieu's *Lettres persanes*," *The Eighteenth Century* 26 (1985); and Lisa Lowe, "French Literary Orientalism: Representation of 'Others' in the Texts of Montesquieu, Flaubert, and Kristeva" (Ph.D. diss., University of California-Santa Cruz, 1986).

30. Edward W. Said, *Orientalism* (New York: Pantheon Books, 1978).

31. See Tzvetan Todorov, "The Morality of Conquest," *Diogenes* 125 (Spring 1984): 89-102.

32. Testud, 656.

33. Tenenbaum also criticizes the narrowly polemical procedures of most

feminist scholarship. She points out that the rigid assumption of an opposition between household and polity has left feminists unable "to take full account of the varied traditions of thinking about the household and its manifold relations to the polity" (91) and results in "the systematic exclusion of theorists [like Montesquieu] who offer a more subtle or positive view of woman's domestic role, and/or proclaim the relevance of domestic values to public life" (102).

34. The phrase comes from Catherine H. Zuckert, *Natural Right and the American Imagination: Political Philosophy in Novel Form* (Savage, MD: Rowman & Littlefield, 1990).

35. Those scholars who have unearthed all the antecedents include: G. L. Van Roosbroeck, *Persian Letters before Montesquieu* (New York: Institute of French Studies, 1932) and Charles E. Kany, *The Beginnings of the Epistolary Novel in France, Italy and Spain* (Berkeley: University of California Press, 1937). Montesquieu offers his own history of the epistle and an assessment of his contribution to it in *Pensées*, no. 892:

> Formerly the epistolary style was in the hands of the pedants, who wrote in Latin. Balzac received the epistolary style and manner from these men. Voiture was disgusted by it, and, as he had a fine spirit, he introduced finesse and a certain affectation, which one always finds in the passage from pedantry to the air and tone of the world. M. de Fontenelle, almost a contemporary of these men, mixed the finesse of Voiture, a bit of his affectation, with more learning and enlightenment, and more philosophy. . . . My *Lettres persanes* showed how to make novels out of letters.

36. Allan Bloom, "Introduction," in Jean-Jacques Rousseau, *Emile*, trans. Allan Bloom (New York: Basic Books, 1979), 6, 21.

37. Cf. Rousseau's criticism of Montesquieu's erotic tale *Le Temple de Gnide* in *Reveries* #4. Montesquieu had already responded to such criticisms in *Pensées*, no. 89:

> Some people have regarded the reading of *Le Temple de Gnide* as dangerous. But they do not realize that they are imputing to a single novel the fault of all. Whatever licentiousness there may be in a line of verse is the vice of the poet. But that the passions would be moved by it, that is the work of poetry.
> The reading of novels is without doubt dangerous. What is not? Would to God that one had to correct only the ill effects of reading novels! But to order a sentient being not to have sensations; to want to banish the passions, without even allowing one to reform them; to propose perfection to a century which is every day worse; among so much wickedness, to be indignant against weakness; I am afraid lest a morality so high become an abstraction, and lest in showing us so far from what we ought to be, we lose sight of what we are.

38. *Pensées*, no. 2095. The other three were Malebranche, Shaftesbury, and Montaigne—three of the four are authors of dialogues.

39. The imagery comes from Erich Heller, *The Artist's Journey into the Interior* (New York: Random House, 1959), 202-3, cited by Hanna Fenichel Pitkin, *Wittgenstein and Justice* (Berkeley: University of California Press, 1972), viii: "'Do you understand Kant?' is like asking 'Have you been to the summit of Mount Blanc?' The answer is *yes* or *no*. 'Do you understand Nietzsche?' is like asking 'Do you know Rome?' The answer is simple only if you have never been there."

40. Janet Gurkin Altman, *Epistolarity: Approaches to a Form* (Columbus: Ohio State University Press, 1982), places dialogic and epistolary exchange at opposite ends of the communication spectrum. In letters, unlike oral exchange, the participants are separated in space and time. The correspondence is a means of engagement, but one that occurs at discrete, staggered, nonshareable moments. In the *Persian Letters* this discontinuity is increased by multiple plots, multiple correspondents (twenty-seven in all), nonchronological ordering of some of the letters (the final batch of harem letters, for instance), and occasional gaps between letters (as when a period of a year goes by with no letters written by Usbek).

41. In his "Essay on Taste" written for Diderot's *Encyclopédie*, Montesquieu had harsh words for the kind of eidetic analysis found in the Platonic dialogue:

> The dialogues, so admired by the ancients, in which Plato caused Socrates to reason are today insupportable, because they are founded on a false philosophy; for all these reasonings drawn from the good, the beautiful, the perfect, the wise, the foolish, the hard, the soft, the dry, the humid, treated as positive things, no longer mean anything.

Although one could conceivably write a non-Platonic or anti-Platonic dialogue, Montesquieu chose not to. He may well have thought it better to reject the dialogic manner of presentation as of a piece with the Platonic investigation of the Ideas. See also *Pensées*, no. 2062.

42. Dena Goodman, *Criticism in Action: Enlightenment Experiments in Political Writing* (Ithaca: Cornell University Press, 1989), 2. While Goodman proceeds by contrasting the *Persian Letters* to Fénelon's *Aventures de Télémaque*, "the last great exemplar of the *speculum principis* in France" (7), it seems to me that Machiavelli looms larger in Montesquieu's mind. Montesquieu's engagement with the thought of Machiavelli begins early and endures. Machiavelli's presence is felt in the first paper Montesquieu presented to the Academy of Bordeaux (*Dissertation sur la politique des Romains dans la religion*, 1716). In his *Considerations on the Causes of the Greatness of the Romans and Their Decline*, Montesquieu is again in Machiavelli's territory, offering a rather different assessment of Roman virtue. In *The Spirit of the Laws*, Machiavelli is the subject of one of Montesquieu's most impassioned and most famous pronouncements:

We begin to be cured of Machiavellism, and recover from it every day. More moderation has become necessary in the councils of princes. What would formerly have been called a master-stroke of politics would be now, independent of the horror it might occasion, the greatest imprudence.

Montesquieu was by no means a simple anti-Machiavel. He did, however, seek to counter Machiavelli's detrimental influence on political practice.

Work has been done to demonstrate Montesquieu's familiarity with Machiavelli, utilizing all the traditional tools of influence-scholarship: the study of Montesquieu's library inventory, compilations of allusions and echoes in language, similarity of theme and argument, etc. (See E. Levi-Malvano, *Montesquieu e Machiavelli* [Paris: Champion, 1912]; A. Bertière, "Montesquieu, lecteur de Machiavel," *Actes du Congrès Montesquieu* [Bordeaux: Delmas, 1956]: 141-58; Robert Shackleton, "Montesquieu and Machiavelli: A Reappraisal," *Comparative Literature Studies* 1[1964]: 1-13.) However, no one has yet done the real work, for instance, a comparative reading of the *Discourses* and the *Considerations*.

43. Thomas L. Pangle, "Montesquieu, Charles Louis de Secondat," in *The Blackwell Encyclopedia of Political Thought*, ed. David Miller (Oxford: Basil Blackwell, 1987), 344.

44. See Thomas L. Pangle, *Montesquieu's Philosophy of Liberalism: A Commentary on "The Spirit of the Laws"* (Chicago: The University of Chicago Press, 1973), 11-19, for a helpful discussion of Montesquieu's manner of writing and, with a few notable exceptions (D'Alembert and Taine), the critics' inability to penetrate it. They have failed to follow Montesquieu's own rules of reading as expressed in *Pensée* no. 833:

In reading a book, one must be willing to believe that the author is aware of what seem, at first glance, to be contradictions. Thus it is necessary to begin by mistrusting one's first judgments, to go back to the passages that seem to contradict one another, to compare them to one another, and further, to compare them with what precedes and follows them. One must determine if the passages in question flow from the same premises—if the contradiction is in the things themselves, or only in the peculiar manner of presentation. When one has done all this, one is able to pronounce imperiously: "There is a contradiction here."

But that is not all. When a work is systematic, it is necessary to be certain one has grasped the system entire. You see a great machine laboring to produce an effect. You see the gears turning in opposite directions; you think, at first, that the machine is bound to self-destruct, that all its workings hinder one another, that the machine will grind to a halt. Yet it keeps on going. Its parts, which appeared at odds, unite for the proposed object.

Pangle explains Montesquieu's style as, in part at least, a mirror of the "complex multiformity of political life" (17). One senses a similarity to Nietzsche whose aphoristic style makes evident his rejection of all previous dogmatic philosophy in an immediately appreciable way. For Nietzsche, it is the mode most suitable to the perspectival nature of truth.

45. Earlier dismissals of coherence have given way to a strong consensus that the *Persian Letters* is a true whole. However, there is not much agreement on what makes it such. The articles usually cited as seminal to this development are Roger Laufer, "La Réussite romanesque et la signification des *Lettres persanes* de Montesquieu," *Revue d'histoire littéraire de la France* 61 (Avril-Juin 1961): 188-203; Roger Mercier, "Le Roman dans les *Lettres persanes*: structure et signification," *Revue des sciences humaines* (Juillet-Septembre 1962): 345-56; and Pauline Kra, "The Invisible Chain of the *Lettres persanes*," *Studies on Voltaire* 23 (1963): 3-55.

Laufer finds the unity of the book to reside in its very disunity: the "increasing contradiction between philosophic inquiry and human blindness constitutes the 'secret chain'" (200). Kra reads the book in linear fashion, rather than dichotomously. For her, the Orient is not crucial; she abstracts from the novelistic elements and instead investigates in detail the ideational sequence of the letters. She discerns a logical progression of themes from the individual to the social to the political. I believe that this categorization does an injustice to the individual letters. Moreoever, it seems to me untrue to the spirit of Montesquieu and his motto: "Tout est extrêmement lié" (*The Spirit of the Laws* XIX.15). Mary M. Crumpacker, "The Secret Chain of the *Lettres persanes*, and the mystery of the B edition," *Studies on Voltaire and the 18th Century* 102 (1973): 121-41, writes in a similar vein, seeing the book as an illustration of the scientific method and finding the same movement from particular to general.

Kra's study includes a preliminary survey of her most important predecessors in the quest for unity. In addition to citing those who have written on the order of *The Spirit of the Laws*, she mentions Pierre Barrière, *Un grand provincial: Charles-Louis de Secondat, baron de La Brède et de Montesquieu* (Bordeaux: Delmas, 1946), 242-44; and Paul Vernière, "Introduction," *Lettres persanes* (Paris: Éditions Garnier Frères, 1960) as having concerned themselves with the plan of the letters. Barrière's approach is similar to her own, while Vernière offers a dual categorization: first dividing the letters into three parts in accordance with chronology and plot (the voyage, Paris or the Occidental world, and the harem drama) and then making a quite separate division in accordance with theme: the primary cleavage here being Orient/Occident. The first schema ignores the appearance of Persian and specifically "harem drama" elements throughout the main "Occidental" section, while the second schema, although taking note of this intercalation, overemphasizes the cleavage between Orient and Occident (by, for instance, dividing the letters on the subject of religion into those two camps—thus Usbek's letter recommending religious toleration and pluralism is placed under the rubric of "L'Orient/Religion" since it discusses Islamic treatment of Armenians and Zoroastrians rather than Christian treatment of Jews).

Since these initial attempts to untangle the chain, everyone has had a try at it. J. L. Carr, "The Secret Chain of the *Lettres persanes*," *Studies on Vol-*

taire 55 (1967): 15-26, discovers a narrowly political and antiquarian chain; he reads the book as an exact and didactic allegory to political events in France, a sort of Freemason guessing game. R. L. Frautschi, "The Would-be Invisible Chain in *Les Lettres persanes*," *French Review* 40 (April 1967): 604-12, links the formal aesthetic principle of variety and surprise to the psychology of the drama and calls it an attitudinal chain. Agnes G. Raymond, "Encore quelques réflexions sur la "chaîne secrète" des *Lettres persanes*," *Studies on Voltaire* 89 (1972): 1337-47, sees the novel as an early exploration of the notion of the general spirit of a nation, and more particularly a demonstration of the infinite chain of interrelated causes that eventuates in the unique (and in the case of both France and Persia uniquely destructive) general spirit. Nick Roddick, "The Structure of the *Lettres persanes*," *French Studies* 28 (October 1974): 396-407, focuses upon the intercalation of Persian and Parisian elements. He shows very clearly Montesquieu's departure from a strict chronological ordering of the harem letters in the last third of the work and the interesting effect that has upon the structure. However, because he regards the harem intrigue as entertainment, he gives but a feeble account of the significance of that departure from chronology. Susan C. Strong, "Why a *secret* chain?: oriental *topoi* and the essential mystery of the *Lettres persanes*," *Studies on Voltaire and the 18th Century* 230 (1985): 167-79, attaches crucial importance to the oriental and literary character of the work. She finds a complex rhetorical strategy, alternating between narrative and miscellany, which lures and frustrates, and along the way educates, the reader.

    46. *Persian Letters*, trans. George R. Healy (Indianapolis, IN: Bobbs-Merrill, 1964), 9n.1; and *LP*, 422.

Chapter Two

    1. For instance, Pangle, "Montesquieu," 344, hazards this description: "The work may be tentatively characterized as presenting the negative or ground-clearing portion of Montesquieu's philosophy: his critique, in a spirit informed by Bayle, Locke, and Spinoza, of the reigning traditions of Judaeo-Christian religion and Aristotelian natural right." I believe Montesquieu's critique is more far-reaching than Pangle allows, extending even to his protomodern forebears. I hope to establish the distinctiveness of Montesquieu's contribution within the tradition of political thought, to show him as something more than the Continental Locke. Montesquieu is too often regarded as a derivative part of hyphenated modernity, an addition to that amalgam of Machiavelli-Hobbes-Locke-Rousseau.

    2. Aristotle, *The Politics*, trans. Carnes Lord (Chicago: The University of Chicago Press, 1984), 1279a17-21. Further, at 1279b15-17, Aristotle defines tyranny as the "monarchic rule of a despot over the political association" (also 1295a17); at 1292a15-25, he describes democracies that become despotic and analogous to tyranny; at 1306b1-6, he speaks of oligarchies being overthrown when they become too despotic. (I have made slight emendations in this and subsequent passages from the Lord translation.)

3. Leo Strauss, *On Tyranny* (Ithaca: Cornell University Press, 1963), 21.

4. For a fascinating philological tour, see R. Koebner, "Despot and Despotism: Vicissitudes of a Political Term," *Journal of the Warburg and Courtauld Institutes* 14 (1951): 275-302; also Melvin Richter, "Despotism," in *Dictionary of the History of Ideas* 2 (New York: Charles Scribner's Sons, 1973): 1-18; and Franco Venturi, "Oriental Despotism," *Journal of the History of Ideas* 24 (Jan.-March 1963): 133-42.

5. Koebner, 288.

6. Thomas Hobbes, *Leviathan*, ed. Michael Oakeshott (New York: Macmillan, 1962), 154.

7. According to Koebner, 300, "For *despotisme* no earlier evidence has been traced than the jesting side-remark of an antiquarian, who in 1698 wrote of 'le despotisme que la grammairiens ont exercé sur les poésies d'Homère.'" I don't know whether Montesquieu knew of this first usage, but he does include a letter (#36) that mocks a disputation concerning Homer (a part of the "Quarrel of the Ancients and Moderns"), and that contains as well a swipe at scholastic Latin.

8. Koebner, 300-301, gives a brief history of the -ism suffix (yet another Greek contribution that Latin purists had long resisted).

9. In the *Spicilège*, Montesquieu notes that in certain cases the religious authorities have been the purveyors of Hobbes: "It is the abbé Dubois [cardinal and prime minister to the regent] who has corrupted the duc d'Orléans and has had him read Hobbes and other authors of that kind" (2:1350).

10. Jean-Jacques Rousseau, *On the Social Contract*, ed. Roger D. Masters, trans. Judith R. Masters (New York: St. Martin's Press, 1978), 127.

11. *Dossier de L'Esprit des lois*, 2:996.

12. See Harvey C. Mansfield, Jr., *Taming the Prince: The Ambivalence of Modern Executive Power* (New York: Free Press, 1989) for an account of the philosophic effort to harness the force unleashed by Machiavelli. Mansfield's short chapter on Montesquieu is, I believe, one of the finest things written on him.

13. Hobbes, 100.

14. Ibid., 101.

15. This is one of two published references to Hobbes. The other, from his *Défense de L'Esprit des lois*, is even more negative, perhaps exaggeratedly so—Montesquieu speaks of the "terrible system" of Hobbes. Among the *Pensées*, there are three more references: nos. 601, 615, 1142. There is also a letter of 8 October 1750 to Monseigneur de Fitz-James where, in defending himself against the charge of irreligion, Montesquieu boasts that "Everyone in England acknowledges that no one better combatted Hobbes, and Spinoza also, than I. In Germany it is admitted that I have better crushed Bayle, in two chapters, than M. Basnage and other theologians have done in books expressly made for that purpose."

16. *Pensées*, no. 1142, points up Hobbes's anthropocentrism: "Hobbes said that curiosity is peculiar to man; in this he deceives himself: each animal having it according to the extent of his understanding."

17. Leo Strauss, *The Political Philosophy of Hobbes: Its Basis and Its Genesis*, trans. Elsa M. Sinclair (Chicago: The University of Chicago Press, 1952), 110-12.

18. This passage was excluded from Montesquieu's *Traité des Devoirs* (1725) and placed in the *Pensées* instead. The *Traité des Devoirs* is now lost; all that remains is an abstract of it and those excisions placed in the *Pensées*, some of which eventually made their way into *The Spirit of the Laws*.

19. Just as Usbek downplays the special providence of the gods, so he downplays heavenly wrath in explaining the demise of the wicked Troglodytes. The plague that finally wiped them out was a recurrence of a disease that had been successfully treated the first time around by a foreign doctor who refuses to return because he wasn't paid for his services. Were he to intervene again, the doctor says he would be opposing the just anger of the gods. Usbek, however, says the Troglodytes were victims of their own injustice. Man has arts with which to counter the violence of nature, but their practice requires certain moral precepts, including the observance of contracts. Had remuneration been forthcoming, the doctor would not have regarded a new epidemic as a judgment of the gods; after all, disease is the condition from which he derives his livelihood.

20. Lack of attention to the conversational context, as well as a simple equation of Usbek with Montesquieu, mars the work of Allessandro S. Crisafulli, "Montesquieu's Story of the Troglodytes: Its Background, Meaning, and Significance," *PMLA* 43 (June 1943): 372-92. Crisafulli was the first to read the story of the wicked Troglodytes as a rebuttal of Hobbes. The bulk of his essay, however, is concerned with the good Troglodytes, whom he takes as evidence of Montesquieu's primitivism. Crisafulli aligns Montesquieu with thinkers like Shaftesbury. He does not consider whether the fable may not raise objections against both sides of the contemporary debate.

21. Most notable of the others are the long series on population #112-22, and Rica's library tour #133-37; there are also other shorter series #89-90, #94-95, #99-100, #102-4. This density of explicitly connected letters is characteristic of the book's second half, a circumstance that has led some commentators (mistakenly I believe) to view the movement of the book as an ascent or progression from the simple to the complex, from the more frivolous to the more weighty. See for instance, Barrière, *Un grand provincial*, 242-44; and Kra, "The Invisible Chain," 11, 13, 40.

22. These captions are not salutations. As the preface makes clear, Montesquieu, in his role as translator, has stripped the letters of such trivialities; rather, these are "editor"-supplied headings. As such, they provide clues to the sometimes shifting character of the relationship between correspondents. For instance, in the first three letters to Rustan (#1,8,19) the caption is "Usbek to his friend Rustan," while the final letter (#91) is simply "Usbek to Rustan." The change is indicative of Usbek's emotional isolation from others, as the harem situation comes to dominate his thoughts.

23. Pauline Kra, "Religion in Montesquieu's *Lettres persanes*," *Studies on Voltaire and the 18th Century* 72 (1970): 40-55.

24. Most available editions append the various unpublished letters and fragments, including the Troglodyte finale. See *Pléiade*, "Dossier des Lettres persanes," 1:383-4, no. 120.

25. See chap. 5, pp. 78-79, for discussion of this subset.

Chapter Three

1. The title is borrowed from one of the more unusual holdings in Montesquieu's own library, a scandalous English novel of monastic life called *Venus in the cloister, or the nun in her smock*. For a full tour of the sex and marriage division of the La Brède catalogue, see Geffriaud-Rosso, 191-99.

2. Usbek/wives: #3, 4, 7, 20, 26, 47, 53, 62, 65, 70, 71, 154, 156, 157, 158, 161; Usbek/eunuchs: #2, 21, 41-43, 64, 79, 96, 147-53, 159, 160; letters in which women figure, sometimes as the sole subject, sometimes as ancillary or illustrative: #1, 6, 9, 11, 12, 22-24, 27, 28, 34, 38, 48, 51, 52, 55, 56, 58, 59, 63, 67, 78, 86, 99, 106, 107, 110, 114, 116, 120, 125, 139, 141, 155.

3. Dauphiné, 91-92, briefly examines the different characters of the wives, as does Sara Ellen Procious Maleug, "Commentary on Papers by Shelby O. Spruell and Ann M. Moore," in *Proceedings of the Annual Meeting of the Western Society for French History* 8 (1980): 159-62. In general, however, commentators have tended to concentrate on the more spectacular Roxane to the exclusion of the other wives. This oversight diminishes the rich variety of the work and, more seriously, can lead one to overstate its pessimism.

4. Crumpacker, 137n.17, gives a very different, and implausibly complicated, account of the quarrel, placing the blame on a second (entirely hypothetical) homosexual slave girl and exonerating the "dutiful and compassionate Zachi."

5. Lowe, 55, argues to the contrary, maintaining that lesbianism, as a sexuality not dependent on men, is the greatest threat to Usbek's rule. As if aware that Zachi is flimsy material on which to base such a claim, Lowe ascribes homosexual behavior to Roxane also. Unfortunately, there is no basis in the text for such an assertion.

6. In his unfinished *Essay on Taste*, written in his last years for the *Encyclopédie*, Montesquieu uses Italy's castrati—"who belong neither to the sex which we love nor to that which we admire"—to illustrate the concept of "sensibility" and the mixed, ambivalent character of pleasure (2:1252).

7. Hegel, as well as Rousseau, is indebted to Montesquieu. Hegel's account of the master/slave dialectic—wherein the master's victory results only in sterility, and the slave's submission provides the ground for the laborious development of higher consciousness—bears a strong resemblance to Montesquieu's account of domestic despotism. Interestingly, the dialectic as originally conceived by Hegel was animated by the desire for love, not recognition; it was romantic rather than historical, erotic rather than polemic. See G. W. F. Hegel, *Early Theological Writings*, trans. T. M. Knox (Philadelphia: Uni-

versity of Pennsylvania Press, 1971), 302-8; and the discussion of this fragment in Alexandre Kojève, *Introduction to the Reading of Hegel: Lectures on
the "Phenomenology of Spirit,"* assembled by Raymond Queneau, ed. Allan
Bloom, trans. James H. Nichols, Jr. (Ithaca: Cornell University Press, 1969),
242-52.

8. Compare Xenophon's treatment in the *Hiero* of the tyrant's neediness,
his desire to be loved by all and sundry, and the commentary on it by Leo
Strauss, *On Tyranny* (Ithaca: Cornell University Press, 1968), 91-94.

9. The son-in-law who employs such proofs is named Suphis, after a
mystical, medieval Muslim sect. Soliman is a modified spelling of both the
Hebrew king Solomon, famous for his wisdom and his seven hundred wives
(plus three hundred concubines), and the Ottoman king Suleiman I, known as
the Magnificent and the Lawgiver. The kingly Soliman is brought low by the
superstitious Suphis—could Montesquieu intend a comment upon church/state
relations as well as upon sexual relations?

10. For this unpublished letter, see "Dossier des Lettres persanes," 1:383-
84, no. 123. Inclusion of this letter would have completed the book's symme-
try: three sets of four letters each (added to the five written by Usbek) for a
total of seventeen letters exchanged between Usbek and his wives. This set
would then have exactly matched the seventeen letters exchanged between
Usbek and his eunuchs. (For those given to numerology, seventeen is the number that represents nature; thus, an appropriate number for the harem correspondence.)

Chapter Four

1. In deploying this horrific image of the charnel house, Montesquieu knew
whereof he spoke. Three of his four aunts and his two sisters (a third died in
infancy) all became nuns, two of them quite prominent, each holding the office of mother superior of the convent of the Filles de Notre-Dame at Saint-
Paulin. Four uncles and his brother were in the Church also.

2. In *Discourses* 2.5, Machiavelli had allotted Christianity a similar life
span.

3. The self-interested revaluation of Christian asceticism is precisely what
Nietzsche praised Martin Luther for: "perhaps Luther performed no greater
service than to have had the courage of his *sensuality* (in those days it was
called, delicately enough, 'evangelical freedom')" (Friedrich Nietzsche, *On the
Genealogy of Morals*, in *Basic Writings of Nietzsche*, trans. Walter Kaufmann
[New York: Modern Library, 1968], 534).

4. David Hume, "Of Polygamy and Divorces" in *Essays Moral, Political
and Literary*, ed. Eugene F. Miller (Indianapolis: Liberty Classics, 1985), 187.
After giving it fair field, Hume goes on to challenge this position with what
he believes to be "three unanswerable objections," first among them the fate
of the children. Hume's other objections take issue with Montesquieu's reading of the human heart:

If it be true, on the one hand, that the heart of man naturally delights in liberty, and hates every thing to which it is confined; it is also true, on the other, that the heart of man naturally submits to necessity, and soon loses an inclination, when there appears an absolute impossibility of gratifying it. (188)

Love may require liberty, but friendship can thrive under constraint. According to Hume, the lasting component in marriage is friendship. See also the essay "Of the Populousness of Ancient Nations," 377-464, where Hume appears as a defender of modernity against the imputation that the ancient world was more populous. Both Montesquieu and Hume regard population as a measure of the happiness of peoples and the wisdom of legislation. Montesquieu, however, is by no means simply a proponent of the manners and institutions of pagan antiquity, as Hume implies.

5. Jean-Baptiste Gaultier, *Les "Lettres persanes" convaincues d'impiété* (Paris: n.p., 1751).

6. Once again, Montesquieu sounds like an anticipation of Nietzsche on the genesis of slave morality. Nietzsche, for instance, says that "the advance toward universal empires is always also an advance toward universal divinities; despotism with its triumph over the independent nobility always prepares the way for some kind of monotheism" (*Genealogy of Morals*, 526).

7. See the article by Richard Myers, "Christianity and Politics in Montesquieu's *Greatness and Decline of the Romans*," *Interpretation* 17 (Winter 1989-90): 223-38.

8. As Rousseau says in the *Emile*, 44: "they turn to the prejudice of the species the attraction given for the sake of multiplying it." Rousseau was to take up at greater length this problem of a vanity-induced rejection of motherhood, although his concern went beyond the practice of abortion (i.e., population) to that of wetnursing (i.e., education). Oddly enough, Montesquieu's source for the statement about savage women cites the encumbrance of nursing (and especially its detrimental effect upon the sexual appeal of a woman's breasts) rather than the pregnancy itself as the motive for aborting (Etienne de Flaucourt, *Histoire de la grand ile de Madagascar* [Paris: Pierre Lamy, 1658], quoted in the Vernière edition of the letters, 253n.1). Alone among mammals, the human female has *double entendre* breasts, possessed of seductive powers as well as a maternal purpose. The inherent danger is that they may be diverted from the sustenance of the young and reserved for the delectation of the adult male.

9. Again, Montesquieu spoke from the experience of those closest to him. His wife, Jeanne de Lartigue was a Protestant. As a result of the civil and legal liabilities that entailed, their marriage ceremony was "quiet, almost clandestine" and, on her death, she was interred "almost surreptitiously." (Robert Shackleton, "Madame de Montesquieu with some considerations on Thérèse de Secondat," in *Woman and Society in Eighteenth-Century France: Essays in Honor of John Stephenson Spink* [London: Athlone Press, 1979]: 232-33.)

10. Usbek actually writes a letter from Paris on the same day (#25). It is a

letter of very few lines, the effect of which is to focus attention all the more on Rica's letter. Usbek writes: "Rica is writing you a long letter and tells me that he extensively described this country. His lively mind draws quick conclusions, but I think slowly, and I cannot tell you anything now."

11. Letter #101 discusses the role that the Christian doctrine of the Holy Ghost plays in augmenting the proselytizing spirit, and #29 discusses the link between the Christian concept of heresy and civil war.

12. Xenophon, *Cyropaedia*, I.i.2-3.

Chapter Five

1. Montesquieu's primary sources are the still well-regarded Jean Chardin, *Voyages en Perse et autres lieux de l'Orient* (Amsterdam: n.p., 1711) and Jean-Baptiste Tavernier, *Les six voyages en Turquie, en Perse et aux Indes* (Amsterdam: n.p., 1676). In #72, Montesquieu pokes fun at his own reliance on this literature: when Rica encounters a "universal decider"—a man with opinions on every question who brooks no dissent—Rica thinks to gain the upper hand by speaking to him of Persia; the man contradicts him twice, "on the authority of Tavernier and Chardin."

2. Parvine Mahmoud, "Les Persans de Montesquieu," *French Review* 34 (Oct. 1960): 47. For an account of other deliberate distortions, see Ahmad Gunny, "Montesquieu's view of Islam in the *Lettres persanes*," *Studies on Voltaire* 174 (1978): 151-66.

3. For treatments of the eunuchs in the *Persian Letters*, see Roger Kempf, "*Les Lettres persanes* ou le corps absent," *Tel Quel* 22 (Eté 1965): 81-86; Michel Delon, "Un monde d'eunuques," *Europe* 55 (Février 1977): 79-88; Alan J. Singerman, "Réflections sur une métaphore: le sérail dans les *Lettres persanes*," *Studies on Voltaire* 185 (1980): 181-98; and Alain Grosrichard, *La Structure de sérail: La Fiction de despotisme asiatique dans l'Occident classique* (Paris: Seuil, 1979).

4. Paul Valéry, "The Persian Letters: A Preface," in *Collected Works*, ed. Jackson Mathews, trans. Denise Folliot and Jackson Mathews (New York: Pantheon, 1962), 10: 225.

5. See also XV.19, and *Considerations on the Romans* XXII.

6. Four of the wives' letters, including both of those that mention trips to the country, are signed from the "seraglio at Fatmé" (#3, 4, 47, 70), rather than from the more usual "seraglio at Ispahan." For the women, this country retreat is associated with freedom and independence. The country figures in Usbek's emotional makeup as well, although it has a somewhat different bearing for him (see chap. 7, pp. 109-10).

7. God himself is not spared. Nietzsche, *Genealogy of Morals*, 1.8, speaks of "that ghastly paradox of a 'God on the cross,' that mystery of an unimaginable ultimate cruelty and self-crucifixion of God *for the salvation of man*."

8. Carr, 336-37.

9. The two different forms of rule by one man, which Montesquieu calls despotism and monarchy, are acknowledged by Machiavelli as well, although

he attaches no moral significance to them: "principalities of which memory remains have been governed in two diverse modes: either by one prince, and all the others servants who as ministers help govern the kingdom by his favor and appointment; or by a prince and by barons who hold that rank not by favor of the lord but by antiquity of blood line." Machiavelli gives the kingdoms of Turkey and France as his examples (*The Prince*, trans. Harvey C. Mansfield, Jr. [Chicago: The University of Chicago Press, 1985], 17).

10. Aristotle unobtrusively makes the same point in his discussion of household slavery in the first book of the *Politics* (1255b30-37):

> The science characteristic of the despot is expertise in using slaves, since the despot is what he is not in the acquiring of slaves but in the use of them. This science has nothing great or dignified about it: the despot must know how to command the things that the slave must know how to do. Hence for those to whom it is open not to suffer ills themselves, a guardian [or administrator] assumes this prerogative, while they themselves engage in politics or philosophy.

11. #41, 42, 64, 79, 96, 147, 149, 151, 152, 159, 160.

12. *The Spirit of the Laws*, V.14.

13. Orest Ranum, "Personality and Politics in the *Persian Letters*," *Political Science Quarterly* 84 (Dec. 1969): 620, illustrates the *roman à calendrier* by comparing #148 (November 1718), the grant of plenary power to the eunuch, with the "promulgation of the *arret* which effectively ended government by council" in France (September 1718).

Chapter Six

1. Believing that "Montesquieu's deepest thoughts on religion" are found in #141, Sanford Kessler, "Religion and Liberalism in Montesquieu's *Persian Letters*," *Polity* 15 (Spring 1983): 380-96, rests his presentation of Montesquieu's critique of religious orthodoxy almost exclusively on an explication of this letter. Goodman (95-98) also stresses its importance. Less attention has been paid to #67.

2. Kra, "Religion," 117-18.

3. When he speaks of "the savages of Louisiana," Montesquieu may be presumed to have reference as much to the tribe of French speculators involved in John Law's Louisiana bubble as to the Natchez Indians. The book's only other mention of Louis XIV's New World territory might be construed to have reference to France also, in this case an attack on the *Roi Soleil* Louis and the divine right of kings:

> The prejudices of superstition are greater than all other prejudices, and its reasons greater than all other reasons. Thus, although savage peoples do not know despotism naturally, these people [the Natchez of Louisi-

ana] know it. They worship the sun, and if their leader had not imagined that he was the brother of the sun, they would have found in him only a poor wretch like themselves. (XVIII.18)

4. Thomas Jefferson perfected this method of critical ventriloquism. His quest for a demystified Christianity culminated in his two extracts of the Gospels, "The Philosophy of Jesus" and "The Life and Morals of Jesus." To produce these abridgments, Jefferson excised all verses with reference to miraculous events, retaining only the moral precepts of Jesus and a considerably curtailed account of his doings. The so-called Jefferson Bible achieves a four-fifths reduction in volume (from 3,778 verses to 737) and an even more drastic revision in content (*The Papers of Thomas Jefferson*, Second Series, ed. Dickinson W. Adams, *Jefferson's Extracts from the Gospels* [Princeton: Princeton University Press, 1983]).

5. In one instance, we are told that "[t]he law of Moses was very crude," for by failing to punish a master who kills his slave, Hebrew law added the loss of security to the loss of liberty and thus violated natural law (XV.17). In another instance, we are told that "[t]he laws of Moses were very wise" because they limited the use of temples as a place of asylum for criminals (XXV.3). In each case, Montesquieu's point is that there should be no immunity from punishment, whether by virtue of one's status or one's religion.

6. *The Prince*, 13. Machiavelli gives an even more audacious treatment of David in *Discourses*, 1.26.

7. In the preface, Montesquieu gives a rather different assessment of the perspicacity of his Persians: "One thing has often astonished me: to see these Persians sometimes as learned as I in the customs and manners of the nation, to the point of knowing the most subtle details and of noticing things which I am sure have escaped many a German who has traveled in France."

8. *Discourses*, 1.introduction.

9. In his "translator's preface" to *Le Temple de Gnide*, Montesquieu offers an elaborate account of that text's line of transmission: written by an anonymous post-Sapphic Greek author, eventually unearthed from the entombment of a Christian bishop's library and sold, presumably by Turkish merchants, to a French ambassador, falling finally into the hands of the present translator. I believe that Montesquieu intends the shifting custody of this text as a pattern for Western culture altogether, which passes from the formative period of Greek antiquity to a Christian era, wherein the classical legacy is both preserved and suppressed, to a period of cross-fertilization with the East, and finally to a period of European enlightenment and ascendancy.

10. Therein Montesquieu ties the prohibition of certain degrees of incest (namely father/children and brother/sister) to the need to preserve natural modesty. While Montesquieu claims both here and in XVI.12 that "nature has spoken to all nations . . . nature has given us modesty," the set of chapters immediately prior to this one paints a rather different picture, giving numerous instances of climates and countries where "nature [i.e., "the lubricity of women"] has a strength, and modesty a weakness that is incomprehensible"

(XVI.10). Nature it seems is contradictory; the natural law that enjoins modesty is at odds with natural desire and natural forces like climate. The intervention of the legislator by means of civil law is necessary to educate men to modesty. Modesty and its corollary, the incest taboo, are what we might oxymoronically call "natural conventions"—the result of the application of foresight and force to the dilemma of human sexuality.

Chapter Seven

1. Rica/Usbek: #45, 49, 52, 54, 59, 63, 68, 72, 78, 126, 128, 140-42.

2. Interestingly, the ascription of these two letters (#74 and #144) to Usbek is dubious. In all editions of the *Persian Letters* during Montesquieu's life, Rica was designated as the author of #74. The reassignment was made in the 1758 edition on the basis, apparently, of "content and style" (see George R. Healy's explanation in the Bobbs-Merrill edition of the *Persian Letters*, 127,n.1). With respect to #144 (a late addition, not appearing until the 1754 version), uncertainty prevails. In the *Pléiade* edition among others, Rica is given as the author. It seems to me entirely possible that Montesquieu intended there to be no response from Usbek to Rica's often pointed missives.

There is one further intriguing detail about the headings affixed to the Rica/Usbek correspondence: Rica's letters are all addressed "Rica to Usbek, at—." Montesquieu, in his guise as translator of the letters, says in the preface that "[t]he Persians who write here were lodged in my home, and we spent our time together." Presumably then, the unnamed location is the residence of our anonymous compiler. (Another possibility is that the unnamed location is Versailles. However, it seems to me unlikely that Usbek would seek out the French court having recently fled from the Persian court. Moreover, Usbek is, according to Rica, in a place where "you can reason altogether at your ease" [#63], hardly a description of court life.) Extrapolating further, we might surmise that the letters addressed "Rica to—" and "Usbek to—" are directed to this provincial friend and editor. Consistent with this speculation is the fact that Rica, who is more frequently away in the city, writes seventeen letters to the unnamed correspondent, while Usbek writes only five to him. Arguing against the hypothesis that Montesquieu has inserted himself into his work in this fashion are the strong hints that the unnamed correspondent is a fellow Moslem. A positive identification is further complicated by the fact that no destination is given for any of the letters to this person (a departure from standard practice). Whoever the mystery man is, both Usbek and Rica write to him about writing. All of the letters on the subjects of authors, scholars, and philosophers; libraries, universities, and academies; books, journals, and memoirs; alphabets and grammar, go to him. Whether a Persian interested in Western learning or a Frenchman fluent in Persian, he is both a bookish man and a man who transcends his own culture.

3. Usbek's letters to Rhédi are #33, 36, 44, 46, 48, 57, 61, 69, 75, 80, 83, 88, 92, 94, 95, 106, 113-22, 124, 129, 146. Usbek writes more to Rhédi than

any other single individual. Moreover, these letters include those on the most serious topics: the nature and justice of God, the disquisition on population, the defense of the arts and sciences. Ibben is next with fourteen, followed by five to the unnamed correspondent, five to Mirza, four to Rustan, three to Nessir, three to the mollah, three to Solim, one or two to a variety of others.

4. Anne M. Cohler, *Montesquieu's Comparative Politics and the Spirit of American Constitutionalism* (Lawrence: University Press of Kansas, 1988), 2.

5. Judith N. Shklar, *Montesquieu* (Oxford: Oxford University Press, 1987), 48, 33-34.

6. Ibid., 34.

7. Usbek is struck by the fact that Italian women wear only one veil (Montesquieu, in his pretended role as translator and compiler of the letters, appends a footnote saying the Persians wear four), that they go out accompanied by old female chaperones (instead of eunuchs), that they can be seen by their male relatives, and that they are permitted to look at men other than their relatives through a "jalousie." What appears to Usbek as the great liberty of Christian women may appear to the reader as different only in degree, not in kind, from the confinement of the harem.

8. There is one letter written by a French actress, but it comes to our attention only because Rica includes it in a letter he sends to "—" (#28); there is also a letter from a Muscovite wife to her mother, included in Nargum's letter to Usbek (#51). These are the only non-Persian women whose letters we see.

9. #24, 28, 38, 52, 55, 58, 63, 78, 82, 86, 99, 107, 110, 125, 139, 141.

10. Oddly enough, Montesquieu finds women unsuited to the rule of households. Household rule requires a stronger executive than political rule.

11. On this point, Nietzsche is in agreement with Rousseau, although he has a rather different understanding of woman's essential nature:

Since the French Revolution, woman's influence in Europe has decreased proportionately as her rights and claims have increased; and the "emancipation of woman," insofar as that is demanded and promoted by women themselves (and not merely by shallow males) is thus seen to be an odd symptom of the increasing weakening and dulling of the most feminine instincts. . . . [viz.,] the genuine, cunning suppleness of a beast of prey, the tiger's claw under the glove, the naivete of her egoism, her ineducability and inner wildness, the incomprehensibility, scope, and movement of her desires and virtues —. (*Beyond Good and Evil*, 7: 239.)

12. Montesquieu hints at the potentially unisex or androgynous tendency of liberty in *The Spirit of the Laws* as well. In a chapter "On manners and mores in the despotic state" (XIX.12), Montesquieu attributes the fixity of manners under despotism to female confinement and the resulting suppression of vanity:

Women are ordinarily enclosed there and have no tone to give. In other countries where they live with men, their desire to please and one's desire to please them too prompt one to change manners continually. The two sexes spoil each other; each loses its distinctive and essential quality; arbitrariness is put into what was absolute, and manners change every day.

The free and public play of natural attraction may lead to the abandonment, or at least the continual modification, of the respective roles of "defense" and "attack" (see XVI.12). Montesquieu was aware that sexual liberation could culminate in a certain sexual homogenization. In his *Pensées*, no. 620, in a discussion of the ways in which *politesse* (that is, the unwritten ceremonial law of a people) might evolve, Montesquieu notes the inclination of French women to reject the prerogatives of the pedestal: "The change has come on the part of women, who regard themselves as the dupes of a ceremonial made to honor them."

13. This chapter is near the center of book XXVIII entitled "On the origin and revolutions of the civil laws among the French." Interestingly, this book contains far more chapters (forty-five) than any other book (more than a third as many as the runner-up) and comes right after the only book (XXVII, "On the origin and revolutions of the Roman laws on inheritance") to consist of a sole chapter, a fact to which Montesquieu draws our attention by affixing it with the words "Chapitre Unique" instead of "Chapitre Premier." The book on Roman inheritance traces the Roman republic's attempt to forbid women access to wealth. The account culminates with the establishment of the Roman empire and its abandonment of that attempt, moved by "reasonings of fairness, moderation, and propriety" as well as "nature itself." The singularity and simplicity of Rome (whether republican or imperial) stand in sharp contrast to the endlessly complex evolution of the French feudal laws and the relation of those civil provisions to the "establishment" and "revolutions" of the French monarchy (recounted in books XXVIII, XXX, and XXXI). Appropriately, book XXVIII bears as its epigraph the opening lines of Ovid's *Metamorphosis*: "My imagination brings me to speak of forms changing into new bodies." *The Spirit of the Laws* contains only two other epigraphs, one to the work as a whole (also from Ovid, also on the subject of creation), and another serving as proem to the subject of commerce in book XX (along with Montesquieu's own "Invocation to the Muses").

14. Interestingly, the only other oath uttered by Montesquieu himself (identical in form—"God forbid!") appears in XII.6 "On the crime against nature." There, before recommending the decriminalization of homosexuality (along with witchcraft and heresy), Montesquieu pleads his innocence of any design to lessen the horror in which homosexuality is held. Putting the two oaths together, I believe Montesquieu's point would be that the real crime against nature lies in repressive definitions of virtue, which, as it happens, have the effect of distorting natural sexuality. Montesquieu says:

> I shall assert that the crime against nature will not make much progress in a society unless the people are also inclined to it by some custom, as

among the Greeks, where the young people performed all their exercises naked, as among ourselves where education at home is no longer the usage, as among the Asians where some individuals have a large number of wives whom they scorn while others can have none.

In each case (gymnastic, religious education, polygamy), it is sexual segregation which conduces to the prevalence of homosexuality. And in each case, sexual segregation is dictated by a certain view of virtue: the manly virtue of the public-spirited citizen-warrior, the Christian emphasis on chastity and suppression of the passions, the Islamic protection of female virtue through imprisonment.

15. Every bit as expert at taking umbrage as Montesquieu describes them to be, the Spaniards struck back, although not, as Rica had hoped, via a traveling Spaniard's letter about France. Instead, in 1761 José Cadalso wrote "A Paper in Defense of the Spanish Nation: Notes on the Persian Letter that President Montesquieu Wrote Insulting the Religion, Valor, Science and Nobility of the Spaniards," a line-by-line refutation of letter #78 so fraught with outraged pride that it confirms much more than it disproves Montesquieu's portrait. Begins Cadalso:

That a French fop of few years, even less judgment and no modesty would affront the honest citizen, ridicule the grave senator, insult the respected prelate and depreciate the gray-haired and scarred war hero, is a very common thing that should not surprise anyone who knows a little about the world. But that the Baron de Secondat, President Montesquieu, magistrate doctor, the glory of his nation, honor of the French robe and author of *The Spirit of the Laws* would employ his erudite pen in spoiling with indecorous calumnies the splendor of a glorious nation is, in my view, a terrible example of the extravagancies of which the human heart is capable.

(José Cadalso, *Defensa de la Nación Española contra la carta persiana LXXVIII de Montesquieu* [texto inédito], edición, prólogo y notas de Guy Mercadier [France-Iberie Recherche Institut D'Etudes Hispaniques, Hispano-Americaines et Luso-Bresiliennes, Universite de Toulouse, 1970], 4. My thanks to Lauren Weiner for supplying the translation from the Spanish.

16. This route of transmission has recently been confirmed by archaeological study of the skeletal traces of the disease in pre-Columbian America (*Washington Post*, 5 Nov. 1989, p. A10).

17. Karl Marx, "On the Jewish Question," in *The Marx–Engels Reader*, ed. Robert C. Tucker (New York: W. W. Norton & Co., 1978), 49.

18. Ibid., 50.

19. Ibid., 52.

20. The subsequent history of this nobly liberal paragraph contains a painful irony: in the next century it served as the inspiration for Maurice Joly's *Dialogue aux enfers entre Machiavel et Montesquieu, ou, La politique de Machiavel au XIXe siècle* (Bruxelles: Imprimerie de A. Mertens et fils, 1864),

a work attacking Louis Napoleon's policy of world domination by the transparent device of making Machiavelli its spokesman and Montesquieu its opponent. It was Joly's *Dialogue in Hell* that was then plagiarized to create the infamous hoax *The Protocols of the Learned Elders of Zion*. Machiavelli's parts went verbatim to the rabbis and Montesquieu's rebuttals were purged. See Herman Bernstein, *The Truth about "the Protocols of Zion"; a complete exposure* (New York: Covici, Friede, 1935). *The Protocols* had considerable influence in stirring up anti-Semitic feeling both in Russia and Germany, where Czarist pogroms and eventually Nazi death camps would prove Montesquieu to have been wrong in his prediction of safety for the Jews and the demise of Machiavellism. Thus, the very Machiavellism that Montesquieu held the Jews to have set in the course of ultimate extinction came to be attributed to the Jews themselves and provided the perverse justification for the exercise of a Machiavellism horrible beyond measure.

Chapter Eight

1. Goodman, 102-3, also 225-26.
2. Myers, 238.
3. Mansfield, 228.
4. No better proof is needed than the fact that Montesquieu offers Plato's *Republic* as the model for a "popular" regime dedicated to virtue (IV.6); in other words, if you pursue the quest for virtue to its logical conclusion, you end up not with a democracy, but with a philosopher-king. Montesquieu introduces William Penn ("a true Lycurgus") and the activities of the *Société* in the New World as modern examples of "that which was extraordinary in the Greek institutions." Both Puritans and Jesuits attempted to found theocratic states—God is the ultimate philosopher-king. Ancient and Christian legislators are "alike in the singular path on which they have set their people, in their ascendancy over free men, in the prejudices they have vanquished [viz., love of one's own in the form of family and property], and in the passions they have subdued."
5. The importance of this question was emphasized by Leo Strauss in the transcript of his "Seminar on Montesquieu, A course given in the Winter and Spring Quarters of 1966 in the Department of Political Science, The University of Chicago."
6. Edward Gibbon, *The History of the Decline and Fall of the Roman Empire* (London: Methuen, 1911), 5: 191-95, summarizes the reign of Justinian II, the last of the Heraclian dynasty. Here is his account of the incident:

> His favourite ministers were two beings the least susceptible of human sympathy, an eunuch and a monk; to the one he abandoned the palace, to the other the finances; the former corrected the emperor's mother with a scourge, the latter suspended the insolvent tributaries, with their heads downwards, over a slow and smoky fire.

I assume that Montesquieu's substitution of the wife for the mother is deliberate. As always, he is more interested in the conjugal relation than the filial.

7. Montesquieu in his *Notes sur l'Angleterre* (1:883) seems to express his own dismay and frustration at the effects of male indifference upon female sensibilities: "The women here are reserved, since the Englishmen scarcely take notice of them; accordingly, the women themselves fancy that a foreigner who speaks to them desires to mount them. 'I do not want, they say, [and here Montesquieu gives his rendition of the English idiom] *give to him encouragement.*'"

8. Like Montesquieu, Nietzsche also voices admiration for the French spirit: "European *noblesse*—of feeling, of taste, of manners, taking the word, in short, in every higher sense—is the work and invention of *France*; European vulgarity, the plebeianism of modern ideas, that of *England.*—" (*Beyond Good and Evil*, #253.) While Montesquieu would never join in Nietzsche's antiliberal and hypertrophic denunciations of "the English-mechanistic doltification of the world" (#252), he would welcome French refinements and recensions.

In his praise of the French in *Beyond Good and Evil*, #254, Nietzsche itemizes France's three claims to cultural superiority. It is worthy of extensive quotation, for it reads like a eulogy of Montesquieu himself:

First, the capacity for artistic passions, for that devotion to "form" for which the phrase *l'art pour l'art* has been invented along with a thousand others: that sort of thing has not been lacking in France for the last three centuries and has made possible again and again, thanks to their reverence for the "small number," a kind of chamber music in literature for which one looks in vain in the rest of Europe.

The second thing on which the French can base a superiority over Europe is their old, manifold, *moralistic* culture, . . . as the most consummate expression of a typically French curiosity and inventiveness for this realm of delicate thrills, one may consider Henri Beyle [alias Stendhal], that remarkable anticipatory and precursory human being who ran with a Napoleonic tempo through *his* Europe, through several centuries of the European soul, as an explorer and discoverer of this soul: it required two generations to *catch up* with him in any way, to figure out again a few of the riddles that tormented and enchanted him, this odd epicurean and question mark of a man who was France's last great psychologist.

There is yet a third claim to superiority. The French character contains a halfway successful synthesis of the north and the south which allows them to comprehend many things and to do things which an Englishman could never understand. Their temperament, periodically turned toward and away from the south, in which from time to time Provençal and Ligurian blood foams over, protects them against the gruesome northern gray on gray and the sunless concept-spooking and anemia—the disease of *German* taste. . . . Even now one still encounters in France an advance understanding and accommodation of those rarer and rarely contented human beings who are too comprehensive to find satisfaction in any fatherlandishness and know how to love the south in the north and the north in the south—the born Midlanders, the "good Europeans."

One couldn't find a better description of the artistry, the insight, and the capacious moderation of Montesquieu.

In a letter to Karl Löwith (26 November 1946), Leo Strauss writes:

Do you know Montesquieu? He is the most perfect gentleman of Continental Europe (he had an English mother). Completely anti-Christian, more humane than Machiavelli, equally attracted by republican Rome and the ancient Germans, benevolent and aristocratically irreverent, etc., etc.—In short, all that Nietzsche and Stendhal *imagined*, but which Stendhal was not. (For Stendhal already descends from Rousseau).

("Correspondence Concerning Modernity: Karl Löwith and Leo Strauss," *Independent Journal of Philosophy* 4 [1983]: 115). My thanks to Michael Franz for alerting me to this passage.

9. Mary P. Nichols, *Citizens and Statesmen: A Study of Aristotle's "Politics"* (Savage, MD: Rowman & Littlefield, 1992), 30-31.

10. Herodotus, *The History*, trans. David Grene (Chicago: The University of Chicago Press, 1987), 2.172-73.

11. In his *Pensées*, no. 109, Montesquieu selected one epigraph for each of his published works. However, none of them was employed as such. The choice for the *Persian Letters* is from the most famous sonnet ("All'Italia") of Vincenzio da Filicaia (known to the English world through Byron's paraphrase of it in Canto IV of "Childe Harold's Pilgrimage"). Filicaia's European reputation dates from his odes commemorating John III's raising of the siege of Vienna (1683), an act which saved Europe from the invading Turks.

12. "The theological-sexual problem" is a phrase borrowed from Pamela K. Jensen of Kenyon College. Her lecture "The Theological-Sexual Problem in Rousseau" was delivered at Fordham University, 27 April 1992.

13. On a wild Montesquieuan hunch, I would say that the fact that France has never had much of a feminist movement might be connected with women's historically great social role there, just as the frequently Antigonic character of feminism in the English-speaking world (from England to the United States to Australia) might be linked to the traditionally stark separation of hearth and home from agora and assembly.

14. This is a lesson with contemporary relevance. Of late, Third World nations have begun to reject statism and embrace the entrepreneurial ethic. Women have been crucial to this economic transformation, though not so much in the role of consumers as in that of the entrepreneurs themselves. For instance, many Latin American microlending programs (in which very small sums of capital are used to open street stands or home-operated businesses) concentrate on lending to women. Women's stronger ties of responsibility to chil-

dren and their freedom from the pathologies of *machismo* have made them better risks. In a modern banking system, the mustaches of Montesquieu's Spaniards (#78) are no longer acceptable as collateral.

15. *The Oxford Classical Dictionary,* 2d ed. (Oxford: Oxford University Press), 139.

Works Cited

Abensour, Léon. *La Femme et le féminisme avant la Révolution*. Paris: Leroux, 1923.

Altman, Janet Gurkin. *Epistolarity: Approaches to a Form*. Columbus: Ohio State University Press, 1982.

Aristotle. *Nicomachean Ethics*. Loeb Classical Library. 1975.

———. *The Politics*. Translated by Carnes Lord. Chicago: The University of Chicago Press, 1984.

Barrière, Pierre. "Les Éléments personnels et les éléments bordelais dans les *Lettres persanes*." *Revue d'histoire littéraire de la France* 51 (1951): 17-36.

———. *Un grand provincial: Charles-Louis de Secondat, baron de La Brède et de Montesquieu*. Bordeaux: Delmas, 1946.

Beauvoir, Simone de. *The Second Sex*. Translated by H. M. Parshley. New York: Knopf, 1953.

Bernstein, Herman. *The Truth about "the Protocols of Zion"; a complete exposure*. New York: Covici, Friede, 1935.

Bertière, A. "Montesquieu, lecteur de Machiavel." In *Actes du Congrès Montesquieu réuni à Bordeaux du 23 au 26 mai 1955 pour commémorer la deuxième centenaire de la mort de Montesquieu*. Bordeaux: Delmas, 1956: 141-58.

Boase, Alan M. "The Interpretation of *Les Lettres persanes*." In *The French Mind*. Edited by Will G. Moore. Oxford: Oxford University Press, 1952: 152-69.

Cadalso, José. *Defensa de la Nación Española contra la carta persiana LXXVIII de Montesquieu* (texto inédito). Edición, prólogo y notas de Guy Mercadier. France-Iberie Recherche Institut D'Etudes Hispaniques, Hispano-Americaines et Luso-Bresiliennes, Universite de Toulouse, 1970.

Carr, J. L. "The Secret Chain of the *Lettres persanes.*" *Studies on Voltaire and the 18th Century* 55 (Jan.-March 1967): 15-26.

Chardin, Jean. *Voyages en Perse et autres lieux de l'Orient.* Amsterdam: n.p., 1711.

Cohler, Anne M. *Montesquieu's Comparative Politics and the Spirit of American Constitutionalism.* Lawrence: University Press of Kansas, 1988.

Crisafulli, Allessandro S. "Montesquieu's Story of the Troglodytes: Its Background, Meaning, and Significance." *PMLA* 43 (June 1943): 372-92.

Cropsey, Joseph. *Political Philosophy and the Issues of Politics.* Chicago: The University of Chicago Press, 1977.

Crumpacker, Mary M. "The Secret Chain of the *Lettres persanes,* and the mystery of the B edition. *Studies on Voltaire and the 18th Century* 102 (1973): 121-41.

Dauphiné, Claude. "Pourquoi un roman de sérail?" *Europe* 55 (Février 1977): 89-96.

Delon, Michel. "Un Monde d'eunuques." *Europe* 55 (Février 1977): 79-88.

Filicaia, Vincenzio da. *Poesie Toscane.* Firenze: Per Niccolo Conti, 1819.

Flaucourt, Etienne de. *Histoire de la grand île de Madagascar.* Paris: Pierre Lamy, 1658. Quoted in *Lettres Persanes*, 253n.1. Edited by Paul Vernière. Paris: Garnier Frères, 1960.

Frautschi, R. L. "The Would-be Invisible Chain in *Les Lettres persanes.*" *French Review* 40 (April 1967): 604-12.

Gaultier, Jean-Baptiste. *Les "Lettres persanes" convaincues d'impiété.* Paris: n.p., 1751.

Geffriaud-Rosso, Jeanette. *Montesquieu et la féminité.* Pise: Libreria Goliardica Editrice, 1977.

Gibbon, Edward. *The History of the Decline and Fall of the Roman Empire.* Edited by J. B. Bury in seven volumes. London: Methuen, 1911.

Goodman, Dena. *Criticism in Action: Enlightenment Experiments in Political Writing.* Ithaca: Cornell University Press, 1989.

Graffigny, Françoise de. *Lettres péruviennes.* Paris: Côte-Femmes, 1990.

Green, F. C. "Montesquieu the Novelist and Some Imitations of the *Lettres persanes.*" *Modern Language Review* 20 (Jan. 1925): 32-42.

Grosrichard, Alain. *La Structure de sérail: La Fiction de despotisme asiatique dans l'Occident classique.* Paris: Seuil, 1979.

Gunny, Ahmad. "Montesquieu's view of Islam in the *Lettres persanes.*" *Studies on Voltaire and the 18th Century* 174 (1978): 151-66.

Hamilton, Alexander, James Madison, and John Jay. *The Federalist Papers.* Edited by Clinton Rossiter. New York: NAL Penguin, 1961.

Hegel, G. W. F. *Early Theological Writings.* Translated by T. M. Knox. Philadelphia: University of Pennsylvania Press, 1971.

Heller, Erich. *The Artist's Journey into the Interior.* New York: Random House, 1959, 202-3. Quoted in Hanna Fenichel Pitkin, *Wittgenstein and Justice,* viii. Berkeley: University of California Press, 1971.

Herodotus. *The History.* Translated by David Grene. Chicago: The University of Chicago Press, 1987.

Hobbes, Thomas. *Leviathan.* Edited by Michael Oakeshott. New York: Macmillan, 1962.

Hume, David. *Essays Moral, Political, and Literary.* Edited by Eugene F. Miller. Indianapolis: Liberty Classics, 1985.

James, Henry. *Literary Criticism: Essays on Literature, American Writers, English Writers.* New York: Library of America, 1984.

Jefferson, Thomas. *The Papers of Thomas Jefferson.* Second Series, edited by Dickinson W. Adams. *Jefferson's Extracts from the Gospels.* Princeton: Princeton University Press, 1983.

Jensen, Pamela K. "The Theological-Sexual Problem in Rousseau." Lecture given at Fordham University, 27 April 1992.

Joly, Maurice. *Dialogue aux enfers entre Machiavel et Montesquieu, ou, La politique de Machiavel au XIXe siècle.* Bruxelles: Imprimerie de A. Mertens et fils, 1864.

Kany, Charles E. *The Beginnings of the Epistolary Novel in France, Italy and Spain.* Berkeley: University of California Press, 1937.

Kempf, Roger. "*Les Lettres persanes* ou le corps absent." *Tel Quel* 22 (Eté 1965): 81-86.

Kessler, Sanford. "Religion and Liberalism in Montesquieu's *Persian Letters.*" *Polity* 15 (Spring 1983): 380-96.

Koebner, R. "Despot and Despotism: Vicissitudes of a Political Term." *Journal of the Warburg and Courtauld Institutes* 14 (1951): 275-302.

Kojève, Alexandre. *Introduction to the Reading of Hegel: Lectures on the "Phenomenology of Spirit."* Assembled by Raymond Queneau, edited by Allan Bloom, translated by James H. Nichols, Jr. Ithaca: Cornell University Press, 1969.

Kra, Pauline. "The Invisible Chain of the *Lettres persanes.*" *Studies on Voltaire and the 18th Century* 23 (1963): 3-55.

―――. "Montesquieu and Women." In *French Women and the Age of Enlightenment.* Edited by Samia I. Spencer, 272-84. Bloomington: Indiana University Press, 1984.

―――. "Religion in Montesquieu's *Lettres persanes.*" *Studies on Voltaire and the 18th Century* 72 (1970): 11-224.

La Harpe, Jean-François de. *Philosophie du dix-huitième siècle.* Vol. I. Paris: Chez Deterville, Libraire, 1818.

Lanson, Gustave. *Histoire de la littérature française.* 3d ed. Paris: Hachette, 1895.

Laufer, Roger. "La Réussite romanesque et la signification des *Lettres persanes* de Montesquieu." *Revue d'histoire littéraire de la France* 61 (Avril-Juin 1961): 188-203.

Levi-Malvano, Ettore. *Montesquieu e Machiavelli.* Paris: Champion, 1912.

Locke, John. *A Paraphrase and Notes on the Epistles of St. Paul.* 2 vols. Edited by Arthur W. Wainwright. Oxford: Oxford University Press, 1987.

———. *"The Reasonableness of Christianity" with "A Discourse of Miracles" and part of "A Third Letter Concerning Toleration."* Edited by I. T. Ramsey. Stanford: Stanford University Press, 1958.

Lowe, Lisa M. "French Literary Orientalism: Representation of 'Others' in the Texts of Montesquieu, Flaubert, and Kristeva." Ph.D. diss., University of California-Santa Cruz, 1986.

Machiavelli, Niccolò. *Discourses on the First Ten Books of Titus Livius.* Translated by Christian E. Detmold. In *The Prince and the Discourses.* New York: Random House, 1950.

———. *The Prince.* Translated by Harvey C. Mansfield, Jr. Chicago: The University of Chicago Press, 1985.

Mahmoud, Parvine. "Les Persans de Montesquieu." *French Review* 34 (Oct. 1960): 44-50.

Maleug, Sara Ellen Procious. "Commentary on Papers by Shelby O. Spruell and Ann M. Moore." *Proceedings of the Annual Meeting of the Western Society for French History* 8 (1980): 159-62.

Mandeville, Bernard. *The Fable of the Bees: or, Private Vices, Publick Benefits.* 2 vols. With a commentary critical, historical and explanatory by F. B. Kaye. Oxford: Clarendon Press, 1924; reprint, Indianapolis: Liberty Classics, 1988.

Mansfield, Harvey C., Jr. *Taming the Prince: The Ambivalence of Modern Executive Power.* New York: Free Press, 1989.

Marx, Karl. "On the Jewish Question." In *The Marx–Engels Reader.* Edited by Robert C. Tucker, 26-62. New York: W. W. Norton & Co., 1978.

Mason, Sheila. "The Riddle of Roxane." In *Woman and Society in Eighteenth-Century France: Essays in Honour of John Stephenson Spink.* Edited by Eva Jacobs, W. H. Barber, Jean H. Bloch, F. W. Leakey, and Eileen LeBreton, 28-41. London: Athlone Press, 1979.

Mercier, Roger. "Le Roman dans les *Lettres persanes*: structure et signification." *Revue des sciences humaines* (Juillet-Septembre 1962): 345-56.

Millett, Kate. *Sexual Politics.* Garden City, New York: Doubleday, 1970.

Montesquieu. *Lettres persanes.* Édition établie et présentée par Jean Starobinski. Paris: Gallimard, 1973.

——. *Lettres Persanes.* Edition de P. Vernière. Paris: Garnier Frères, 1960.

——. *The Persian Letters.* Translated by George R. Healy. Indianapolis: Bobbs-Merrill, Library of Liberal Arts, 1964.

——. *Persian Letters.* Translated by C.J. Betts. NY: Penguin, 1973.

——. *Oeuvres complètes.* 2 vols. Édition établie et annotée par Roger Caillois. Paris: Gallimard, "Bibliothèque de la Pléiade," 1949-51.

——. *The Spirit of the Laws.* Translated and edited by Anne M. Cohler, Basia Carolyn Miller, and Harold Samuel Stone. Cambridge: Cambridge University Press, 1989.

Myers, Richard. "Christianity and Politics in Montesquieu's *Greatness and Decline of the Romans.*" *Interpretation* 17 (Winter 1989-90): 223-38.

Neumann, Franz. "Montesquieu." Introduction to *The Spirit of the Laws,* ix-lxiv. New York: Hafner Press, 1949.

Nichols, Mary P. *Citizens and Statesmen: A Study of Aristotle's "Politics."* Savage, MD: Rowman & Littlefield, 1992.

Nietzsche, Friedrich. *Basic Writings of Nietzsche.* Translated by Walter Kaufmann. New York: Random House, Modern Library, 1968.

Oake, Roger B. "Polygamy in the *Lettres persanes.*" *Romanic Review* 32 (Feb. 1941): 56-62.

Okin, Susan Moller. *Women in Western Political Thought.* Princeton: Princeton University Press, 1979.

O'Reilly, Robert F. "The Artistry of Montesquieu's Narrative Tales." Ph.D. diss., University of Wisconsin, 1967.

——. "Montesquieu: anti-feminist." *Studies on Voltaire and the 18th Century* 102 (1973): 143-56.

Ovid. *Metamorphoses.* Translated by Rolfe Humphries. Bloomington: Indiana University Press, 1955.

Oxford Classical Dictionary, 2d ed. Oxford: Oxford University Press.

Pangle, Thomas L. "Montesquieu, Charles-Louis de Secondat." *The Blackwell Encyclopedia of Political Thought.* Edited by David Miller, 344-47. Oxford: Basil Blackwell, 1987.

———. *Montesquieu's Philosophy of Liberalism: A Commentary on "The Spirit of the Laws."* Chicago: The University of Chicago Press, 1973.

Plato. *Republic.* Translated by Allan Bloom. New York: Basic Books, 1968.

———. *Symposium.* Loeb Classical Library. 1975.

Pollock, M. J. "Montesquieu on the Patriarchal Family: A Discussion and Critique." *Nottingham French Studies* 18 (1979): 9-21.

Pucci, Suzanne L. "Orientalism and Representations of Exteriority in Montesquieu's *Lettres persanes.*" *The Eighteenth Century* 26 (1985): 263-79.

Ranum, Orest. "Personality and Politics in the *Persian Letters.*" *Political Science Quarterly* 84 (Dec. 1969): 606-27.

Raymond, Agnes G. "Encore quelques réflexions sur la 'chaîne secrète' des *Lettres persanes.*" *Studies on Voltaire and the 18th Century* 89 (1972): 1337-47.

Richardson, Samuel. *Pamela; Or, Virtue Rewarded.* New York: Penguin, 1980.

Richter, Melvin. "Despotism." In *Dictionary of the History of Ideas,* Vol. 2. New York: Charles Scribner's Sons, 1973.

Roddick, Nick. "The Structure of the *Lettres persanes.*" *French Studies* 28 (Oct. 1974): 396-407.

Rogers, Katherine M. "Subversion of Patriarchy in *Les Lettres Persanes.*" *Philological Quarterly* 65 (Winter 1986): 61-78.

Rousseau, Jean-Jacques. *Emile or On Education.* Introduction, translation, & notes by Allan Bloom. New York: Basic Books, 1979.

———. *Oeuvres complètes,* vol. 1. Édition publiée sous la direction de Bernard Gagnegin et Marcel Raymond. Paris: Gallimard, "Bibliothèque de la Piéiade," 1959.

————. *On the Social Contract*. Edited by Roger D. Masters, translated by Judith R. Masters. New York: St. Martin's Press, 1978.

Said, Edward W. *Orientalism*. New York: Pantheon Books, 1978.

Sainte-Beuve, Charles-Augustin. "Montesquieu." In *Portraits on the Eighteenth Century: Historic and Literary*, vol. 1. Translated by Katherine P. Wormeley, 109-56. New York: Frederick Ungar Publishing, 1964.

Saintsbury, George. "Montesquieu." In *French Literature and Its Masters*. Edited by Huntington Cairns, 84-93. New York: Knopf, 1946.

Shackleton, Robert. "Madame de Montesquieu with some considerations on Thérèse de Secondat." In *Woman and Society in Eighteenth-Century France: Essays in Honour of John Stephenson Spink*. Edited by Eva Jacobs, W. H. Barber, Jean H. Bloch, F. W. Leakey, and Eileen LeBreton, 229-42. London: Athlone Press, 1979.

————. *Montesquieu: A Critical Biography*. London: Oxford University Press, 1961.

————. "Montesquieu and Machiavelli: A Reappraisal." *Comparative Literature Studies* 1 (1964): 1-13.

————. "The Moslem Chronology of the *Lettres persanes*." *French Studies* 8 (Jan. 1954): 17-27.

Shanley, Mary, and Peter Stillman. "Political and Marital Despotism: Montesquieu's *Persian Letters*." In *The Family in Political Thought*. Edited by Jean Bethke Elshtain, 67-79. Amherst: University of Massachusetts Press, 1982.

Shklar, Judith. *Montesquieu*. Oxford: Oxford University Press, 1987.

Singerman, Alan J. "Réflections sur une métaphore: le sérail dans les *Lettres persanes*." *Studies on Voltaire and the 18th Century* 185 (1980): 181-98.

Sorel, Albert. *Montesquieu*. Translated by Melville B. Anderson and Edward Playfair Anderson. Port Washington, NY: Kennikat Press, 1969.

Spinoza, Benedict de. *A Theologico-Political Treatise*. Translated by R. H. M. Elwes. G. Bell & Son, 1883; reprint New York: Dover, 1951.

Spruell, Shelby O. "The Metaphorical Use of Sexual Repression to Represent Political Oppression in Montesquieu's *Persian Letters.*" *Proceedings of the Annual Meeting of the Western Society for French History* 8 (1980): 147-58.

Starobinski, Jean. *Montesquieu par lui-meme*. Paris: Seuil, 1953.

Strauss, Leo. "Correspondence Concerning Modernity: Karl Löwith and Leo Strauss." *Independent Journal of Philosophy* 4 (1983): 105-15.

———. *On Tyranny*. Ithaca: Cornell University Press, 1963.

———. *The Political Philosophy of Hobbes: Its Basis and Its Genesis*. Translated by Elsa M. Sinclair. Chicago: The University of Chicago Press, 1952.

———. Transcript: "Seminar on Montesquieu, A course given in the Winter and Spring Quarters of 1966 in the Department of Political Science, University of Chicago."

Strong, Susan C. "Why a *secret* chain?: oriental *topoi* and the essential mystery of the *Lettres persanes.*" *Studies on Voltaire and the 18th Century* 230 (1985): 167-79.

Tavernier, Jean-Baptiste. *Les six voyages en Turquie, en Perse et aux Indes*. Amsterdam, 1676.

Tenenbaum, Susan. "Woman Through the Prism of Political Thought." *Polity* 15 (Fall 1982): 90-102.

Testud, Pierre. "Les *Lettres persanes*, roman épistolaire." *Revue d'histoire littéraire de la France* 66 (Oct.-Dec. 1966): 642-56.

Tocqueville, Alexis de. *The Old Régime and the French Revolution*. Translated by Stuart Gilbert. Garden City, New York: Doubleday, 1955.

Todorov, Tzvetan. "The Morality of Conquest." *Diogenes* 125 (Spring 1984): 89-102.

Valéry, Paul. "The Persian Letters: A Preface." In *Collected Works*. Edited by Jackson Mathews, translated by Denise Folliot and Jackson Mathews, 215-25. Vol. 10, *History and Politics*. New York: Pantheon, 1962.

Van Roosbroeck, G. L. *Persian Letters before Montesquieu*. New York: Institute of French Studies, 1932.

Vantuch, Anton. "Les éléments personnels dans les *Lettres persanes*." *Annales de la Faculté des lettres et sciences humaines de Nice* 8 (1969): 127-42.

Vartanian, Aram. "Eroticism and Politics in the *Lettres persanes*." *Romanic Review* 60 (Feb. 1969): 23-33.

Venturi, Franco. "Oriental Despotism." *Journal of the History of Ideas* 24 (Jan.-March 1963): 133-42.

Virgil. *The Aeneid*. Translated by W. F. Jackson Knight. New York: Penguin, 1956.

Xenophon. *Cyropaedia*. Loeb Classical Library. 1983

———. *Hiero*. Loeb Classical Libary. 1968.

———. *Oeconomicus*. Loeb Classical Libary. 1979.

Zuckert, Catherine H. *Natural Right and the American Imagination: Political Philosophy in Novel Form*. Savage, MD: Rowman & Littlefield, 1990.

Index

Abbas I, shah of Persia; compared to Henry IV, king of France, 68–69

abortion, xi, 66–68, 169n.8

absolutism: and fear, in Hobbes, 21–22; French, 16, 79, 81, 124; fundamental law of, 83; and moderate government, 24, 148. *See also* despotism, tyranny

Achilles, and the problem of flux, 135

adultery: compared to lesbianism, 49; in French and English novels, 61; French tolerance of, 118, 119; in harem, 42, 47; and women's liberation, 54

Aiguillon, Anne-Charlotte de Crussol-Florensac, duchesse d', 4

Alembert, Jean Le Rond d', 162n.44

Amasis I, king of Egypt, 146

Antigone: and relation of public and private realms, 148

Aquino, Corazon, 116

Aristophanes: plays of female insurrection, 113; view of sexuality, 77

Aristotle, 16, 26; compared to Montesquieu, 24–25, 61, 108; on despotism, 20–21, 164n.2, 171n.10; on kingship and tyranny, 23–24;

on male supremacy, 146; on moderation, 24–25; relation of household and *polis/politeίai* in, 42, 108; on sexual pleasure, 96; on spiritedness, 99

Armenians: persecution of, 68–69, 106

Athena, 150–51

Athens: compared to France, 143; and philosophy, 19

Austen, Jane, 61

Avesta, 106

Babylonians: female supremacy among, 93; fertility goddesses, 93, 106, 148

Barrière, Pierre, 6

Bayle, Pierre: and atheism, 149; on China, 140; and *querelle des femmes*, 93

beauty: contest, 45–46, 72; empire of, 117; among English and French, 143; and race prejudice, 81–82

Beccaria, Cesare, 158n.7

Bhutto, Benazir, 116

Bible: covenant of circumcision in, 79; divorce in, 52; eunuchs in, 73; and philosophers, 101–3, 104; primogeniture in, 66; story of

191

About the Author

Diana J. Schaub is Assistant Professor of Political Science at Loyola College in Maryland. She received her A.B. from Kenyon College and her M.A. and Ph.D. degrees from The University of Chicago. In 1994–95 she was the postdoctoral fellow of the Program on Constitutional Government at Harvard University.